JOURNEY THROUGH DARKNESS

Peggy Nightingale, PhD and MA (Hons) from Macquarie University School of English and Linguistics, is a lecturer at the Tertiary Education Research Centre, University of New South Wales. She is a member of the executive committee of the Higher Education Research and Development Society of Australasia and editor of *HERSDA News*. Previously she was secretary of the Macquarie Unit for the Study of New Literatures in English, and a teacher at the University of the West Indies and the Government Training College, Trinidad. She has written journal articles on V.S. Naipaul, George Lamming, Albert Wendt, and Anantha Murthy, as well as publications on higher education, student writing and problem solving. She is the editor of *A Sense of Place in the New Literatures in English* (UQP 1986).

PR
9272.9
.N32
Z79
1987

JOURNEY THROUGH DARKNESS

THE WRITING OF V.S. NAIPAUL

Peggy Nightingale

University of Queensland Press

ST LUCIA • LONDON • NEW YORK

WITHDRAWN

GOSHEN COLLEGE LIBRARY
GOSHEN, INDIANA

First published 1987 by University of Queensland Press
Box 42, St Lucia, Queensland, Australia

© Peggy Nightingale 1987

This book is copyright. Apart from any fair dealing for the
purposes of private study, research, criticism or review, as
permitted under the Copyright Act, no part may be reproduced
by any process without written permission. Enquiries should
be made to the publisher.

Typeset by University of Queensland Press
Printed in Australia by Australian Print Group, Maryborough

Distributed in the UK and Europe by University of Queensland Press
Dunhams Lane, Letchworth, Herts. SG6 1LF England

Distributed in the USA and Canada by University of Queensland Press
250 Commercial Street, Manchester, NH 03101 USA

Cataloguing in Publication Data

National Library of Australia

Nightingale, Peggy, 1942–
    Journey through darkness: the writing of V.S. Naipaul

    Bibliography.

    1. Naipaul, V.S. (Vidiadhar Surajprasad), 1932–
    – Criticism and interpretation. I. Title.

823'.914

British Library (data available)

Library of Congress

Nightingale, Peggy, 1942–

    Journey through darkness.

    Bibliography: p.
    1. Naipaul, V.S. (Vidiadhar Surajprasad),
1932–   – Criticism and interpretation. 2. Colonies in literature. 3. Culture
conflict in literature. I. Title.

PR9272.9.N32Z79   1986   823'.914   86-13231

ISBN 0 7022 2016 7

Contents

Acknowledgments

Because this book resulted from postgraduate study at Macquarie University, I must thank first of all Yasmine Gooneratne who, in official terms, supervised my work. She did far more than such a phrase can suggest, and my debt to her is enormous. Other members of the School of English and Linguistics, especially those associated with the Macquarie Unit for the Study of New Literatures in English, were unfailingly encouraging and helpful, but I would like to name Elizabeth Liggins, Gareth Griffiths, MayBrit Akerholt, Rosemary Colmer, and Mark Macleod.

A few years after submission, most thesis writers feel profoundly embarrassed by their production. I am no exception, but I was fortunate to have examiners who offered genuinely constructive criticism – Edward Baugh, Ken Goodwin, and Mark Kinkead-Weekes. I hope this book corrects some of the deficiencies they pointed out.

There are many others – family (Kate, Jean, Peter), friends and colleagues to whom I am grateful. Doug Killam and Helen Tiffin offered hard-to-obtain materials as well as their friendship. My colleagues at the Tertiary Education Research Centre of the University of New South Wales were understanding while I struggled to meet this commitment, even though it was part of a different professional life from the one we share. As for all the others, I cannot name everyone but sincerely thank you all.

For permission to quote freely from V.S. Naipaul's works, thanks to Gillon Aitken. Other permissions were received for a passage from "New Concepts of Person and

Place in *The Twyborn Affair* and *A Bend in the River"* by Helen Tiffin, in *A Sense of Place in the New Literatures in English*, edited by Peggy Nightingale, University of Queensland Press; a passage from *The Hero and the Crowd in a Colonial Polity* by A.W. Singham, Yale University Press; and a passage from U.R. Anantha Murthy's *Samskara* (translated by A.K. Ramanujan), Oxford University Press. For financial assistance, my gratitude to Macquarie University and the Commonwealth Postgraduate Research Award Scheme.

Most of all, I thank V.S. Naipaul for writing the books which have given me and many other readers great pleasure.

Key to abbreviations of titles (in order of publication)

MMas	*The Mystic Masseur* (1957)
SE	*The Suffrage of Elvira* (1958)
MS	*Miguel Street* (1959)
HB	*A House for Mr Biswas* (1961)
MP	*The Middle Passage* (1962)
SKC	*Mr Stone and the Knights Companion* (1963)
AD	*An Area of Darkness* (1964)
MimM	*The Mimic Men* (1967)
FI	*A Flag on the Island* (1967)
LED	*The Loss of El Dorado* (1969)
FS	*In A Free State* (1971)
OB	*The Overcrowded Barracoon* (1972)
G	*Guerrillas* (1975)
IWC	*India: A Wounded Civilization* (1977)
CP	*Critical Perspectives on V.S. Naipaul* (Hamner, ed. 1977)
BR	*A Bend in the River* (1979)
REP	*The Return of Eva Peron* (1980)
CD	*A Congo Diary* (1980)
AB	*Among the Believers* (1982)
FC	*Finding the Centre* (1984)

Introduction

From the edge of a constricted circle of dim light surrounding a hut, a child peers into the darkness. A decrepit bus with failing headlamps rattles out of the twilight on its journey to a destination of which the child knows nothing. To V. S. Naipaul the child in the dark represents the colonial dilemma. The image is most fully developed in *A House for Mr Biswas* (1961) but appears also in *An Area of Darkness* (1964), *The Mimic Men* (1967), and *A Bend in the River* (1979). The vision it expresses colours all Naipaul's writing, since the child becomes a man whose experience is equally restricted. Knowing only the area around his hut, the child cannot envisage the enormous outside world in which the road originates and into which it disappears. Time is meaningless; the child knows only the present and has no conception of his own past or future. He has not learned to ask why his hut is at that particular isolated spot in the bush.

The descendants of slave or bondman in a newly independent colony ask the question, and in spite of such historical explanations as voyages of exploration, wars between imperial powers, economic factors in the sugar cane industry, and the demand for labour, they are left unconvinced that there is a valid explanation for their presence in this part of the world. They feel victims of cosmic whimsy. The bus represents the colony itself rattling along on its erratic course, poorly equipped for the night-time journey. To the individual, its destination is as obscure as that of the bus to the child.

In *An Area of Darkness* Naipaul spells out the significance
of the darkness.

> To me as a child the India that had produced so many of the
> persons and things around me was featureless, and I thought
> of the time when the transference was made as a period of
> darkness, darkness which also extended to the land, as
> darkness surrounds a hut at evening, though for a little way
> around the hut there is still light. The light was the area of
> my experience, in time and place. And even now, though
> time has widened, though space has contracted and I have
> travelled lucidly over that area which was to me the area of
> darkness, something of darkness remains, in those atti-
> tudes, those ways of thinking and seeing which are no
> longer mine. (AD 32)

The dislocation of which Naipaul, and so many other
West Indians, write originates in the last darkness – "ways
of thinking and seeing which are no longer mine." Indian
and African alike were removed from their ancient cultures
and placed in a void, denied full participation in the white
master's culture and simultaneously denied access to their
own. In a few generations old traditions might lose their
meaning but are not replaced by new ones that are of sufficient coherence. The emerging nation rings with a caco-
phony of voices. Further, the old ways are often deemed to
be inferior to the ways of the master; there is shame attached to the past. So the past is both wrenched away and rejected.

The colonial present has little, however, to offer. In
Naipaul's image the road is bad, the bus rickety, the sun
and the sky seem to be falling, and canefields with their
past of inhumanity and their present of economic uncertainty surround the hut.

> Once, years before, [Mr Biswas] was conducting one of
> Ajodha's motorbuses that ran its erratic course to remote
> and unsuspected villages. It was late afternoon and they
> were racing back along the ill-made country road. Their
> lights were weak and they were racing the sun. The sun
> fell; and in the short dusk they passed a lonely hut set in a

clearing far back from the road. Smoke came from under the ragged thatched eaves: the evening meal was being prepared. And in the gloom, a boy was leaning against the hut, his hands behind him, staring at the road. He wore a vest and nothing more. The vest glowed white. In an instant the bus went by, noisy in the dark, through bush and level sugar-cane fields. Mr Biswas could not remember where the hut stood, but the picture remained: a boy leaning against an earth house that had no reason for being there, under the dark falling sky, a boy who didn't know where the road, and that bus, went. (HB 171)

Former colonies are painfully aware of their insignificance in world affairs. Even when the colony is the prize in an ideological tug-of-war, it has little control over its own destiny. Economics become a joke when a population is too small and too poor to support its own institutions. Knowing all this, ex-colonials look to the metropolis, the former master, and seek to identify themselves with the "glory that was Rome", but too often they find the glory is past. The legacy of imperialism is exhaustion and demoralization of the master. Even if colonials were able to identify completely with the metropolitan culture, they would find it limited. Past, present, and future are all denied them. Naipaul's fiction investigates the possible responses an individual may make to the dilemma of existence in the post-imperial world.

Naipaul discerns the forces that shape the human sensibility as lurking in the social structure – particularly that left by colonialism. Imperialism, expansionism, paternalism are the arch-villains, the corruptors of both colonized and colonizer. In emphasizing the deprivation of the colonized, one may neglect the effect on the colonizers. Joseph Conrad preceded Naipaul when he fictionalized the converse effect of colonialism in *Heart of Darkness*; removed from the vital stimulus of a creative and productive environment, Kurtz's idealism turns to materialism, his humanity to brutality, and the society that he seeks to create or reform is corrupted by his corruption.

V. S. Naipaul's nonfiction explicitly states the reasons for
the rootlessness, corruption, and violence which he believes characterize modern existence. The inter-relationship
between Naipaul's studies of various societies and his attempt to come to terms with what he sees through fictional
writing is one of the central concerns of this book. But this
is not a one-way process: Naipaul's nonfictional writing is
shaped by his novelist's techniques. While the nonfiction
frequently defines the attitudes and investigates the situations that later become the major themes and elements of
the plots of Naipaul's fiction, the nonfiction itself is often,
if less obviously, shaped by the fiction which precedes it.

The evolution of Naipaul's oeuvre shows the movement
outward from the West Indian settings of his early work, to
the metropolis, and finally to the rest of the post-colonial
world. The child outside the hut surrounded by darkness
may represent the writer himself, who first studies the
area illuminated by the glow from inside. First with
humour and sympathy in short stories (*Miguel Street*, 1959,
and the early stories collected in *A Flag on the Island*, 1967)
then more critically, with satiric revelations of political
corruption (*The Mystic Masseur*, 1957, and *The Suffrage of
Elvira*, 1958), then with a sense of personal tragedy and cultural loss and poverty (*A House for Mr Biswas*), Naipaul
writes fictional accounts of life in Trinidad. Finally, his rejection of the whole Caribbean area is made explicit in *The
Middle Passage* (1962). Many critics have condemned Naipaul's apparent lack of compassion in this first phase of his
work; certainly *The Middle Passage* is not a sympathetic account of the culture and politics of the societies Naipaul
visited. Nor does the fiction gloss over the failings of Trinidadian society. But it is hard to sustain a charge of lack of
compassion in the treatment of Mr Biswas or the residents
of Miguel Street. Perhaps satire failed to provide the protection needed by a writer whose development was shaped
by watching the suffering of Mr Biswas's prototype, and
writing out the tragedy was too harrowing to be cathartic;
the result could have been a profound need to sever all links

with the past and move into the darkness surrounding the lighted clearing of experience.

So Naipaul looks up the road seeking the point of origin of the bus. In the second phase of his career, he investigates the two separate metropolitan models with which his Trinidadian Indian background provided him. Significantly, he writes of an English character in an English setting (*Mr Stone and the Knights Companion*, 1963) while he is physically in India collecting the material for his personal response to the area of darkness from which his family emerged. Briefly, Naipaul has a look at the influence of the United States on Trinidad ("A Flag on the Island", 1965). However, it would seem that he did not find that metropolis to be of significance to the island, for his next major work is *The Mimic Men* in which the narrator/protagonist finally turns away from his West Indian island home and flees to London. Echoing Naipaul's schoolboy enjoyment of the study of ancient history, Ralph Singh turns to Rome for relief from the present and for an explanation of current political events. Naipaul, too, turns to history at this time and writes *The Loss of El Dorado* (1969), seeking in Trinidad's past the patterns which may order the chaos of the present.

After these investigations of the points of origin, Naipaul seems to begin to suggest what may lie in the future, the destination of the bus on which we hurtle through the darkness. The legacy of colonialism is fearful: deracination, disengagement and violence, the heart of darkness itself. *In a Free State* (1971) and *Guerrillas* (1975) offer very dark visions of the modern world, as do Naipaul's articles of this period, which report on Argentinian terrorism, Mobutu's Congo, and the life and times of a Trinidadian murderer, collected in *The Return of Eva Peron* (1980). Naipaul's next published work is a reinvestigation of India, subtitled *A Wounded Civilization* (1977). The book is far less personal than *An Area of Darkness* and more analytical; the title itself seems to suggest a change in Naipaul's perspective toward a greater sympathy for the civilization which has been

so terribly wounded by outside forces over such a period of
time. And in his last published novel, *A Bend in the River*
(1979), Naipaul seems better able to accept chaos, less in-
clined to try to affix blame for the state of the world, but at
the same time more fearful than ever. The source of that
fear, the Arab world, becomes the subject of his next nonfictional work, *Among the Believers* (1982), a study which
though more tolerant of individual limitations, rejects fundamentalist Islamic faith as totally inadequate as the basis
of a modern state. One cannot know, of course, but it may
be that the recently published *Finding the Centre* (1984)
marks the beginning of a new stage in Naipaul's career as a
writer, for in it he recovers both balance and a sense of his
identity as a writer. Perhaps his investigations of so many
of the dark places outside the child's circle of light has at
last enlarged the perimeters of the clearing, illuminating
both points of origin and possible destinations so that the
unknown is, if not less frightening, at least more manageable.

Naipaul emphasizes, in fiction and in nonfiction, the problems of individuals struggling to maintain their integrity
as independent persons while still functioning as cogs in
the wheels of a social structure. The background is always
clearly defined; even when the setting is a creation of the
author, as is the island of Isabella in the novel *The Mimic
Men*, it is recognizable as a historical possibility, typical of
the region in which events are said to take place. But the
most important issue is the response of individuals to the
society in which they are enmeshed and which often seems
totally unaware of their struggles to survive.

> Mr Biswas could never afterwards say exactly where his
> father's hut had stood or where Dhari and the others had
> dug. He never knew whether anyone found Raghu's money.
> It could not have been much, since Raghu earned so little.
> But the ground did yield treasure. For this was in South
> Trinidad and the land Bipti had sold so cheaply to Dhari
> was later found to be rich with oil. And when Mr Biswas
> working on a feature article for the magazine section of the

Sunday Sentinal – RALEIGH'S DREAM COMES TRUE, said the headline, 'But the Gold is Black. Only the Earth is Yellow, Only the Bush Green' – when Mr Biswas looked for the place where he had spent his early years he saw nothing but oil derricks and grimy pumps, see-sawing, see-sawing, endlessly, surrounded by red No Smoking notices. His grandparents' house had also disappeared, and when huts of mud and grass are pulled down they leave no trace. His navel-string, buried on that inauspicious night, and his sixth finger, buried not long after, had turned to dust. The pond had been drained and the whole swamp region was now a garden city of white wooden bungalows with red roofs, cisterns on tall stilts, and neat gardens. The stream where he had watched the black fish had been dammed, diverted into a reservoir, and its winding irregular bed covered by straight lawns, streets and drives. The world carried no witness to Mr Biswas's birth and early years. (HB 38)

Both fiction and nonfiction deal with particular and disturbingly immediate situations in order to reveal the general malaise of our times. Personal relationships may occasionally provide some shelter and protection from the harsh conditions of the society but more frequently they reflect the tensions and patterns of the society. Mr Biswas's struggle to become independent of the Tulsi family into which he has married parallels the efforts of many former colonies to break the ties with the metropolis. Salim's love affair in *A Bend in the River* forms part of a complex pattern of dependent relationships and, with the steamer on the river, provides an extended metaphor for colonial and post-colonial experience. Many characters become involved in politics, but even men like Ralph Singh in *The Mimic Men* who are capable of seeing the corruption about them are unable to effect reforms; more often they are themselves defeated or corrupted, as is Ganesh in *The Mystic Masseur*. Other characters seek personal freedom, significant and culturally liberated lives in exile, but they fail to become part of the new worlds they enter and end in limbo as do the characters of *In a Free State*. Individuals have few satisfactory defences against the forces that seek to entrap and destroy their personalities. Various types of withdrawal seem to be all that Naipaul offers in the end: withdrawal into the eccentricity of Man-Man in *Miguel Street,* or that of Mr Biswas as he tries to defend himself against the Tulsis; withdrawal into a personal creative world such as Jimmy Ahmed's in *Guerrillas* or (more satisfactorily) Ralph Singh's in *The Mimic Men;* or the complete withdrawal of Mr Stone or Salim in *A Bend in the River* as each resigns himself to the impossibility of altering his fate. Only Mr Biswas fights back with limited success and undoubted, if comic, heroism against the forces that seek to deny his intrinsic worth as an individual.

Re-entering the argument about the "truth" of Naipaul's condemnation of postcolonial societies seems pointless at this stage. Certainly he frequently manipulates facts of geography or even political events in his fiction to provide coherent patterns of imagery, and just as certainly his non-fiction is a very personal account of his observations. He never pretends otherwise. But his writing is so confident, his style so authoritative that it is easy to be seduced into believing that he thinks he is offering absolute truth. Closer consideration of the themes of his work over a period of nearly thirty years makes one aware of Naipaul's distrust of imagination's tendency to fantasy, of his profound understanding of the distortions of nonfiction and the reality captured by fiction. His early hope that history would provide the answers to his questions about how humankind reached its present state may be giving way to distrust of history. Once he exclaimed in *The Middle Passage*, "How can the history of this futility be written?" Then he himself wrote it, emphasizing parallels and cycles repeating themselves. Finally, he creates fictional historians who doubt the possibility of learning the truth about or from the past.

Choosing to base his fiction on fact and to make apparently uncomplicated metaphors out of reality, Naipaul exposes himself to another, much more serious criticism. In

1979 (Lecture, Macquarie University), Wilson Harris spoke of the bridge one tries to cross in order to come to an understanding of the irrational roots of experience. If the bridge breaks, one can be left dangling precariously over the stream of life or one can fall into it. Harris suggested that Naipaul dangles, that he is a spectator afraid to become immersed in life itself; Harris believes that Naipaul suffers from the "self-deceiving lucidity of the journalist/spectator" who can be suddenly thrown into the stream with disastrous results. Reason, according to Harris, can be a valuable tool but it can also become a kind of hubris if one fails to recognize the essential irrationality of experience. In terms of literature, a deeper clarity of image is possible if the writer is receptive to the complex of images that springs from within and cannot be entirely comprehended in a rational manner. While *Finding the Centre* seems to acknowledge some of the possibilities of irrational experience, Naipaul's technique remains that of a logician, an analyst.

The problem is that Harris is asking that Naipaul abandon his conviction that it is the writer's duty to order experience, that he must bring his powers of reason to bear on what is essentially chaotic so that readers may better understand the fearful failures of our era. In 1973, having been a writer for over fifteen years, Naipaul tells Ronald Bryden his goal is to order experience, to make a whole of it and to present "a very ordered total philosophy" (370). This theme recurs in Naipaul's critical writing and in interviews from the early 1960s to the present. In his nonfiction Naipaul writes of societies ostensibly as disparate as Argentina and India, Zaire and and Mauritius, and he sees in them and their politics a legacy of imperialism. Drawing parallels, making historical comparisons, he imposes on the apparent chaos an order. But even more urgently, Naipaul seems to be compelled to use writing as a life-line to keep himself afloat in times of stress, as do many of his fictional creations. When it seems impossible to find order in events, it is still possible for Naipaul to order words. Perhaps Naipaul's control over the words, the structures of his writing only create an illusion of order of the content. But if illusory, it is a comforting illusion not only for the writer but also for many of his readers. The difficulties Mr Biswas, Ralph Singh, Mr Stone, Ganesh, Jimmy Ahmed, and Salim encounter in their writings and their frequent failures to master reality suggest that Naipaul is aware both of the irrationality of which Harris speaks and the formidable task of imposing order on it. Naipaul's observation of Trinidad society brought to his attention the fact that fantasies based on Hollywood films or mass media advertising assumed greater reality than the facts of island life. At the same time his father's short stories demonstrated to him the manner in which fiction can enhance one's perception of reality. Time and again the reader discovers in Naipaul's fiction an imaginative recreation of people and events he has previously observed and recorded as a journalist. Conversely, in his nonfiction Naipaul often notes the fantasies or fictions which have come to be accepted as fact. Fact becomes fiction; fantasy becomes history. To understand experience, to comprehend reality, one must come to terms with these paradoxes; it is unlikely that anyone will achieve full understanding or comprehension but Naipaul continues to attempt to do so through a series of steps into the darkness surrounding an individual's limited experience.

Part One

Within the Circle of Light

Humour and Sympathy: *Miguel Street* and other stories

The first book Naipaul wrote (but the third published), *Miguel Street* (1959), is a collection of short stories which are unified by the presence of a single narrator, a single setting, and a group of characters who individually become the focus of separate stories. The stories are further unified by themes of postcolonial futility, brutality, and lack of creativity which are lightened by humour and irony. The lightly ironic tone is reinforced by lines from calypsos quoted as comments on events in the stories and by subjecting the narrator himself to irony. The narrator unselfconsciously includes himself among admirers of Big Foot, the coward who achieved fame by throwing a stone through a Radio Trinidad window "to wake them up", and Man-man who "had seen God after having a bath". Nor is he surprised at this sighting: "Seeing God was quite common in Port of Spain, and indeed, in Trinidad at that time . . . I suppose it was natural that since God was in the area Man-man should see Him." (MS 50–51) There is development in the narrator's appreciation of the eccentricity of his surroundings as the book progresses, so that such statements become more tongue-in-cheek in later chapters than in early ones. The comic effect of these stories is also enhanced by Naipaul's use of a slightly modified form of Trinidad's racy and amusing dialect. An example is in the account of Man-man's crucifixion: when the people begin to take seriously his request to be stoned, "Man-man looked hurt and surprised. He shouted, 'What the hell is this? What the hell you people think you doing? Look, get me down from this thing quick, let me down quick, and I go settle with that son of a bitch who pelt a stone at me'" (MS 54). Naipaul's timing is that of a skilled comic as well: "The police took away Man-man. [New paragraph] The authorities kept him for observation. Then for good." (MS 55) The cadence set up by the arrangement of these short sentences is perfect for the understated effect of the conclusion of this episode.

However, the humour of these stories is deceptive. On reflection, one realizes that the residents of Miguel Street fail to achieve their dreams, and that even the dreams are limited. The *Miguel Street* stories are typical of the sort of story Naipaul claims in *The Middle Passage* is always told in Trinidad. "It was a place where the stories were never stories of success but of failure: brilliant men, scholarship winners, who had died young, gone mad, or taken to drink; cricketers of promise whose careers had been ruined by disagreements with the authorities" (MP 41). While his first two novels, *The Mystic Masseur* and *The Suffrage of Elvira*, satirize West Indian society, emphasizing elements of farce, the *Miguel Street* stories establish Naipaul's deep concern for the individual in a limited and limiting milieu, regardless of his treating them with humour. Miguel Street is a microcosm of Trinidad society – " . . . we, who lived there, saw our street as a world . . . " (MS 79) – and for Naipaul, Trinidad in turn becomes representative of postcolonial societies everywhere. Here at the beginning of his career, Naipaul adopts the perspective of the child outside his hut at the end of day. The circle of light defines his world. The young narrator of the short stories demonstrates the growing awareness of one approaching maturity. At first he knows the people around him only as they wish to be known; later he begins to see their fragility. Knowledge of the society that shapes them comes later still. The narrator of *Miguel Street* seems to stand between these last two stages of awareness. At the end of the book after Hat's imprisonment, the young man writes, " . . . it was just three years, three years in which I had grown up and looked critically at the people around me. I no longer wanted to be like Eddoes. He was so weak and thin, and I hadn't realized that he was so small. Titus Hoyt was stupid and boring, and not funny at all. Everything had changed" (MS 213–14). But he is still drawing no conclusions about why the driver of a scavenging cart is the best hero-figure the street can find and why Titus Hoyt cannot be more than a figure of fun, ultimately only stupid and boring.

Even in the account of bribing Ganesh to obtain a scholarship, the young narrator seems unaware of the social implications of the corruption of public figures or the results for a whole society of buying qualifications rather than earning them. Throughout the book, characters make highly critical remarks about Trinidad that seem to be habitual rather than reasoned judgments about what is missing from the society. It is Naipaul, the author, creator of narrator and stories alike, who questions the values of the society and uses the limited understanding of the narrator to imply the effects of such values on individual lives.

The dwellers on Miguel Street lack a sense of personal identity. Their concepts of self are formed by imitation of American film stars or by playing stereotyped roles approved by their peers. "I don't know if you remember the year the film *Casablanca* was made. That was the year when Bogart's fame spread like fire through Port of Spain and hundreds of young men began adopting the hardboiled Bogartian attitude" (MS 9). The narrator's neighbour "Bogart" has no name of his own and no profession despite the sign declaring him to be a tailor. He becomes a bigamist when his need to prove his masculinity causes him to desert his barren first wife, but it seems that without the external reinforcement of the men on Miguel Street, he still lacks a sustaining self-concept. He must return to the street "'to be a man, among we men.'" (MS 16) Similarly Big Foot has no name of his own and plays a role – the bully – to hide his underlying fear of physical pain. Even Hat who leads the street society and stands as interpreter of it for the narrator, in his youth copies the style of Rex Harrison and finally proves not to be as self-sufficient as he seems. Linked to these images demonstrating failure to establish identities are those concerning language. When Edward goes to work at the American base at Chaguaramas, he adopts American styles of dress and behaviour and alternates between a Trinidadian and an American accent. While the contrast of Titus Hoyt's florid, over-written literary efforts with his day-to-day dialect is in itself amusing, it also reveals his failure to find the level of usage which would indicate success in his efforts to educate himself and become upwardly mobile in social status.

In these stories Naipaul dramatizes another of his observations of Trinidad: although some men may attempt to be creative, to make something with either their hands or their minds, most of their efforts are futile. No number of Edward's paintings of brown hand clasping black will solve Trinidad's racial rivalries; Bogart and Popo seem to be instinctively aware of this futility when they refuse to make the items their signs advertise. Popo has found a safe way to satisfy his own creative urge when he makes "the thing without a name": it cannot be disparaged if it is never finished and no one ever knows for what it is intended. When Popo is forced to conform and make the things his society demands, he is no longer the cheerful, easy-going man with time for talk of "serious things" with a boy. Ironically, Bhakcu whose efforts result only in the destruction or mutilation of the vehicles he loves is "also an artist" (MS 157); the outcome of his tinkering, though not productive or creative, makes him happy. Morgan is less satisfied with the realization of his ambitions: although finally the whole street both laughs at him and recognizes his artistry as a "pyrotechnicist", he must flee. Hat serves as commentator and interpreter of these events for the youthful narrator, expressing the cynicism of these people about the likelihood of actually enjoying the fulfilment of their aims: "But as Hat said, when a man gets something he wants badly, he doesn't like it" (MS 91). Only a few lines later, the narrator reveals his own more mature perspective at the time of writing: "They said Morgan went to Venezuela. They said he went mad. They said he became a jockey in Colombia. They said all sorts of things, but the people of Miguel Street were always romancers" (MS 92). One begins to appreciate that the people of Miguel Street need to be romancers.

Another romancer and the true artist of Miguel Street is B – for Black – Wordsworth who identifies himself as the spiritual brother of White Wordsworth. Because of Naipaul's compassion, this story of a man who might have appeared as a ridiculous, lying fraud becomes one of the most moving of the collection. B. Wordsworth awakens in the narrator the sense of wonder which is essential to poetry, and he transports the narrator from Miguel Street into a lush and fruitful paradise in the middle of the city. While staring at the starry sky with the poet, the boy discovers both his own insignificance and his greatness. Although he never writes his poem, B. Wordsworth attains the perspective of a true poet, but the fate of his little garden of Eden symbolizes the likely fate of all poetic insight in this sterile society. B. Wordsworth seems to recognize something special about the boy's capacity to judge the people around him, a talent the narrator displays in a comment like the following which reveals a perception he had as a boy, not one developed later as the writer of the story. "You felt that George was never really in touch with what was going on around him all the time, and I found it strange that no one should have said that George was mad, while everybody said that Man-man, whom I liked, was mad" (MS 26).

George is one of the characters who represent the brutal and violent side of life on Miguel Street. People there accept many kinds of violence as a natural response to certain situations; children are severely beaten for misdemeanors, wives are made aware of their subservience by regular beatings, and revenge is usually sought at a physical level. It is only when George and Toni carry their beatings of women and children to extremes, or when Morgan ridicules his family by staging a trial and public flogging, that the Street condemns them. But George is also disliked because he cannot carry his liquor, and Toni Hereira cannot fit in because he is white and demeans himself in the eyes of other residents by living on Miguel Street. In *The Loss of El Dorado*, Naipaul traces the source of their brutality not only to the slave era but to the earlier period of exploration and European settlement. Incidentally, there is a hint of his interest in Trinidad's history in this book when Titus

Hoyt teaches the children the history of Fort George: " 'This fort was built at a time when the French and them was planning to invade Trinidad.' . . . 'That was in 1803, when we was fighting Napoleon.' " The boys are impressed because "We had never realized anyone considered us so important" (MS 103), foreshadowing Naipaul's claim that the history of Trinidad is unknown on the island. The use of the third person plural illustrates the colonial need to be identified with important metropolitan events past or present.

Women on Miguel Street can also become tragic figures — not because they are the objects of violence but because there is so little outlet for their human needs. Toni's woman, Angela, has fled from the suffocation of the good life as a doctor's wife in Mucurapo; she returns to the clean antiseptic smell which chokes her and to a life of inactivity and boredom with a big, new black car (that resembles a hearse) for solace. "The Maternal Instinct" is the most tragic of the stories which seem, despite the comedy of *Miguel Street*, to foreshadow the tragedy of *A House for Mr Biswas*. Laura's dreams of a better life for her eight children (of seven fathers) are shattered when her eldest daughter Lorna comes home pregnant. "And for the first time I heard Laura crying. It wasn't ordinary crying. She seemed to be crying all the cry she had saved up since she was born; all the cry she had tried to cover up with her laughter. I have heard people cry at funerals but there is a lot of showing-off in their crying. Laura's crying that night was the most terrible thing I had heard. It made me feel that the world was a stupid, sad place, and I almost began crying with Laura" (MS 115–15). When Lorna drowns, a suicide according to Hat, "Laura said, 'It good. It good. It better that way.' " (MS 117) A world where casual sex and too many children are the only outlets for the joy and loving warmth of a woman like Laura, a world where there is no other relief from poverty and no other type of creativity is, indeed, a stupid, sad place.

So, in many ways in *Miguel Street* Naipaul studies the responses that West Indian society forces upon its members. Bolo is ultimately driven into total withdrawal. Bolo's constant refrain through the story, "Caution", is that black people or Trinidad people are worthless, liars and cheats who are in turn duped by the rest of the world, a refrain that is picked up by Eddoes in this story and by other characters elsewhere. This is the self-denigration Naipaul sees as a natural legacy of slavery and colonial domination. Elias is also forced to abandon ambition and hope and to accept "His Chosen Calling"; his failures are primarily the result of the brutality of his home and the deficiencies of Titus Hoyt's schooling, but he has also set himself unrealistic goals in his efforts to refute the world's judgment that all who live in an unimportant place are themselves unimportant and worthless. Naipaul discovers in Trinidad a constant need for the reassurance of superlatives to ward off the pressing fear of nonentity. It lies behind B. Wordsworth's claim to be writing the greatest poem in the world and Morgan's desire to make the most beautiful fireworks. In *A House for Mr Biswas*, Mohun Biswas is constantly given journalistic assignments to find those who are neediest or most evil, richest or tallest, thinnest or fastest. It is also symptomatic of the constriction of island existence that people believe it is possible to find or be the most anything.

Man-man is the first of Naipaul's characters to take refuge in the written word. Like Ganesh in *The Mystic Masseur* who takes pleasure in the feel of paper and the look of certain typefaces, Man-man is obsessed by the shape of letters and will spend a day writing one word, repeating a letter until the stimulus which suggested the word is withdrawn. Shaping a word is for him an attempt to order experience, to give a form and with it meaning to institutions like school and cricket which are essential parts of experience in Trinidad. With limited success, B. Wordsworth also seeks the solace of writing to ease the painful awareness of disorder and disharmony in his society. The young narrator of *Miguel Street* becomes the first of Naipaul's writer narrators, using writing as a way of exploring the sensibility of his society. Like Mr Biswas he starts as a sign-painter concerned with the physical shape of words rather than the concepts they express, but he becomes increasingly aware of changes in his evaluation of Miguel Street's characters and its culture; while the perspective is most often that of a boy, uncritical and easily impressed, the narrator frequently offers a more mature judgment as a comment on his own youthful simplicity which he is re-creating. As Michael Gilkes says in the 1974 Mittelholzer Lecture: "Certainly it is in the work of V. S. Naipaul that the West Indian's sense of inner division, of self-alienation, achieves its most precise and disturbing expression. The young hero and narrator in *Miguel Street* (1959), like Lamming's 'G', learns as he grows up that people's personae — their apparent self-confidence and stability — are only facades behind which their fragile, inner selves crouch in fear"

It is evident that in this narrator Naipaul has portrayed a young man very much like himself. He has told Adrian Rowe-Evans (1971, 57) that his writing has helped him establish an "intellectual stance". "In writing my first four or five books (including books which perhaps people think of as my big books) I was simply recording my reactions to the world; I hadn't come to any conclusion about it. (It was the reviewers who came to a conclusion!) But since then, through my writing, through the effort honestly to res-pond, I have begun to analyse. First of all, the deficiencies of the society from which I came; and then, through that, what goes to make this much more complex society in which I have worked so long." The progression from sign-painter to writer (or in *The Mystic Masseur*, from Ganesh's obsession with the appearance of words to the understand-ing of how to use them for his own purposes) is an image which expresses Naipaul's concept of the development of a writer. "As you get older you begin to write more profound-ly; you think less of the way words lie on paper, and more of meaning." Perhaps this statement helps to explain why

Salim, the narrator of Naipaul's latest novel *A Bend in the River*, is the least self-conscious (as a writer) of all Naipaul's narrators. Like Ralph Singh in *The Mimic Men*, Salim reviews his life in a postcolonial society, but while Singh emphasizes society's impact on himself as an individual and regards the act of writing as a means of defining himself to himself, Salim is more outward-looking. He tries to formulate a view of the world and to communicate it as he analyses his own experience; writing seems to be less therapy and more communication for him, as perhaps writing is now for Naipaul himself.

Although discussion of *Miguel Street* must take account of the negative aspects of the society Naipaul portrays, the limitations it imposes on individuals, and their generally futile efforts to break free of those restrictions, it should be noted at the same time that the Miguel Street community frequently rallies to support its members in times of trouble and that there is an element of chivalry in the behaviour of these rough people despite the narrator's disclaimer: "We were none of us chivalrous, but Nathaniel had a contempt for women which we couldn't like . . . And when Miss Ricaud, the welfare woman, passed, Nathaniel would say, 'Look at that big cow.' Which wasn't in good taste, for we all thought that Miss Ricaud was too fat to be laughed at, and ought instead to be pitied." (MS 110–11) Compassion plays a part in keeping the narrator from revealing Big Foot's cowardice to the others, and ensures that there are no jokes on the street when Laura's grandchild and Eddoes's daughter arrive. Landeg White, in *V. S. Naipaul: A Critical Introduction* (1975, 49), concludes from these episodes that "no one actually helps anyone else, and sympathy is limited to this occasional suspension of laughter." However, I think this unduly underrates the importance of the community, which often replaces family. Although Popo had been judged "too conceited" by the men of the street, they try to cheer him by offering friendship when his wife deserts him. The boy narrator turns to other Street residents for comfort and "wisdom" rather than to his mother, with whom he seems to have little contact except when she chastises him. Significantly, Naipaul omitted the story "The Enemy" from *Miguel Street*. Written in 1955 and later included in the collection *A Flag on the Island* (1967), it tells of the boy's constant battles with his mother after his father's death during a storm (which is the precursor of the storm scene in *A House for Mr Biswas*). He discovers her love and concern for him when he sees her tears after he is injured. The sentimentality of the conclusion — "I wished I were a Hindu god at that moment, with two hundred arms, so that all two hundred could be broken, just to enjoy that moment, and to see again my mother's tears." (FI 87) — would have been out of keeping with the tone of *Miguel Street*. Thematically the story's suggestion of stronger family ties would have weakened the narrator's identification with the street and with Hat.

"The Mourners" (1950), "My Aunt Gold Teeth" (1954) and "The Raffle" (1957) also date from the period when *Miguel Street* was written, and are told by a boy who seems to be the *Miguel Street* narrator, referring to Ganesh and to the street. They, too, would weaken the unity and coherence of the earlier collection, which is so tight as to make the book more a novel than a collection of short stories. In this respect, this early work anticipates some of Naipaul's most sophisticated technical achievements, such as the structure of *The Mimic Men* and *In a Free State*. Adding to his observations of life in urban Trinidad, "My Aunt Gold Teeth" and "The Mourners" portray in fairly simple terms the erosion of Hindu life in rural Trinidad as it meets Christian and European styles, a theme fully developed in *A House for Mr Biswas*. Except for "Greenie and Yellow" and "The Perfect Tenants", the other stories in *A Flag on the Island* are set in Trinidad and were written after Naipaul's return to the West Indies to gather material for *The Middle Passage*. In general the themes are similar to those of the *Miguel Street* stories; it seems that the return reinforced Naipaul's earlier observations.

The consciousness of race as a handicap for Negro and

Indian alike is one of these themes. "The Baker's Story" in which the Negro narrator needs a Chinese to sell the bread he bakes because black people "don't like to see black people meddling with their food" (FI 144) is a highly amusing presentation of the way in which race restricts the individual's choices in Trinidad society. Even in the purely comic "The Night Watchman's Occurrence Book", the diary entries of Charles Ethelbert Hillyard show the self-deprecation of a black man of little education whose job depends on a somewhat overbearing white boss.

In "A Christmas Story" the theme of self-denigration is treated in a much more serious fashion: whatever their motives, colonial missionaries foster a profound sense of worthlessness in their converts which leads to the loss of identity represented by the narrator's change of name from Choonilal to Randolph. For this Randolph is to be pitied, but he is also a victim of Naipaulian irony. The indictment of the narrator is all the more devastating because Naipaul achieves it through the character's own words. Far from a confession, the story becomes a series of rationalizations and justifications for a career of petty graft and bribery. Naipaul has managed the difficult task of suggesting that this unattractive character is himself the victim of social forces in a colonial society, forces that have created moral and ethical confusion and the loss of a consistent self-concept. However, by the time Randolph regrets being denied the chance to expiate his sin, one believes him to be simply too weak and self-seeking to confess when it is no longer necessary. Perhaps this is why the story, though technically accomplished, is not entirely successful: it is hard to care that anyone so unsympathetically portrayed is the victim of colonial domination.

"A Christmas Story" and "The Heart" both lack the humour and compassion of the other stories. In tone, they are more like *The Middle Passage*: exasperated, angry, fearful but aggressive. In its economical delineation of character, "The Heart" seems to achieve its purposes, but it remains a rather distasteful portrait of human weakness and viciousness. This story is one of the weak points of *A Flag on the Island*, which is itself a failure as a book because of its lack of unity. Perhaps it is unfair to expect fifteen years' oddments to be unified, but Naipaul has achieved coherence in most of his collections. Even *The Overcrowded Barracoon* arranges its articles chronologically within thematically defined sections, and *The Return of Eva Peron*, for all the variety of its parts, achieves strong thematic unity.

In the *Miguel Street* stories Naipaul takes a fairly sympathetic look at individuals in urban Trinidad. His writing records a familiar milieu and allows readers to form judgments for themselves about the conditions which produce the characters and their responses to the conditions. Naipaul does not enter into the social analysis characteristic of his later fiction, perhaps because he has not yet begun the nonfiction writing which often defines objectively the difficulties faced by characters in his fiction. It is as if he has only just begun to investigate the illuminated circle around the hut, and has not yet discovered enough weakness and corruption to be jolted out of compassion and humour into the bitterness of "A Christmas Story" and "The Heart".

The Satiric View: *The Mystic Masseur*

The Mystic Masseur (1957) and *The Suffrage of Elvira* (1958), like *Miguel Street*, deal with comic and eccentric characters in Trinidad. In these two novels Naipaul moves from the relatively simple observation of individuals and situations characteristic of the short stories to satiric consideration of the society itself. Both novels reveal his developing interest in the politics of colonies but maintain the exuberant humour of the stories. At this stage of his career, Naipaul has not yet begun his extended nonfiction studies of various societies and his fiction is performing the function his nonfiction gradually assumes: the portrayal of social conditions as he observes them. Primarily on the basis of these

books, critics of the 1960s discuss Naipaul as a "social satirist" [See Lee 1966, Rohlehr 1968, Wyndham 1971]. Most are
more approving than George Lamming who attacks Naipaul in *The Pleasures of Exile* (1960, 225), claiming that his
"books can't move beyond a castrated satire". Surely publication of *A House for Mr Biswas* in the next year disproved
this charge, but it is worth remembering that similar rejec-
tions of Naipaul's work have persisted.

Naipaul himself has declined the label "satirist", arguing
that "true satire is impossible when values have been rejected" (1969b, 303). He says elsewhere: "I am not a satirist.
Satire comes out of a tremendous impulse of optimism.
One simply does not indulge in satire while one is awaiting
death. Satire is a type of anger. Irony and comedy, I think,
come out of a sense of acceptance" (Walcott 1965, 5). The
dates of these statements place them in the period of time
after his exasperated rejection of the Caribbean and India
and when he is beginning to explore various non-Caribbean
societies. In 1958, he discusses "The Regional Barrier"
which separates him from the English public and reviewers
who evaluate his work on political, rather than on literary
grounds (OB 9–16); he understands that this is almost inevitable as he is as yet unprepared to write of other societies. At the time of writing *The Mystic Masseur* and *The Suffrage of Elvira*, Naipaul considers that he was not angry
enough for satire, nor had his political understanding progressed very far; he simply reported what he observed
without the optimistic hope of bringing about reform. In
this respect he had, at that time, a sense of acceptance, but
investigation of *Miguel Street* has already demonstrated his
awareness of the limitations of Trinidadian society. Exas-
peration and rejection seem to come after facing the tragedy
of Mr Biswas and after the return to the West Indies to research *The Middle Passage*. A short time later, while struggling with his intense reaction to India, he was writing *Mr
Stone and the Knights Companion* which portrays a different
type of acceptance, one that has elements of withdrawal
and self-protection. In his next novel, *The Mimic Men*,

Ralph Singh also accepts his condition and withdraws. These are the books that show Naipaul's frame of mind at the time he was claiming not to be a satirist, neither angry nor optimistic enough for satire.

Possibly in defining these first two novels as satires we use the term more in the sense Naipaul does in *A House for Mr Biswas*: "'Though no one recognized his strength, Anand was among the strong. His satirical sense kept him aloof. At first this was only a pose, an imitation of his father. But satire led to contempt, and at Shorthills contempt, quick, deep, inclusive, became part of his nature. It led to inadequacies, to self-awareness and a lasting loneliness. But it made him unassailable" (HB 372). The tone of the pre-*Biswas* books places them in the "Horatian" tradition rather than the "Juvenalian": there is more amusement than indignation; more a sense of the foibles and the folly of humankind than a sense of vices and corruption deserving contempt. So Naipaul's description of the growth of Anand's contempt seems to capture the essence of the evolution of his own perspective. And since no such evolution occurs in a straight line of development, it also seems to explain the breaches of the genial tone of the early books. In *The Mystic Masseur*, the dinner party at Government House is overdone in the assembly of characters and their collected faux-pas, for instance. And more significantly, the Epilogue of *The Suffrage of Elvira* seems to strike a jarring note. In terms of theme, it seems consistent with the rest of the novel (showing the candidate and the electorate alike to be sullied by the planting of democracy in tainted and inadequately prepared soil), but in terms of style, the ugliness and violence of the mob, the threatening and grim comic tone are out of keeping with the lighter, cynical satire of the novel as a whole. Although the people of Elvira are a fickle lot, easily swayed by rumour and mood, the motives for their violence in burning the Jaguar are neither clear nor convincing. There has been no earlier evidence of envy of the benefits accruing to the committee, and previously the people have been well aware of and accepted shady dealings throughout the campaign. Nor is there any reason to think they would be surprised to learn that Harbans expected to profit from his election success. His lack of interest in Jordan's illness is surely no more surprising than his unwillingness to accept Nelly as his daughter-in-law. In the Epilogue, Naipaul abandons the distancing techniques of irony and understatement which preserved the lighter tone of the rest of the novel.

To distance himself from the subject matter of *The Mystic Masseur*, Naipaul creates a narrator who has a slight but memorable acquaintance with Ganesh in his early days and subsequently follows his career with interest. Naipaul also invents an autobiography (suppressed in its first year of publication but known to the narrator) to emphasize satirically the inflation of Ganesh's importance and prominence. Like Ganesh, the narrator is a member of the East Indian sub-society of Trinidad. (One must surmise this fact from his statement that his mother probably heard of Ganesh from the Great Belcher when they met at an Indian wedding or funeral [MMas 113]. His statement about "how Trinidad doctors like cutting off black people feet" [MMas 7] is not necesssarily evidence of Negro ancestry as "black" is sometimes used quite loosely in Trinidad, despite the colour hierarchy that operates and the rivalries between Indians and Negroes.) Also like Ganesh, he finally journeys to the metropolis as he improves his status in the colonial society. However, more knowing than the boy who recounts the *Miguel Street* stories, the *The Mystic Masseur* narrator is capable of quite sophisticated judgments of Ganesh's character; readers who view the narrator as one of Ganesh's uncritical admirers fail to pick up the many indications of his conscious use of irony in telling the tale.

The narrator establishes his own credentials as a mature and reasonable judge by evaluating his own attitudes as a youth: "Thinking now about that visit I made to Ganesh as a boy, I am struck only by my egotism. It never crossed my mind then that the people I saw casually all around me had their own very important lives; that, for instance, I was as

unimportant to Ganesh as he was amusing – and puzzling
– to me. Yet when Ganesh published his autobiography,
The Years of Guilt, I read it half hoping to find some reference to myself. Of course, there was none" (MMas 113).
A. C. Derrick (1969, 35) calls attention to passages in which
the narrator employs unexpectedly inflated language to
achieve a sardonic tone which accentuates the "mock
heroic terms of portrayal in the novel". This device is particularly effective when the narrator quotes an anonymous
Nicaraguan critic of Ganesh's autobiography or turns literary critic himself to discuss Ganesh's personal revelation
What God Told Me. The wonderfully comic first lines of
Ganesh's book – " 'On Thursday, May 2, at nine o'clock in
the morning just after I had had breakfast, I saw God. He
looked at me and said . . . ' " – contrast hilariously and to
satiric effect with the narrator's appraisal of the book as a
"classic in Trinidad literature", making possible a neat
double-parody of what passes for literature in Trinidad,
and what passes there for literary criticism: "Its stark simplicity, almost ingenuousness, is shattering. The character
of the narrator is beautifully revealed, especially in the
chapters of dialogue, where his humility and spiritual bewilderment counterpoint the unravelling of many knotty
metaphysical points" (MMas 159). The sudden shift in style
calls attention to the narrator's intended irony. Passages
like this confirm Landeg White's (1975, 64) assessment of
the narrator as "an intelligent observer who understands
very well what is happening. If he frequently appears to be
going along with the accepted view of Ganesh, this is not
because he is taken in but because he is delighted and intri-
gued and because it is only by talking with his tongue in
his cheek that he can explore the whole situation and at the
same time convey the full flavour of his delight."

At times the intrusions of this narrator seem, though
comic, somewhat heavy-handed, but generally Ganesh is
allowed to speak for himself and then the ironic under-
cutting of his position is most effective. When he refuses to
allow people in Fourways to call him "Teacher Ganesh"

after his argument with Miller over his students' lack of progress under Ganesh's tutorship, he says: "'It is wrong to call me that,' . . . adding cryptically, 'I feel I was teaching the wrong things to the wrong people'" (MMas 27). The irony is that in trying to "form not inform", Ganesh could have been doing the right thing for the right people, but being ill-prepared himself, *he* was the wrong person. Naipaul's characterization of Ganesh is no simple satiric portrait. The clash with Miller sympathetically reveals the forces that motivate Ganesh. As a student at Queen's Royal College, Ganesh had been subjected to ridicule and humiliation for his dress, his lack of ability at sport, his rural Indian speech, and his participation in the Hindu ritual of initiation, but had not been moved to anger. Miller's remark in dialect (which ironically places him close to Ganesh) elicits the first angry outburst of his adult life. He was willing to accept humiliation to earn his way out of Fourways, but resents the continuing identification with it.

The change in Ganesh's character as his success increases is the measure of the threat Naipaul feels living in Trinidad constitutes to those virtues of sympathy and humanity Ganesh once possessed. The threat is masked by humour in *The Mystic Masseur* but spelled out explicitly in *The Middle Passage*. As a pundit, Ganesh is successful, chiefly because he is sympathetic, approachable and hard-working. He is truly disturbed by the sheer terror he sees in the eyes of the boy who is "chased" by a black cloud. Ganesh may be a fake in that he stages the scene of vanquishing the cloud cleverly but he has his psychology right, puts effort into the case, and his intentions are both humane and honourable. The ironic tone of the narrator is dropped throughout this passage. Later cures of the Woman Who Couldn't Eat and Lover Boy are more comic and opportunistic, but not this one. Even as Ganesh becomes increasingly clever at self-promotion, he is worthy of some respect. Perhaps he was clever in realizing that he would make more by not having a fixed fee, but he was also charitable enough not to turn away someone who had nothing. Perhaps it was clever of him to use formal speech in addressing people who needed to be impressed, and dialect in conversation with simple folk, but it also made him approachable to all types.

At last, however, Ganesh loses his ability to communicate with the simple people who made him a success; the contrast between accounts of his speech as a successful pundit and those of his performance as a would-be labour mediator is extreme, and again confirm that the narrator is aware of Ganesh's "fall". In the midst of the pretentious display of books and learning, the early Ganesh had something meaningful to say.

> At other times he said that happiness was only possible if you cleared your life of desire and looked upon yourself as part of Life, just a tiny link in the vast chain of Creation. "Lie down on the dry grass and feel Life growing out from the rocks and earth beneath you, through you, and upwards. Look at the clouds and sky when it isn't hot and feel that you are part of all that. Feel that everything else is an extension of you. Therefore you, who are all this, can never die."
>
> People sometimes understood and when they got up they felt a little nobler. (MMas 157)

What little irony is operative in that last comment is very wistful. On the other hand, at the strikers' meeting Ganesh "missed his cue. Stupidly, completely missed his cue. He forgot that he was talking to a crowd of impatient strikers as a man of good and God. He talked instead as though they were the easy-going crowd in Woodford Square and he the fighting MLC and nothing more" (MMas 211). He has not troubled to assess the situation or listen to the mob. He relies on his own position and reputation and that is not enough to placate the angry men who have been duped by their dishonest union leaders. After that experience, Ganesh identifies himself with the Establishment which repays him with appointed positions when the people will no longer elect him. He becomes the cold and unattractive "statesman" the narrator meets on a station platform in

England. Leela, Beharry, the Great Belcher, all the amusing characters who cared for him and encouraged him in his rise to fame have been left behind, and Ganesh is the isolated G. Ramsey Muir, Esq, MBE. Looking back with knowledge of Naipaul's later work, we see that this is the tragedy of *The Mystic Masseur.* In success, Ganesh continues to be haunted by his origins. Dining at Government House, he cannot manage the cutlery and is nauseated by the non-vegetarian food. "The meal was torture to Ganesh. He felt alien and uncomfortable. He grew sulkier and sulkier and refused all the courses. He felt as if he were a boy again, going to Queens Royal College for the first time" (MMas 204). At home he eats his rice and dahl and curry with his fingers, and vows, "going to show them". And indeed he does. But at what price? The question dominates Naipaul's writing. The person in a colonial society who tries to live by the standards of the colonizer is left without any standards, an outsider in both the original society and the adopted one.

Naipaul's work consistently illustrates the ways in which people are shaped by the societies in which they dwell. Social forces act as if they were agents of fate. In *The Mystic Masseur*, Ganesh rarely initiates activity to improve his position, he reacts to situations as they occur. In the terms of the novel, fate is all-important in his career. Over and over again Ganesh almost involuntarily makes the promise to write books; he announces "stupidly almost without knowing what he was saying" (MMas 40) that he is going to write a book; " . . . so far as this business of writing books was concerned he seemed to have no will: . . . It all seemed pre-ordained" (MMas 45). Eventually books are written but only when Narayan's taunts as The Little Bird force the issue. Each time Ganesh's career is advanced it is because of some external event. His aunt gives him his uncle's books on mysticism, and Ganesh ceases to be an unsuccessful masseur and becomes a successful mystic. He decides to fight Narayan only after the latter is romanticized by an English newspaper. He decided to stand for elec-

tion only because Indarsingh chooses to seek nomination
in Ganesh's ward. He gains his MBE only because he earns
the distrust of the labour unions. The summation of this
theme occurs in a passage which refers to Ganesh's autobiography.

> Here it might be well to pause awhile and consider the cir-
> cumstances of Ganesh's rise, from teacher to masseur, from
> masseur to mystic, from mystic to MLC. In his autobiogra-
> phy, *The Years of Guilt,* which he began writing at this time,
> Ganesh attributes his success (he asks to be pardoned for
> using the word) to God. The autobiography shows that he
> believed strongly in predestination; and the circumstances
> which conspired to elevate him seem indeed to be provi-
> dential. If he had been born ten years earlier it is unlikely,
> if you take into account the Trinidad Indian's attitude to
> education at that time, that his father would have sent him
> to the Queen's Royal College. He might have become a pun-
> dit, and a mediocre pundit. If he had been born ten years
> later his father would have sent him to America or Canada
> or England to get a profession – the Indian attitude to
> education had changed so completely – and Ganesh might
> have become an unsuccessful lawyer or a dangerous doctor.
> If, when the Americans descended on Trinidad in 1941,
> Ganesh had taken Leela's advice and got a job with the
> Americans or become a taxi-driver, like so many masseurs,
> the mystic path would have been closed to him for ever and
> he would have been ruined. (MMas 199–200)

Naipaul's use of a concept of fate which could be rooted
in Ganesh's Hindu background suits the context of the book
admirably, but the satiric tone with which predestination
is invoked makes perfectly clear that Naipaul intends these
passages as implied critical comment on Trinidad society.
Ganesh is not destined for his great "success" by fate but by
the attitudes of his society. His strong sense of the inferiority of his origins is shaped by the tendency of everyone
around him to denigrate Trinidad in general and Trinidad
Indians in particular. Failure is always excused as the
result of another's trickery or the backwardness of Trinidad. Naipaul portrays Trinidadians as a pragmatic people,

lacking in ideals, to whom bribery is a way of life and to whom the successful fake or trickster is a hero, statements he makes explicit in *The Middle Passage*. So someone who can win notoriety by publishing a book on the relief of constipation has his reputation established forever. There is a lot of talk about education but most of it is meaningless. Indarsingh, who is apparently genuinely "educated", ends up representing Ganesh's old constituency while Ganesh becomes a Statesman. So Naipaul establishes his view that while Trinidad society pays lip service to the values of education, it mistrusts those who truly have it and elevates those who are "semi-educated". The reverence Ganesh feels for the look and feel and smell of print and paper is part of this attitude. It is not the content of a book which impresses him but its size. The failure of his first book is attributed to the printer's trickery in using small type and thin paper to restrict the text's size. The developing character of Ganesh and the saga of his rise to fame are used to reveal what Naipaul diagnoses as the failure of Trinidad. The prejudices and expectations of his wife, father-in-law, friends and clients influence Ganesh's development in directions that satisfy and reflect the prejudices and expectations of Trinidad society. Ganesh is a "man of the people" in the same sense as Chief the Honourable M. A. Nanga in Chinua Achebe's novel (1966). Achebe places responsibility for Nanga's political survival on the electorate who accept his well-known corruption as part of the bribery, immorality, trickery and violence that constitute a way of life inherited from now-departed colonial masters. In *The Mystic Masseur* and more explicitly in *The Suffrage of Elvira*, Naipaul expresses a similar view.

The narrator of *The Mystic Masseur* is further removed from his subject than the narrator of *Miguel Street*. Despite his disclaimers, he has become capable of satire and of consciously employing irony. The changes in Naipaul's two narrators' perspectives parallel the development of his own understanding of conditions within the society in which he was raised. The adoption of an omniscient third person narrator for his next two novels appears to indicate Naipaul's growing confidence as an analyst of character and society. However, *The Suffrage of Elvira* remains in the satiric mode, tied to observation of events and actions. But shortly, with *A House for Mr Biswas*, Naipaul achieves a depth of understanding that captures the internal and external turmoil as he links the breakdown of an individual with the disintegration of his society.

The Satire Darkens: *The Suffrage of Elvira*

Although *The Suffrage of Elvira* (1958) is an energetic and delightfully amusing satire on political activity in a post-colonial society, Naipaul's picture of Trinidad is less charming and endearing than that offered in *The Mystic Masseur*. It also presents events and situations which can be verified as essentially accurate, despite satiric exaggeration, in non-fictional sources, though not Naipaul's own. He himself is not very revealing in a *Times* article published in early 1964, when he says, "I wrote *The Suffrage of Elvira* to prove to myself that I could invent, invent a story constructed around a given incident." Naipaul was in Trinidad for three months in 1956 during the election period and his uncle, Dr Rudranath Capildeo, once leader of the East Indian Democratic Labour Party, has bitterly complained that many elements of Harbans' story are based on his own election campaign. There may be an echo from further back in Naipaul's family history: in *Finding the Centre*, he mentions in passing that in the 1930s, two senior sons-in-law in his mother's family were concerned with establishing the Local Road Board and with the politics of the island Legislative Council. Additionally, sociologists and political scientists have described other election campaigns, the structures of the Indian community and how they affect politics in Trinidad in terms which validate Naipaul's observations upon which he builds the comic exaggerations of Elvira's political life. (See Klass 1961, Malik 1971, Lewis 1962)

The litany intoned by Chitteranjan and Rampiari's husband which culminates in

"When you want *any* sort of help, Rampiari husband, who you does come to?"
"I does come to you, Goldsmith."
"So when *I* want help, who I must come to?"
"You must come to me, Goldsmith." (SE 88)

illustrates an observed structural relationship in the organization of Hindu society. A relationship in which one person is acknowledged to be superior and assists another who thus admits his inferiority and binds himself to the superior is called a *praja* relationship. The superior looks on the other as his responsibility and while the inferior may repay favours with gifts or labour, he or she will continue to be guided by the superior. Morton Klass (226) observed an election while conducting his field study in Trinidad and notes that the leaders of "Amity" were able to swing their followers' vote to the leading Hindu figure on the island to whom they themselves felt a sense of obligation for services rendered. In contrast villagers from two districts where strong *praja* relationships had not formed (for complicated economic and social, especially caste, reasons) tended to vote for the other candidate, another Indian, to whom *they* felt under obligation.

Similarly, the reality behind Naipaul's invented story is confirmed by Y. K. Malik's study of East Indian political history in Trinidad which offers an explanation of the source of the community's mistrust of each other. According to Malik (29), "amoral familism" is often a by-product of the joint family scheme: "Amoral familism is based on the belief that everybody in the society is pursuing the interests of his own family, and that whoever seeks public office seeks it for his own good and not for the good of the community. There is always distrust of the outsider. In such societies organization of effective leadership is very difficult to achieve". Naipaul has been criticized for misrepresenting Trinidad and other postcolonial societies so it

seems worth noting that trained professionals observe and
comment similarly, though much less amusingly and colourfully.

The situations which Naipaul ridicules contain serious
abuses of the democratic process. Where *The Mystic Masseur* traces the process by which an individual is reduced
by entering the political arena, *The Suffrage of Elvira* emphasizes the two-way process which sees both candidate
and electorate demeaned. Probably the seeds have been
sown over many years of colonial government, and have
lain dormant in Elvira's soil waiting only for "this universal
suffrage nonsense" to bring them to life. This is not an in-
nocent electorate defrauded by a clever crook; on the contrary, before the election, the society is free-wheeling and
amoral. However, after the campaign it turns destructive
and vicious and drives the successful candidate away. The
book's title carries an echo of "suffering", and Elvira does
suffer from her bout of election fever as families divide,
neighbours feud, and people become increasingly greedy.
Behind the light and cynical humour of the novel is the implied judgment that Elvira deserves little better than the
MLC she elects. In fact, Naipaul shows the distortion of
those elements of human life which are frequently used to
prove nobler instincts. Charity is mocked by Mahadeo's
lists of sick or dying residents of Elvira who may be used as
objects of vote-getting gestures. Religious principle is
mocked when leaders of Muslims turn over the group vote
to a Hindu for personal gain, or when Naipaul ironically
portrays how "the people of Elvira putting God in their
heart" (SE 235) as Harbans buys three separate religious
services to pray for divine guidance on his behalf. Values
based on family love and loyalty are equally flawed; the
Baksh family fights an endless war of words, punctuated
by frequent blows, in which adults constantly demand respect and love which they have not earned, and children become the victims of their struggle and frustration.

Despite these serious statements, most of this novel comprises sheer farce. Race is the dominant factor in deciding

an elector's vote, and on this count, Harbans is assured election from the start because of the 62.5 per cent Indian population of Elvira. (Although only 36 per cent of the island's population, at the 1960 census, was Indian, they were concentrated in rural areas like Elvira.) However, personalities and superstition complicate the division of votes and the substance of the novel is concerned with the perilous swings of public opinion. The farcical web of events in Elvira demonstrates the way in which the election campaign is influenced and its outcome determined by communal loyalties, superstition and personal ambitions of the most petty kind. At the centre of the cynical tale, not unlike a trapped fly in a web, is an unexpected real sufferer — a starving puppy who unconsciously triggers off and connects the scattered incidents of the novel. Tiger's tottering progress through the village provoking fear, love, pity and rage in various of its citizens, provides the novel with much of its humour and acts as a unifying element. The drunken Baksh encounters Tiger — a huge beast with red eyes which shrinks to pitiful proportions in the light of day, obviously the result of *obeah* (Trinidad voo-doo) — and rumours of candidates using witchcraft to frighten supporters of opponents abound.

Naipaul skilfully plays off readers' expectations against the "actuality" of Elviran politics. As Harbans approaches Elvira in the Prologue, the reader is informed that "It was the roads of Elvira that interested Harbans. Even the election didn't make him forget to count the ruts and trenches and miniature ravines that made it hell to drive to Elvira." The reader interprets this as a creditable interest in improving his ward. But the next sentence contains the reversal: "So far he had counted seven, and noted the beginning of what promised to be a good landslide." A *good* landslide? "This consoled him . . . " Consoled? The source of Harbans' wealth is soon explained: his Transport Service derives its business from carrying the materials to patch the roads, so Harbans "persuades" public officials to undertake no permanent improvements. (SE 9).

Similarly, the words "democracy" and "the people" evoke certain expectations, memories of phrases such as "government of the people, by the people and for the people." But Elvirans have their own views, colourfully expressed in Trinidad's lively dialect: "Dhaniram, who had been promised something – contracts for his tractor – pulled at his cigarette. 'Is not as though you giving things to we pussonal, Mr Harbans. You must try and feel that you giving to the people. After all, is the meaning of this democracy'" (SE 55). Racial mistrust causes Chittaranjan's suspicions: "'This democracy just make for people like Baksh. Fact. I say it just make for negro and Muslim. They is two people who never like to make anything for theyself, and the moment *you* make something, they start begging. And if you ain't give them, they vex'" (SE 161). If "the people" stand to gain something, speakers count themselves as members of the group, but if "the people" are behaving foolishly or include groups with which they do not wish to be associated, speakers divorce themselves from them with ease. Finally the people are dehumanized votes to be counted and cynically rearranged and realigned over and over again. The third person narrator of *The Suffrage of Elvira* observes and tells all, adopting a moral tone characteristic of Elvira – chatty, familiar, cynical, pitiless – for ironic purposes. According to him, the people of Elvira learned the "possibilities" offered to them by universal suffrage, "And so democracy took root in Elvira" (SE 223).

The tools of Naipaul's comedy are individual eccentricity in characters, comically incongruous situations, and most effectively, unfailingly inventive manipulation of the spoken word. Naipaul's ability to capture the rhythms and flavour of Trinidadian speech enriches this novel perhaps more than any of his other writings. Many of the characters demonstrate an almost Welsh fondness for rhetoric. Dhaniram's Presbyterian school of the Canadian Mission gave him access to the vocabulary of Christianity and he relishes "Armageddon" and "Render unto Caesar". The word "pussonal", which the narrator comments "had enormous vogue in Elvira in 1950" (SE 19), punctuates conversation throughout the book, and emphasizes each individual's need to feel central to the action, vital to the election, a close confidante of the candidate. Yet, ironically, people are treated as objects to be bought, sold, and counted. One of Naipaul's deftest comic touches is Foam's imitation of Lorkhoor — "'this is the voice of Foam Baksh asking you — not begging you or beseeching you or entreating you — but asking you and telling you to vote for the honourable and popular candidate, Mr Pat Harbans'" (SE 106). This is followed by Baksh's imitation of both — "'This is the voice of Baksh begging you and beseeching you to corporate with the Highway Code and keep death off the roads'" (SE 220). Lorkhoor is universally unpopular because of his "stringent determination to speak correct English at all times" (SE 75–76), which makes people outside Elvira believe him to be a tourist from Bombay and which offends Elvirans as pretentious.

Undeniably a comic novel, *The Suffrage of Elvira* holds implications for Trinidad and the "democratic" world which are far from humorous, and again Naipaul's satire is supported by Malik's assertion (88) that before 1956 there was no real difference between parties, no ideology was expressed, and personalities and particular interests dominated campaigns. Additionally, Naipaul's satire darkens in this novel as the squalor of setting and bitterness of racial rivalries assume more prominence. Baksh's home and Ramlogan's rum shop are ramshackle, dilapidated, dirty structures, in which the filthy personal habits of individual characters are hardly surprising but still repulsive. Twice Naipaul describes Mrs Baksh removing greasy hair from her comb, rolling it into a ball and spitting on it, before throwing it into a corner. While racial differences contribute to the satire, the exchange between Chittaranjan and Baksh is evidence of the loathing groups have for each other. "'What is Muslim?' Chittaranjan asked, his smile frozen, his eyes unshining, his voice low and cutting. 'Muslim is everything and Muslim is nothing.' He paused. 'Even negro is Muslim'' (SE 129). Baksh counters, "'All you is just a pack of *kaffir*, if you ask me'" (SE 130). The most insulting thing that either can call the other is Negro, and each feels justified, for the Hindu generally has darker skin, but many more Negroes have been converted to Islam.

To this point in his career, Naipaul does not state explicitly his understanding that the failure of democracy in Elvira is a legacy of Trinidad's history. In *The Middle Passage* he describes the distortion of the colonial parent society which became the imperfect model for the West Indian colonies. The role of bribery and personal power politics in the history of colonial Trinidad are exposed in detail in *The Loss of El Dorado*. Neither by the example of honest administration nor by political education were people prepared for the responsibilities of self-government. Elvira adopts the attitude that there is nothing wrong with taking a bribe as long as one keeps one's side of the bargain. Baksh is universally censured for asking for more after having agreed to terms with Harbans, but when Lorkhoor attacks Harbans by charging that "'A man who gives bribes . . . is also capable of taking bribes,'" Chittaranjan comments, "'This Lorkhoor is a real jackass . . . if he thinks that by saying that he is going to make Harbans lose. People *like* to know that they could get a man to do little things for them every now and then'" (SE 175). The public media are frequently the butts of Naipaul's satire, and clearly will not bring about a reform in the electorate. The *Trinidad Sentinal* publishes enlightening material of the uselessly abstract variety, such as Lorkhoor's poem, and is put to good use as a bed and litter box for Tiger, as wallpaper (behind which cockroaches rustle) for Ramlogan, and as pressing cloths for Chittaranjan's trousers. The radio could be a most effective educational medium in a society still largely illiterate, but advertising jingles and programs portraying "faraway places" do little but offer vicarious escape.

Superficially, *The Suffrage of Elvira* resembles *The Mystic Masseur* in being a comic success story, a similarity ironically emphasized by the list of "winners" recorded at the end. In fact, however, the novel tells a tale of failure – the failure of genuine democracy to take root in Elvira and implicit in the telling, are the reasons for this failure. At this stage Naipaul has not begun to analyse in extended non-fiction how the society was doomed by its beginnings to failure and mediocrity, unredeemed by its later history, and why it may remain unredeemable, but his fiction is directing him toward that task. But over-emphasizing the condemnation of the society distorts the primary effect of the book and its intention to amuse. *The Suffrage of Elvira* remains, most of all, a funny novel, although there is, indeed, a sharper edge to the satire than there was in *The Mystic Masseur*.

Cultural Loss and Poverty: *A House for Mr Biswas*

Throughout his career, Naipaul has acknowledged his debt to his father. Not only did Seepersad Naipaul instill in his son the ambition to become a writer, he also gave his son the vision, the perspective from which he was finally able to capture Trinidadian subjects. But only recently has V. S. Naipaul (1983, 22) written at length about the personal significance of *A House for Mr Biswas* (1961). In Cyprus, he accidentally heard a broadcast of a reading from the novel and found himself profoundly moved both by the subject matter and by the memories of the time of the writing. "Of all my books *A House for Mr Biswas* is the one closest to me. It is the most personal, created out of what I saw and felt as a child . . . The book took three years to write. It felt like a career; . . . The labour ended; the book began to recede. And I found that I was unwilling to reenter the world I had created, unwilling to expose myself again to the emotions that lay below the comedy. I became nervous of the book. I haven't read it since I passed the proofs in May 1961."

The bare facts on which the novel is constructed are well-known. Seepersad Naipaul was a reporter and author of short stories. *Gurudeva and Other Indian Tales* was published privately in Trinidad in 1943; V. S. Naipaul edited these stories to make up *The Adventures of Gurudeva and Other Stories,* published by Deutsch in 1976. A poor Brahmin, Seepersad Naipaul married into the large and prominent Capildeo family. Situated with their store in the central Trinidad village of Chaguanas, the Capildeo family home, Lion House, is still recognizable from the descriptions in the novel. The family's moves, the father's financial dependence on the Capildeos and his attempts to break free, the son's scholarship and depression are all documented. So are the bitter reactions of the Capildeo family who claim that portraits in the novel are libellous distortions and intended to damage reputations of prominent members of the family (see, for example, Oxaal no date). Such feelings may still exist, for in a television program broadcast in Australia in 1985, Shiva Naipaul revisits Lion House and his mother but never mentions the novel.

Naipaul's foreword to *The Adventures of Gurudeva* (1976) reveals a remarkable father-son relationship, in which the father appears to have disclosed much more of his own vulnerability than is usual, and in which father and son encouraged each other in the struggle to reach the shared goal of becoming a writer. Naipaul (19) admits "cannibalizing 'They Named Him Mohun' [one of his father's stories] for the beginning of one of my own books"; drawn from his own experience, Seepersad Naipaul's account of his father's meanness and cruelty, becomes the story of Mr Biswas's birth. Reading the *Gurudeva* stories after *A House for Mr Biswas* produces a curious sense of deja vu. Fact and fiction merge more profoundly than in V. S. Naipaul's writing before this novel: fact producing fiction that yields a clearer picture of reality for the young writer, which he in turn transmutes into another fiction to convey his own version of the reality of life in Trinidad and its effect on the sensibility of a man like his father. Because this is such an important theme in Naipaul's whole oeuvre, the following quotation from his retrospective contemplation of the writing of the novel seems worthwhile:

So the idea for this big book came to me when I was ready for it. The original idea was simple, even formal: to tell the story of a man like my father, and, for the sake of narrative shape, to tell the story of the life as the story of the acquiring of the simple possessions by which the man is surrounded at his death. In the writing the book changed. It became the story of a man's search for a house and all that the possession of one's own house implies. . . . The second idea, about the house, was larger, better. It also contained more of the truth. The novel, once it had ceased to be an idea and had begun to exist as a novel, called up its own truth.

For me to write the story of a man like my father was, in the beginning at any rate, to attempt pure fiction, if only because I was writing of things before my time. The transplanted Hindu–Muslim rural culture of Trinidad into which my father was born early in the century was still a whole culture, close to India. When I was of an age to observe, that culture had begun to weaken; and the time of wholeness had seemed to me as far away as India itself, and almost dateless. I knew little about the Trinidad Indian village way of life. I was a town boy; I had grown up in Port-of-Spain. I had memories of my father's conversation; I also had his short stories. . . . They were my father's way of looking back, in his unhappy thirties and forties. This was what my fantasy had to work on.

So the present novel begins with events twice removed, in an antique, "pastoral" time, and almost in a land of the imagination. The real world gradually defines itself, but it is still for the writer an imagined world. The novel is well established, its tone set, when my own wide-awake memories take over. So the book is a work of the imagination. It is obviously not "made up", created out of nothing. But it does not tell a literal truth. The pattern in the narrative of widening vision and a widening world, though I believe it to be historically true of the people concerned, derives also from the child's way of experiencing. It was on the partial knowledge of a child – myself – and his intuitions and emotion that the writer's imagination went to work. There is more fantasy, and emotion, in this novel than in my later novels, where the intelligence is more in command. (1983, 22)

The play of fantasy and imagination on experience and its fictional recreation produces a complex and paradoxical picture of one man's life in Trinidad. Often forced into absurdity and humiliated by his wife's stifling family, the Tulsis, and by the sterile cultural milieu which his writings support, Biswas is, at the same time, a tragic hero who achieves through his undaunted quest for independence, a victory for the human spirit. Like the earlier fiction, this novel chronicles and exposes flaws in Trinidad society, but this time, in spite of humorous treatment of separate incidents and characters, the effect of the society as a whole on an individual's life is seen as deeply tragic. And yet, Mohun Biswas's struggle for self-respect and freedom provides one of the most optimistic notes in Naipaul's writing.

The experiences of Biswas reflect in small the dilemma of the deracinated ex-colonial: time breaks down the Hindu subculture within Trinidad, but the multiracial society into which Biswas is driven does not provide a viable alternative way of life. Biswas's moves from his rural birthplace to Hanuman House and then to the establishments the Tulsis provide for him allow a detailed picture of village and plantation life in rural Trinidad to emerge. The Chase, described in such a way that the reader becomes quickly familiar with the topography both of the town and of the citizens' minds, is typical of villages all over Trinidad as are the Green Vale barracks typical of those provided for estate labour. When Biswas moves on to Port of Spain, passages of description reveal the chasm opening between his aesthetic/romantic ideals and the squalor of slum life, which it is his task to report for the *Sentinel*. (For typical passages, see HB 21, 127, 185–86, 279, and 398.) Such descriptions simultaneously reveal the nauseating aspects of Trinidad from which Naipaul fled as a young man, and reinforce the reader's awareness of the central impulse of the book, the intensity of Mr Biswas's longing for a home at once private and secure. They also reveal the subtle form of torture the society itself unwittingly imposes on Biswas making him acutely aware of his own physical vulnerability and awakening in him the same mixture of dread and disgust at concerns of the flesh that becomes a major theme of Naipaul's later fiction. Later passages pile phrase upon phrase, building an effect of hysteria suppressed only with the greatest difficulty and capturing Biswas's precarious mental balance.

The highly emotive imagery of these passages suggests disgust and fear while also contributing to the unity that is a striking feature of the novel. Images of transience and promiscuity, of illness, and of filth, and suggestions of bestiality are thrown up by city and country alike. Nowhere is there a permanent, planned structure. Towns like the Chase are "ramshackle"; Biswas's shop walls "lean" and "sag", and their plaster "cracks" and "flakes off"; in Woodbrook — an area that fails dismally to live up to the pastoral promise of its name — lots are unfenced and cluttered with unpainted houses and makeshift sheds. Even the children in city slums are unplanned, illegitimate, and seem to have been brought into the world "with haste and disgust"; there is not time enough to tie and cut an umbilical cord properly, much less plan and construct a home or provide the economic planning that will build an orderly community. Other unifying images suggest illness in degenerating, rotting structures. The stains on barrack walls are "mildewed and sweated and freckled with grey and green and black", associations reinforced by the city's "sweating concrete caverns", "scabbed and blistered facades", and "choked" yards. Related phrases describe filth, unhealthy darkness and confinement. The rough concrete shop floor is "encrusted with dirt" and flaking plaster reveals mud walls under the rusting iron roof. Biswas's view is blocked out by a barracks window nailed shut and plastered over with newspapers. People live in "perpetual shadow; crowded, choked, constricted and suffocating". Further, images of bestiality are subtly generalized to include and diminish humanity. Wooden sheds are referred to as "kennels" and children are said to come in "litters"; the "fowl-coops of wire-netting" offer accommodation hardly less desirable than that offer-

GOSHEN COLLEGE LIBRARY
GOSHEN, INDIANA

ed by the sheds with which they share the yards. Naipaul
cannot allow themes of comradeship cemented by shared
poverty and agony, or compassion developed in extreme
misery which are typical of Mulk Raj Anand's *Coolie* or
Banerjee's *Pather Panchali*: Biswas fights desperately for
privacy and self-respect, finding his rewards in the affec-
tions and respect of his immediate family.

The novel's indictment of Trinidad as doomed, diseased,
and defeated is not based solely on Naipaul's powerful
evocation of these aspects of its physical poverty; the
system of education and the newspapers as they touch Biswas's life fail either to discourage superstition and the
cruelty it fosters, or to encourage the national pride and
consciousness which might lead to social reform. In his list
of curriculum items covered by a country school (HB
42–43), Naipaul demonstrates the narrow perspective of
the individual whom colonialism has robbed of a sense
either of history or of the world outside his limited territory, a theme that dominates much of his nonfiction.
Anand's education with its single-minded pursuit of good
marks on an examination devised in England is equally ir-
relevant to the colony. From this education emerges "a
society unable to face its own image or barely
comprehending that image: the Negress, appalled that she
has been offered black stockings when she asked for flesh-
coloured ones, or Mr Biswas painting 'Santa Clauses and
holly-berries and snow-capped letters; the finished signs
quickly blistered in the blazing sun' " (Davies 1972, 292).

The newspapers that provide a continuous motif in Mr
Biswas's life from the time he reads Dr Pitkin's health col-
umn to his uncle, fail to heal or enrich the Trinidad society
that history and economics have so mistreated and mal-
formed. Its battles to increase circulation lead the *Sentinel*
to concentrate on scandal, morbidity and sensation dis-
regarding the truth about events and the feelings of those
involved. Biswas wins a permanent place on the staff with
his tasteless report "DADDY COMES HOME IN A COFFIN/
U.S. Explorer's Last Journey/ ON ICE/ by M. Biswas", and

is set the task of reporting on Trinidad's oddities. Eventually Editor Burnett's policy of letting other papers report real news is replaced by an austere regime which insists on accuracy and straightforward reporting. Burnett's prototype was Gault MacGowan, whom Seepersad Naipaul revered as the man who taught him to write (see FC). V. S. Naipaul describes him as a much better editor than the fictional character, but MacGowan got into trouble with business interests in Trinidad and was replaced at the end of his contract. This is a fairly simple example of the way the fiction evolves from the facts. The story of MacGowan's run-in with his directors has wonderful comic possibilities – they were afraid stories of vampire bats would scare away the tourists – but it would have misdirected attention away from Biswas, so the situation is simplified, Biswas suffers the indignities of being a "stringer" until the paper loses too many readers with its Panglossian policy that "this was the best of all worlds and Trinidad's official institutions its most magnificent aspects" (HB 338) and Biswas returns to the sensationalism of finding Deserving Destitutes, whose plights are discomfortingly like his own. Like the relationship between the electorate and the candidates in *The Suffrage of Elvira*, the relationship between the press and the public is a mutually destructive one in which the demands and expectations of the latter reinfect and inhibit the former even as it attempts to raise public standards.

Mr Biswas's term as a civil servant points up the failure of the government to create an effective public service to deal with the problems of the community. Postwar development plans require a Community Welfare Department, but the agency is unplanned, aimless, makeshift and transient. Biswas has little idea of his task: "He believed it was to organise village life; why and how village life was to be organised he didn't know" (HB 447). His survey proves only that classification and analysis of data become impossible in a society lacking rules and patterns. Soon the Department is dissolved for the simple reason that it is seen to be archaic, not needed in a society so influenced by contact with America during the war that "everyone had the urge, and many the means, of self-improvement" (HB 527). Ironically, one form of imitation is replaced by another.

Against the background of the failures of Trinidad culture as a whole Naipaul outlines the breakdown of the Hindu subculture into which Biswas is born. As Naipaul himself discovers painfully in *An Area of Darkness,* Indians in Trinidad can neither find their identity in India, nor maintain their identity in Trinidad. His observations and experience are supported by David Lowenthal (1972, 156): "East Indians who have gone home are most keenly aware of being, if not fully West Indian, at least no longer Indian in any traditional sense. Yet East Indian ways of life and thought differ subtly from Creole patterns. Although little traditional remains and creolization is pervasive, East Indian culture and social organization, personality traits and values are markedly unlike those of other West Indians". So the old men gather every evening in the arcade of Hanuman House to speak in Hindi of India, but in a later passage of biting irony recounting Owad's assumption of British middle-class prejudices against Indian immigrants to England, Naipaul reveals the colonial's psychological need for self-assertion at the expense of the mother country. Owad judges the "Indian-ness" of Indians by Trinidadian standards − their food, their Hindi, their ritual, their attempts to be modern − but Naipaul has repeatedly stressed the bad food served by the Tulsis, the loss of Hindi, the empty ritual observances, and the acceptance of modern ways when they are advantageous. To ensure that the reader is not taken in by Owad, Naipaul reports the sisters' reaction to his diatribe; if they are the "last representatives of Hindu culture", it may be considered well and truly finished.

Owad's comments quite unintentionally illustrate that surviving elements of Hindu culture in Trinidad have become hollow and mechanical. Malik (41–42) observes that caste is important even though the social organization that requires it no longer exists: "Though most of the religious and ceremonial functions such as those related to food, occupational division, and touch and pollution have almost disappeared from the Hindu society of the island, caste as a status symbol, and pride in higher-caste origin, still persist". Brahmin birth is the only qualification sought by Mrs Tulsi in the men she chooses as husbands for her daughters; dishonesty, violence, rebelliousness, inability or unwillingness to earn a living may be overlooked, as long as they are safely Brahmins. Biswas sees caste as a game and the playfulness of his character helps him through a series of inescapable mental conflicts. He does not question the deference shown him, a labourer's child, and gifts of food when he is called upon to play his part in Hindu ritual, though he realizes that the home of his sister's low-caste husband indicates lowness in no way. Nevertheless, his Brahmin sensibility renders him unwilling to stock lard or salt beef in his shop even though he would like the profits. Devotees who do not know the prayers and only make hollow gestures go through rituals such as the morning *puja* at Shorthills, or they accumulate prayer flags in a front garden to impress the neighbours. Modern customs – such as Mr Biswas's dowry-less marriage in a registry office – are acceptable when they save money.

School games demonstrate the frantic desire of the young to take on the glamour of American modernity and success revealed by war-time contacts. Anand is surprised when his cousin Vidiadhar, after only a short stay in their school, describes his father as working for the Americans rather than admitting that he is a taxi-driver: "For these boys, who called their parents Ma and Pa, who all came from homes where the sudden flow of American dollars had unleashed ambition, push and uncertainty, these boys had begun to take their English compositions very seriously: their Daddies worked in offices, and at week-ends Daddy and Mummy took them in cars to the seaside, with laden hampers" (HB 397). In a discussion of Gerald Moore's *The Chosen*

Tongue, Kenneth Ramchand (1970, 156) makes a pertinent distinction: "Mr Moore rightly reports that creolisation is one of the principal themes of Naipaul's novels but alleges that Naipaul laments the process as one of loss. No, it is lamented as a growth into mimicry. Negro creolisation is seen by Naipaul as a treading of the weary road to whiteness; Indian creolisation is an imitation of this imitation."

For these characters between cultures, Hindi is the language of intimacy, of shared experience and emotion, while English is the language of law and insult. Naipaul presents conversation in dialect if it is conducted in English and in formal English if the speakers use Hindi. One example of how the languages are used to indicate the seriousness or regard of the speakers is in the conversations concerning Biswas's marriage. Seth uses English (dialect) when he summons Mr Biswas to explain the note he wrote Shama, but the conference with Mrs Tulsi and Seth leading up to his betrothal is conducted in Hindi (formal English), and over a meal. Biswas marries Shama in a registry office where the ceremony would naturally be in English and fail to foster the sense of commitment a Hindu ceremony might have developed. Within a fortnight he flees from Hanuman House, but his mother and aunt intercede on his behalf. His aunt reports her discussion of his prospects with the Tulsis in Hindi even though she is reproachful that he has not told them he made a "love match" and agreed to do without a large wedding and dowry. He denies this allegation. "In a disappointed, tired way Tara said, 'They showed me a love letter.' She used the English word; it sounded vicious" (HB 91). So Mr Biswas returns to Hanuman House and Shama. "But there was as yet little friendliness between them. They spoke in English" (HB 94). Similar passages recount the discovery of Biswas's unflattering names for family members; one mark of his rebellion is that most of the time he refuses to speak Hindi in Hanuman House, but occasionally he is taken in by Mrs Tulsi's melodramatics and led to express (false) emotion in Hindi. Throughout the book, changes in mood and complex relationships are delineated by the choice of language for an occasion (see HB 493–94 and 514–15 for examples).

In *The Time of the Peacock* (1974, 87) Mena Abdullah's characters (who have made the passage from the Punjab to Australia) are aware of the same possibilities. In a delightful comic episode, a Hindu Babu, who does accounts and writes letters for the Indian settlers in a rural Australian community, starts a feud between two Muslims in order to get them to exchange letters of insult — which he will write for a fee. He advises, "'If you write in your language, you must preserve the forms. You must begin with greetings, with blessings on his house and family. You should write in English. That is the language for business and rudeness. If you wrote in English, he could not mistake your feelings'".

Language also reveals the way in which acculturation takes place. There are some discussions which simply cannot be conducted in Hindi, a humorous example being the technical discussions between Biswas's sisters-in-law of their husbands' disabilities,

> "He got one backache these days."
> "You must use hartshorn. He did have backache too. He try Dodd's Kidney Pills and Beecham's and Carter's Little Liver Pills and a hundred and one other little pills. But hartshorn did cure him."
> "He don't like hartshorn. He prefers Sloan's Liniment and Canadian Healing Oil."
> "And he don't like Sloan's Liniment." (HB 95)

Although the names of remedies force this discussion into English, the sisters carry over into the adopted language the traditional habit of never referring to one's husband by name. Similarly, legal proceedings must be conducted in English. Authorities in Trinidad for a long time forced this point by refusing to recognize marriage by Hindu rites until 1946 (Klass, 109). Births are registered and "buth suttificates" obtained for school registration. When Moti touts for lawyer Seebaran, he woos Mr Biswas's business in Hindi, but when he brings the papers which threaten lax creditors with legal action, he uses English, "the language of the law" (HB 158).

The double mimicry so repugnant to Naipaul is further reinforced by the influence of the Canadian Presbyterian Mission which ran most rural schools at the time of Mr Biswas's childhood. It was only later that the orthodox Hindu organization, the Sanatan Dharma Maha Sabha, established many schools. In stories in *A Flag on the Island*, Naipaul shows the divisive force of this influence on the characters of the schoolteacher Lal and the narrator of "A Christmas Story": "Lal had been converted to Presbyterianism from a low Hindu caste and held all unconverted Hindus in contempt. As part of this contempt he spoke to them in broken English" (FI 39). For Lal conversion was a means to a teaching appointment and freedom from the stigma of low-caste birth. Malik reports that unconverted Hindus still believe most converts were low-caste, a point of view Naipaul's narrative does not seek to correct, as he emphasizes the disintegration of the structures of traditional Indian life. His own attitudes toward caste are implied in his portrayal of the conflicts between reformer Biswas and orthodox Tulsis, however, and are articulated in *An Area of Darkness*.

Further evidence of the disintegration of tradition in a colonial setting is offered in the structure of the Tulsi family. Klass describes in detail kin relationships and associated behaviour from which the Tulsis depart. Reversing the practice of daughters' joining their husbands' extended families, Mrs Tulsi seems to seek protection from the threatening creole culture by surrounding herself with an insulating buffer of daughters. Biswas and the other sons-in-law are despised for having no homes to offer and are absorbed into the amorphous conglomeration of Tulsis. The Tulsi sons leave to set up their own establishments with vaguely Christian wives, proving their modernity, further improving their social status, and avoiding the stigma of dependence. Because of this pattern, the dilemma of Biswas within the Tulsi family may be seen as a metaphor for the colonial situation. At the centre of everything is the "old queen", Mrs Tulsi, dispensing discipline and largesse. Her daughters and their families are dependent on her and on the concept of a united family she symbolizes in much the same way that West Indian islands are dependent for their sustenance and their identity on their connections with the metropolitan "mother" country. Even more damaging to its self-image than the fact of economic dependence is its cultural dependence on the traditions of the colonizer. It is for this reason that Naipaul condemns the Caribbean as a sterile wasteland without history or culture in *The Middle Passage*. The Tulsis, like many colonial forces, are frighteningly destructive: in the Shorthills episode, they settle upon rich land, which becomes barren almost overnight in their hands. At the end of the novel, the family has disintegrated in ways that parallel the disintegration of the Empire. The educated sons Shekar and Owad are economically safe, if bourgeois and philistine. Mr Biswas, after his rebellion, is physically exhausted and in dire financial straits, although within his small family circle he has achieved a victory of a sort.

Extending the parallel suggested by George Lamming and Landeg White among others, Biswas becomes a symbol of the colonial society struggling toward independence and freedom. For traditional societies of Asia or Africa, the task is to recover a half-forgotten identity. For Trinidad, it is to forge a viable identity from a group of shattered cultures, the disintegration of which Naipaul writes in *The Loss of El Dorado*. As Biswas enters adulthood, his own family has become fragmented and he has no idea where his childhood home actually stood, the exact plight of Negro slaves and Indian indentured labourers when they were brought to Trinidad. Biswas is unaware that in escaping Bhandat, he has sold himself into bondage to the Tulsis; in a situation analogous to that of workers on the sugar plantations owned by absentee English landlords – indeed the Tulsis are themselves estate owners and put Mr Biswas to work on their holdings – Biswas is expected to work for his subsistence and tiny sums of money. When Biswas is finally driven into some act of defiance or rebellion, he is charged

with disloyalty or ingratitude and prevailed upon to remain with the family. He tries to turn such situations to
victories at least in his own mind, but his victory is far from
pure. At the moment of triumph when he has outraged the
Tulsis with some great heresy, he often feels that "All his
joy . . . had turned into disgust at his condition. The campaign against the Tulsis which he had been conducting
with such pleasure, now seemed pointless and degrading"
(HB 118). Such ambivalence frequently occurs in an emerging nation's attitudes toward the metropolis which exploi-
ted the colony but also developed its concept of national
identity and often provided its form of law and government.
Even when Biswas wins his first taste of freedom and takes
over the shop at the Chase, the old queen emerges trium-
phant; the subject proves incompetent to manage his own
affairs.

In a position redolent of colonial themes, the closing
years of the Green Vale period mark the beginning of Mr
Biswas's mental decline: this culminates during a cataclys-
mic storm that rips apart the half-finished ruin which is the
first house he can call his own. Fear of the future con-
sumes him: "The future wasn't the next day or the next
week or even the next year, times within his comprehension and therefore without dread. The future he feared
could not be thought of in terms of time. It was a blankness, a void like those in dreams, into which, past tomorrow and next week and next year, he was falling" (HB 171).
Mr Biswas sees himself watching life go by as uncompre-
hendingly as the child outside a hut in a clearing, and finds
no more reason for his existence than for that child's at that
place and time. Such a passage sums up a cosmic ignorance
as part of the human condition, but it seems here to have a
special reference to colonial territories. To this point in his
career Naipaul has confined himself to investigation of his
territory, Trinidad, but with the development of the extended comparison between Biswas's situation and the colonial
dilemma, he is moving out of the enclosing clearing and
beginning to draw conclusions about the world outside and

its effect on his world. Even more importantly, he is moving out of the restrictions of satire, and while still writing
comic passages, he is fully engaged with his subject, and
engaging readers' sympathies. *A House for Mr Biswas* deals
with fundamental human fears – the fear of extinction, of
the abyss beneath reality: "The image changed. It was no
longer a forest, but a billowing black cloud. Unless he was
careful the cloud would funnel into his head. He felt it
pressing on his head. He didn't want to look up" (HB 239).

The structure of Part Two parallels that of Part One, and
so implies that human cycles, historical cycles repeat, a
theme which Naipaul explores explicitly in *The Loss of El
Dorado*: Biswas sets out to win independence, achieves at
least partial success, suffers a series of set-backs, and
undergoes a period of terrifying humiliation. Instead of col-
lapsing under the pressure, however, Biswas's rebellion
ends this time in his establishing himself and his family in
an independent home, while the Tulsi family disintegrates.
Significantly, the final break occurs only after they attempt
to humiliate his son as they have humiliated him. Gordon
Rohlehr comments (1968, CP 137): "An interesting ambivalence emerges from the book. First there is the dependence
of the individual upon society for his sense of being; where
by society one means not only other people, but a whole
concrete world with which the consciousness establishes
some deep intimacy, and claims as its own. . . . Secondly
there is the necessary rebellion which the individual must
make against society and the void which must be confront-
ed. In the void are meaninglessness, non-entity, fear,
lunacy and chaos, the storm within and the storm without.
It is out of this confrontation that the new personality
grows."

Robert Morris (1975, 33) sees Biswas's struggle as one to
find order in his life but asserts that paradoxically Biswas
does not know what the order is. The Hindu background
which might have taught him acceptance and given him
standards proves unreliable: it is itself corrupted and disintegrating under the pressure of deracination and creoliza-

tion, and no alternative way of life offers itself to change the dismal conditions of existence. Even those personal relationships which should enrich existence and help to compensate for poverty and discomfort are themselves impoverished as Biswas moves from feud to feud, permitted only brief interludes of comparative peace with his wife and children. Like Ganesh, Biswas rarely initiates action, and when he does, fate seems to have planned some new disaster. In his attempts to retain or regain his equilibrium, literature (in the broadest sense) contributes positively to Biswas's search for order. On the advice of his friend Misir, Biswas tries to write himself but managed only "distorted and scurrilous descriptions of Moti, Mungroo, Seebaran, Seth and Mrs Tulsi" (HB 165) or the wish-fulfilling story *Escape*. Twice, prompted by his mother's death, Biswas seems to capture real emotion on the page: his letter to her doctor and his prose-poem for his literary group. In his reading, too, Biswas seeks primarily escape or comfort, but as his mind disintegrates, meanings are unimportant, and the shape of a word or a letter is the only reality that does not threaten (in echo of Man-Man's madness in *Miguel Street*). Finally, he discovers Dickens: "Without difficulty he transferred characters and settings to people and places he knew. In the grotesques of Dickens everything he feared and suffered from was ridiculed and diminished, so that his own anger, his own contempt became unnecessary, and he was given strength to bear with the most difficult part of his day: dressing in the morning, that daily affirmation of faith in oneself, which at times was for him almost like an act of sacrifice. He shared his discovery with Anand . . . " (HB 337–38). Facts again inform the fiction: Naipaul's father introduced him to many authors including Conrad as well as Dickens. "My father was a self-taught man picking his way through a cultural confusion of which he was perhaps hardly aware and which I have only recently begun to understand; and he wished himself to be a writer. He read less for pleasure than for clues, hints and encouragement; and he introduced me to those writers he had come upon in his own search. Conrad was one of the earliest of these: Conrad the stylist, but more than that, Conrad the late starter, holding out hope to those who didn't seem to be starting at all" (REP 207).

With this novel Naipaul is not at all restricted in range by the facts on which the story is built; fiction now transcends reality to capture a greater truth. The reality of the political situation of postcolonial Trinidad serves as a metaphor for unaccommodated man; Biswas is any individual struggling for self-definition, and a place in the chaos. All that remains for Naipaul is to articulate (in *The Middle Passage*) what he has learned about conditions within the circle of light before he will be ready to move out into the darkness, exploring in fiction the English metropolitan model and in nonfiction the Hindus' other metropolis, India.

Rejection of the Caribbean: *The Middle Passage*

In writing *The Middle Passage* (1962), Naipaul stands within the circle of dim light, restricted to the West Indian locale, but the adult, unlike the child, is beginning to examine closely the social milieu which surrounds him. The preceding four fictional works reveal a development in his understanding of the tensions and complexities of life in Trinidad which is reflected in the maturing perspectives of the young narrators of three of the four books. Forced by the act of writing *The Middle Passage* to confront and analyse the reasons for his well-known decision to leave Trinidad, Naipaul found that he feared returning: "I had never examined this fear of Trinidad. I had never wished to. In my novels I had only expressed this fear; and it is only now, at the moment of writing, that I am able to examine it" (MP 41). He also feared the task of preparing a nonfictional statement of his conclusions: "The novelist works towards conclusions of which he is often unaware; and it is better that he should. To analyse and decide before writing would rob the writer of the excitement which supports him during his solitude, and would be the opposite of my method as a novelist. I also felt it as a danger that, having factually analysed the society as far as I was able, I would be unable afterwards to think of it in terms of fiction and that in anything I might write I would be concerned only to prove a point" (MP 5). Nevertheless, after this experience Naipaul's fictional and nonfictional writings are closely interrelated, complementing and enhancing one another. Interestingly, much of the time the novelist Naipaul continues to work towards the conclusions which are explored in subsequent nonfiction, while the journalist Naipaul observes the scenes, characters, and situations which provide the raw material of the fiction.

While the societies discussed in *The Middle Passage* exhibit different variations on postcolonial themes, Naipaul finds certain common denominators in their experiences. His portrait of an aged Indian in a Negro town in Surinam comes to personify the plight of all those imported to labour in the cane fields and left to seek self-definition in alien surroundings: "A derelict man in a derelict land; a man discovering himself, with surprise and resignation, lost in a landscape which had never ceased to be unreal because the scene of an enforced and always temporary residence; the slaves kidnapped from one continent and abandoned on the unprofitable plantations of another, from which there could never more be escape: I was glad to leave Coronie, for, more than lazy Negroes, it held the full desolation that came to those who made the middle passage" (MP 190). Wherever colonialism has stranded its transplanted people, these conclusions are reinforced: the adjectives "derelict" and "desolate" recur throughout Naipaul's writings, dominating *Guerrillas* thirteen years after publication of *The Middle Passage*. His career has taken Naipaul out of the lighted circle around his own Trinidadian home to retrace the road that brought people to that point, and to try to foresee the destination toward which not only former colonials but civilization as a whole seems to be hurtling in its rickety bus. In both fiction and nonfiction, Naipaul concentrates on individuals and their responses to the pressures and frustrations of their imperfect societies. Because he is such a good reporter — compiling facts, recording details, describing with minute accuracy what he observes, and writing with complete command and control of language and style — Naipaul seems to set himself up as an authority, when in fact, he never claims to offer more than personal impressions which may even appear self-contradictory. (For instance, he comments that Trinidad society denies itself heroes (MP 41–42), but later laments that it wishes to be heroically portrayed (MP 68–69) without attempting to reconcile the two assertions — not a difficult task.) When the strain of a prolonged journey begins to tell on Naipaul, making him testy, impatient and withdrawn, he does not claim to be a balanced or even diligent reporter. The structure of the book reflects his weariness: Chapters 5 and 6 have no inscriptions: "Martinique" does not even have a subtitle — it is as if that very French name says enough for Naipaul who rejects that island society as the most closed of all.

The carefully selected epigraphs for earlier chapters and for the book as a whole may be misunderstood by some readers. Naipaul's ironic intention in quoting Trollope's lyricism regarding Demarara is hard to miss, but in quoting Froude's unflattering statements, Naipaul is not necessarily invoking him as a corroborating witness. In *An Area of Darkness* Naipaul contrasts Jane Austen's use of the word "British" with E. M. Forster's, showing how a geographical designation has come by degrees, in the writings of a series of intervening authors, to describe an entire way of life. Froude is one of the writers who have lost the talent for discovering a new perspective on changing society and who accept unquestioningly the English national myth. A symptom of English narcissism, this failure restricts English awareness of the effects of imperial expansion on their own attitudes. Froude's indictment of the West Indies is an indictment of English colonialism whether he was aware of it or not. Critics such as Gareth Griffiths (1978, 83) believe that Naipaul "seems to accept a West Indian responsibility for the futility he discovers . . . and, implicitly, to blame this futility on the pettiness and self-lacerating snobbery of the West Indians themselves". He goes on to present as a contrast the attitudes of George Lamming. I am not convinced, however, that Lamming's assessment is so different from Naipaul's although their differences of style may make them seem so. Like Lamming, Naipaul pins responsibility on colonial policy, the suppression of identity and the encouragement of a sense of guilt and shame at not being English. Naipaul's view of history lifts the burden of blame for the sterility of island life from the shoulders of contemporary islanders. What Naipaul does blame them for is their failure or refusal to recognize cultural barrenness. The epigraphs to the second chapter of *The Middle Passage* demonstrate Naipaul's awareness that long before the West Indians, the Israelites and the Britons were doubly enslaved as they attempted to absorb the cultures of their masters. In an approach that may originate in his Hindu background, Naipaul often looks on the present moment as a very brief stage in an endless chain of events: cycles repeat themselves, the end of one triggers the beginning of the next. In *The Mimic Men*, Ralph Singh's tormenting vision of disorder and chaos is relieved only by his discovery of the roots of the present in the soil of the past.

Chapter 4's epigraph – James Joyce's words, "My soul frets in the shadow of his language" – raises another issue on which Naipaul has been misunderstood. Despite possessing a more truly cosmopolitan society, featuring a far greater degree of racial equality and assimilation than the other colonies, the Negroes of Surinam advocate the adoption of a local dialect as the national language in place of Dutch. *Talkie-talkie* seems incapable, however, of the subtlety required by people who have moved in wider circles, and would cut Surinamers off entirely from communication with the rest of the world. Naipaul's attitude to Trinidadian dialect is similar. He is well aware of the role language plays in establishing and reinforcing colonial supremacy over various peoples, of how using another's language robs people of their identities; he is also aware of how the tension between dialect and formal English reinforces class barriers. References to language abound in "A Flag on the Island": Selma's admiration of Priest's ability to "use language well" and to sound educated is contrasted with his flair for slipping in and out of dialect; the theme is developed as Blackwhite abandons his English settings to write about the people who "don't exist". Frankie urges Blackwhite to stop trying to be white but then finds him too black when he announced: " . . . I begin to feel that what is wrong with my books is not me, but the language I use. You know, in English, black is a damn bad word. You talk of a black deed. How then can I write in this language?" (FI 204). Clearly, as Naipaul parodies the representatives of Foundationland, we are to see the impossibility of any of Blackwhite's perspectives leading to self-definition and recognition for his people. In his early novels, Naipaul's use of Trinidadian dialect – albeit in a modified form – shows that he can delight in its colourful and expressive qualities; using dialect for comic effect does not denigrate it when the author regards the achievement of comedy as among his highest goals. On the other hand, Naipaul is unable to join West Indian writers like Samuel Selvon (1972, 124) who advocate the additional use of dialect for narrative and descriptive functions to promote self-respect in their people by encouraging them to regard dialect as a rich and expressive idiom, rather than as the outcome of years of illiteracy and cultural deprivation. It is in fact both a gift and a curse, in that it does express the identity of the society in which it grew and, at the same time, restricts that society's communication with the rest of the English-speaking world. Naipaul's expressed objectives as a writer, that he must try to be a clear-sighted observer and ordering chronicler of experience, do not allow Selvon's use of dialect for it would require limiting the perspective of narrator and the accessability of text.

Language is only a symptom of the lack of identity, of

pride and of self-confidence which, in Naipaul's view is the inevitable outcome of the founding of a colonial society, and especially one based on slavery. Slavery is at once the cornerstone on which the West Indian colonies were built and the rock on which their various societies foundered. The strength of Naipaul's conviction is demonstrated by the intensity with which he writes of the torture of slaves in the Luisa Calderon section of *The Loss of El Dorado*, and makes reference to the slave period in *The Mimic Men* and to the slave trade in *A Bend in the River*. To Naipaul, the emigrants from St Kitts are voluntarily undertaking another middle passage; he implies that these anxious, frightened people cannot rediscover in England the identity left behind in Africa, that they are running from one slavery into another without even knowing what it is they are seeking. The St Kitts section of *The Middle Passage* abounds in statements and images that will later provide the basis of the story "Tell Me Who to Kill" (*In a Free State*): the view of London's grimy backyards and busy streets from the Southhampton train, the madmen and their keepers who may have contributed to the concept of Frank's character, the working class faces and clothes in the wedding picture of Philip's daughter which seem to foreshadow the milieu Dayo enters in the story. Most of all, Dayo's brother's story demonstrates that "the West Indian, knowing only the values of money and race, [a phrase that is repeated often in *The Loss of El Dorado*] is lost as soon as he steps out of his own society into one with more complex criteria" (MP 22).

Naipaul is scathingly bitter about the atmosphere created by slavery in the West Indies and about the stratification of relationships based on gradations of colour.

> There is a myth, derived from the Southern states of America of the gracious culture of the slave society. In the West Indian islands slavery and the latifundia created only grossness, men who ate "like cormorants" and drank "like porpoises"; a society without standards, without noble aspirations, nourished by greed and cruelty; a society of whose illiteracy metropolitan administrators continued to

complain right until the middle of the last century; illiteracy which encouraged Governor Vaughan of Jamaica to suggest the placing of a collection of books in the English language "in the most conspicuous places where such of the gentry as are studious may always resort, since there is nothing more ridiculous than ignorance in a person of quality"; grossness to which traveller after traveller testifies ... (MP 28)

Naipaul himself recognizes the hysteria in this outburst; he fled these attitudes and feared meeting them again, but now he recognizes their roots in slavery. In each of the countries he visited, Naipaul found slight variations on the theme composed by slavery. Trinidadians have hardly any memory of slavery, but in places where slavery was long established and more brutally administered, such as British Guiana (Guyana) or Surinam, attitudes are different: "The very word 'Negro', because of its association with slavery, is resented by many black Guianese; the preferred word is 'African', which will cause deep offence in Trinidad" (MP 99). Independence to a black Guianese means simply that he will be left alone to withdraw from society as the prospectors of the interior or the residents of Negro fishing villages have done, but in Surinam only a few, *de luie neger van Coronie,* follow the pattern of withdrawal and indolence. Following the example of the escaped slaves who became bush-Negroes, recalling and recreating their religion, language and pride, the metropolitan Negro leads a Nationalist movement rejecting the borrowed Dutch culture. Jamaica's Ras Tafarianism is to Naipaul only a proletarian extension of Nationalism in Surinam, carried to its crazy and logical limit; the real tragedy of the Caribbean is in the conflict between these attitudes and those of the middle-class West Indian nationalist who "is concerned only to deny the existence of a specially Negro personality" (MP 219).

Naipaul found the effects of slavery most stifling in Martinique. In *The Loss of El Dorado* Naipaul insists that the worst brutality towards slaves was brought to Trinidad when immigrants from Martinique arrived, and in his fiction the descendants of former masters carry French names, Deschampneufs in *The Mimic Men* and Grandlieu in *A Flag on the Island*. In Martinique every variation of colour is noted and catalogued so that no one who carries the slightest trace of Negro blood is allowed to pass for white. As he watches a folk dance rehearsal where old women practise the bel-air, Naipaul is appalled that "to this mincing mimicry the violence and improvisation and awesome skill of African dancing had been reduced" (MP 209). So the former masters seek to retain their superior position. Ex-slaves knew nothing of Africa, even felt contempt for the image of it presented by white society, but their whiteness was second-hand and no alteration could make it fit. In *The Mimic Men* Ralph Singh recalls Browne's delight with his success as a singer of coon songs and his later anguish at having been part of this mockery of his race.

The condition of Guyana's Amerindians parallels that of the slave for they are also being dragged into a European society and deprived of their own culture. The amusing details of Naipaul's guide's pyjamas, toothbrush and Colgate carried to the middle of dense forest reveal the very serious loss of culture, confusion and self-contempt which lead the boy to reject Amerindian girls as possible wives. Such is the harm done by well-meaning Christian missionaries echoing the whole colonial experience. The importance of this view to Naipaul is apparent in that he closes the book with the attempt of a Gideon to convert him to Christianity. The irony is obvious, for Naipaul is at once extremely vulnerable in lacking any faith of his own and deeply aware of the need to reject an identity destroying faith that belongs to someone else.

All of these observations lead Naipaul to conclude that the problem addressed by Black Power or nationalist movements is not political, economic, or racial. It is the bewilderment and irritability of people whose identity has been so profoundly distorted. After the 1970 Black Power riots in Trinidad, he wrote for the *New York Review of Books* that it is not black political power the islanders want, since they already have a black government, but the glamour of a cause, a crusade and messiahs (OB 246). Similarly, in *Guerrillas* the slogan "After Israel, Africa" means nothing more than a vague Biblical promise to the people. Again we reach the essence of the problem of language: equality and assimilation are "attractive but only underline the loss, since to accept assimilation is in a way to accept a permanent inferiority"; on the other hand, the alternatives are also unacceptable in that Europe is now so much "in the Nationalist's bones [that] he feels Africa and Asia are contemptible and ridiculous" (MP 165).

The parish pump politics Naipaul observes in his journey through the Caribbean seem unlikely to unite the people. Politicians are petty at best, predatory and corrupt at worst, playing on and inflaming racial antagonisms. Voters, like those in Elvira, demand paternalism. Naipaul's irony, wry humour and gift for phrase-making are evident in the line, "every new voter regards himself as a pressure group" (MP 120). But he seems to genuinely regret a lost chance in British Guiana where the split, along racial lines, between Jagan and Burnham builds "pressures which might easily overwhelm the country" (MP 133). At Oxford in 1953, these men had impressed Naipaul; they had a case to present and the country seemed to have some forward impetus. A similar situation is at the thematic centre of *The Mimic Men* where (unlike the early satirical fiction) humour does not mask the author's conviction that such conditions open the gates to devastating corruption and possible violent confrontation.

Trinidadians attempt to create an identity that is unique and whole by the creation of what Naipaul believes to be an artificial local culture from the steel band, calypso and limbo. He objects to it as the bastard offspring of a local prostitute and an American tourist – and explores the processes of this mating, with foreign grant-givers as midwives, in "A Flag on the Island". He does not believe that these are the elements of the day-to-day life of ordinary people which is the only valid source of culture; ordinary day-to-day living is done in a cheap imitation of an American advertising agency's model home. What was vital and exciting about calypso – its savage satire, or about steel bands – their violence, has been watered down for tourist consumption and has lost contact with reality. The new colonialism, the new enslavement is the result of tourism which, like the old, even deprives peasant farmers of their land as it is sold to developers.

In his fiction, Naipaul had already portrayed the low standards of the mass media in Trinidad. In *The Middle Passage* he makes explicit his objections to syndicated columns from England and America, Hollywood gossip columns, radio soap operas, and old American films which surround Trinidadians with escapists' dreams of a world they desperately try to emulate. While Naipaul's account of the reactions of movie-goers to certain lines of dialogue are amusing – "When Bogart, without turning, coolly rebuked a pawing Lauren Bacall, 'You're breathin' down mah neck,' Trinidad adopted him as its own. 'That is man!' the audience cried" (MP 59) – it is easy to understand that this media-created, imitative society stifled him personally and poses a real threat to anyone who strives for excellence. These cheating fantasies in his background create an important theme in his work, one born of anxiety which he shares with Frankie in "A Flag on the Island": " . . . the blurring of fantasy with reality . . . gives me the feeling of helplessness . . . " (FI 158). He realizes that in their identification with nonheroic fantasy heroes, Trinidadians are contributing to their own frustrations: "They can never completely identify themselves with what they read in magazines or see in films. Their frustrations can only deepen, for their minds are closed to everything else. Reality is always separate from the ideal; but in Trinidad this fantasy is a form of masochism and is infinitely more cheating than the fantasy which makes the poor delight in films about rich or makes the English singer use an American accent" (MP 65). In his novel *Fireflies* (1971), Shiva Naipaul's character Romesh is entirely predicated on his addiction to movies – to the point that he eventually disappears. These cheating fantasies are different, however, from the proper exercise of fantasy, described by Naipaul elsewhere (OB 23–29). Despite the danger of allowing fantasy to become dominant, the exercise of the imagination involves readers in active participation in a book and turns the fiction into a reality greater than the mere recognition of elements of readers' experience. A word like "Jasmine" may have a life of its own divorced from the common reality of everyday existence, so Naipaul discovers that he is unable to bring the word and the object together after years of knowing only the word. He warns that turning English literature to social comment excludes fantasy until "Writing will become Arthur Miller's definition of a newspaper: a nation talking to itself. And even those who have the key will be able only to witness, not to participate" (OB 28). One must judge the context to decide whether Naipaul's use of the word "fantasy" is pejorative – those cheating fantasies – or whether he intends to invoke the imagination; most often he employs the negative connotations.

When considered together, Naipaul's fiction and nonfiction provide a very profound statement of the interrelation of fact and fiction, of the existence of an element of fantasy in many views of reality. In writing of Negro attempts to join the mainstream of Christian–Hellenic tradition, to ignore the brutality, the insults and the prejudices of past and present, Naipaul says, "this willingness to forget and ignore is part of the West Indian fantasy" (MP 67). Always he seems concerned to show the brutality behind the romance, the unpleasant reality behind the gracious myth: as the *Francisco Bobadilla* enters the Gulf with its load of St Kitts emigrants from Eden, Naipaul repeats Columbus's belief that in the Gulf of Paria he had discovered "the approaches of the terrestrial paradise". Again and again he counterpoints story against story to reveal the society's conflicting visions of reality. The constant use of newspaper stories, quotations from speeches, repetition of

conversations with people at all levels, and references to
Caribbean journals make it easy to share Naipaul's sense
that there is no one truth, one reality in this world. "'The
Land of Calypso is not a copy-writer's phrase. It is one side
of the truth, and it was this gaiety, so inexplicable to me
who had remembered it as the land of failures, which now,
on my return, assaulted me" (MP 54). The two sides of truth
are also apparent when Naipaul condemns Trinidadians
for provincialism and closed minds (MP 61) and shortly
later delights in their cosmopolitan tolerance of all sorts of
people and behaviour (MP 77). The provincialism is more a
quality of the society as a whole and the cosmopolitanism
an individual trait, but they are contradictory impulses of
the sort that may be observed in all human gatherings. So,
in "factually analysing" the societies of the West Indies,
Naipaul articulates the conclusions he reached in his fiction, the conclusions that were the source of both satire
and tragicomedy. The contradictory impulses of provincialism and cosmopolitanism created Ganesh, in whom readers delight even as they condemn what he becomes. The
tragic legacy of the slave society and the indenture are Mr
Biswas's inheritance. *The Middle Passage* is Naipaul's first
attempt to explore his observations of society in nonfiction;
it is also an indication of his growing political concern.

Part Two

Point of Origin

Turning to the Metropolis: *Mr Stone and the Knights Companion*

In 1962 V. S. Naipaul went to India and lived for four months at Srinagar where, while he continued to collect material for *An Area of Darkness,* he wrote *Mr Stone and the Knights Companion* (1963). In this novel the ex-colonial Naipaul abandons the postcolonial setting to which he had hitherto confined himself, and turns for the first time to the metropolis for his subject. Following *A House for Mr Biswas, Mr Stone* shows Naipaul's growing compassion for individuals and continues his investigations of the effects of social pressures on them. Not surprisingly, given the circumstances of writing, neither the novel nor the protagonist seem particularly "English" despite the author's typically accurate and detailed description of setting and characters. Rather, Mr Stone's way of thinking and the "philosophy" from which the novel thematically proceeds seem, in many ways, Indian or Hindu. Mr Stone's attempt to change the pattern of events and assert the individual's importance is Western; his acceptance of the impossibility of the task is Hindu. In a way Naipaul seems to be trying to trace to their sources two contradictory streams of Trinidad's cultural amalgam, and in doing so to penetrate the historical darkness in which, generally, the colonial pursues his existence.

While Mr Biswas had a limited and personal goal — to obtain a home for his family and a place within it for himself — Mr Stone seeks, in the outcome unsuccessfully, to fulfil the larger ambition of immortalizing himself by leaving behind a noble scheme which will benefit all the retiring employees of the firm for which he has worked in obscurity for many years. Spurred on by his own awareness of approaching uselessness and death, Mr Stone formulates a program to hold at bay the end of an active life for himself and others. Despite the nobility of his goals, Mr Stone is not a protagonist of heroic proportions: he is a self-centred, fearful, fanciful, fussy and habit-ridden man. His name, suggesting impassivity and permanence, is belied by his inner turmoil and awareness of transience. Naipaul makes him appear ridiculous in his encounters with the black cat, and insensitive and envious in his outburst against Whymper, whose name appropriately suggests childish clinging despite his busy bluster and assumed sophistication. When Stone's neighbours, the Midgeleys (the name suggests their smallness of mind), announce their plan to destroy the black cat which is no longer wanted and with which Mr Stone has come to identify himself, his pity is only the expression of his self-centred emotionalism. When the cat is gone, he feels horror at his failure to protect it, self-disgust, and fear, yet within minutes he is listening to Margaret's plan to knock down the Midgeleys' derelict fence so the new occupants will have to effect repairs.

Although revealing weakness in his character in accordance with Naipaul's intentions, Mr Stone's thoughts while shaving do not ring quite true: "And gradually, what he had at first thought with such anger and pity – 'You will soon be dead; – became mere words, whose import he had to struggle fully to feel, for they released only a pure sweet emotion of sadness in which the object of his thought was forgotten, a short-lived emotion that he sought to stimulate by additional words, which he at first rejected but later came to accept with sad satisfaction: 'You will soon be dead. Like me'" (SKC 142). These reflections are more appropriate to Forster's Dr Aziz in *A Passage to India* than to the English Mr Stone, for whom feeling might be present but not, probably, articulated. In contrast, Doris Lessing's convincing character Rose (*In Pursuit of the English*, 1960) states merely that she's "got the 'ump" and lapses into silence, begging the narrator not to make her think of disturbing things. Naipaul offers his own comment on his apparent inability to penetrate the closed facades of English streets: "It is a matter of climate. In a warm country life is conducted out of doors. Windows are open, doors are open. People sit in open verandas and cafes. You know your neighbour's business and he knows yours. It is easy for the visitor to get to know the country. He is continually catching people in off-duty positions. In England everything goes on behind closed doors. The man from the warm country automatically leaves the door open behind him. The man from the cold country closes it: it has become a matter of etiquette" (OB 14). Consequently Mr Stone is not so much a character as an evocation of the stereotype of middle-class British white-collar respectability, with tensions and insecurities which seem more Naipaul's vision of the abyss than his own. In contrast, Lessing starts with her awareness of her essential difference from fellow boarder Rose and then puts aside all stereotyped views of English working class girls to reveal a paradoxical mixture of sincere honesty and profound cynicism, warm tolerance and cold prejudice, vulnerability and opportunism, miserliness and petty extravagance. Naipaul's accounts of English boarding house life – in short stories "Greenie and Yellow" and "The Perfect Tenants" (*A Flag on the Island*) or in *The Mimic Men* – seem never to go beyond detailed, but still superficial, observation. In *The Mimic Men* he calls attention to this deficiency himself when Ralph Singh repeatedly describes fellow boarders as having only two dimensions. Naipaul's accurate observation and scrupulous recording of detail force belief in the characterization, but he fails to achieve here the intimacy with his characters that is a feature of *A House for Mr Biswas*.

Naipaul may offer his version of the myth of English reticence in Mr Stone's belief that to reveal a true emotion is to betray it, but this theme has far greater importance in coming to an understanding of the darkness of Naipaul's vision. As Mr Stone plants out seedlings, he is moved to speak of the changes in nature:

> "Doesn't it make you think, though?" he said. "Just the other day the tree was so bare. And the dahlia bush. Like dead grass all winter. I mean, don't you think it's the same with us? That we too will have our spring?"
>
> He stopped. And there was silence. About them outlines blurred, windows brightened. The words he had just spok-

en lingered in his head. They embarrassed him. The silence of the women embarrassed him. (SKC 146)

Margaret's only comment, behind his back, is in her "party voice", "'Well, I think it's a lotta rubbish.'" And Mr Stone recalls another effort he made to communicate true feeling – to capture the magic of his first glimpse of Cobh – which drew the comment, "'Too self-conscious and namby-pamby'". The tragedy for Mr Stone lies in his feeling that the Knights Companion project has been similarly corrupted by being exposed. Essentially this is the fear of the writer or any creator whose work may be misunderstood, but at the same time their creativity is an attempt to achieve immortality. Naipaul recognizes this impulse in his father's attempts to write and in his own: " . . . what is astonishing to me is that, with the vocation, he so accurately transmitted to me – without saying anything about it – his hysteria from the time when I didn't know him: his fear of extinction" (FC 84). In this context, Mr Stone's anxiety becomes an expression of existential angst, and this somewhat ridiculous man becomes one of Naipaul's most sympathetic portraits.

> And now he saw that in that project of the Knights Companion which had contributed so much to his restlessness, the only pure moments, the only true moments were those he had spent in the study, writing out of a feeling whose depth he realized only as he wrote. What he had written was a faint and artificial rendering of that emotion, and the scheme as the Unit had practised it was but a shadow of that shadow. All passion had disappeared. It had taken incidents like the Prisoner of Muswell Hill to remind him, concerned only with administration and success, of the emotion that had gone before. All that he had done, and even the anguish he was feeling now, was a betrayal of that good emotion. All action, all creation was a betrayal of feeling and truth. And in the process of this betrayal his world had come tumbling about him. There remained to him nothing to which he could anchor himself. (SKC 149)

The novel closes with a statement of the impossibility of

making one's mark through creation, a theme in which the Indian perspective of this book again seems apparent.

Structurally, this novel recalls the Hindu emphasis on cyclical repetition which is both more specific and more encompassing than a simple recognition of seasonal cycles or Christian concepts of life-death-rebirth. Mr Stone was not always alarmed by the passing of time: reminders – changes in the tree which is a central image of the novel, for example – had been "reminders of solidity, continuity and flow" (SKC 20). Before meeting Mrs Springer, he had been accustomed to counting years and tabulating experiences, hoarding them and reliving them, caring little for the present until it was past. Mr Stone's reaction to the triumph of having his cat and cheese story taken up by Mrs Springer followed by the disgrace of his failed pun on nuts, the experience of exhilaration followed by dissatisfaction foreshadows the outcome of the Knights Companion project. The first Tomlinson party foreshadows the second. Between them Mr Stone makes his bid to overcome his fear of the vulnerability of the flesh, the terror of mortality – fears he shares with many of Naipaul's protagonists.

His first step is to marry Mrs Springer, whose name ironically suggests the life, vitality, and seasonal renewal Mr Stone tries to capture, but immediately he finds the responsible role of protector thrust upon him. He realizes that tampering with the patterns of existence threatens continuity itself: " . . . communing with his tree, he could not help contrasting its serenity with his disturbance. It would shed its leaves in time; but this would lead to a renewal which would bring greater strength. Responsibility had come too late to him. He had broken the pattern of his life, and this break could at best be only healed. It would not lead to renewal. So the tree no longer comforted. It reproached" (SKC 45). Marriage does not bring the protection Mr Stone sought. In fact, on their delayed honeymoon trip to Cornwall, he has the most upsetting experiences of all. Lost, he and Margaret try to ask directions of a farm labourer who disappears into the smoke of a fire; enveloped in the smoke themselves, "They were robbed of earth and reality. He was robbed of judgment, of the will to act." Even after reality reasserts itself, "Mr Stone never doubted that the incident could be rationally and simply explained. But that hallucinatory moment, when earth and life and senses had been suspended, remained with him. It was like an experience of nothingness, an experience of death" (SKC 64). One might add that it is like an experience of Hindu Maya, the Illusory.

Also on the honeymoon trip, Mr Stone encounters a double in the "mouse", recently retired and in the keeping of fat and complacent women. The scene releases his ambivalent feelings about women; loathing and fearing them, he still clings to the comfort of Margaret and his sister. A constant image in *Mr Stone and the Knights Companion* is the threatening, idle woman. Mr Stone's neighbour, the Monster who is "enormously fat" and whose only function seems to be daintily to water her flower garden contrasts with the Male who is always at work on his house. Tony Tomlinson's widow Grace blooms almost obscenely. Besides these two and Margaret, there are his widowed sister Olive, Gwen and Miss Millington. Surrounding him, it seems that these women are in some way responsible for the death or absence of their men, as if they outlive them only because their parasitic existence conserves their life force. Images of rapacious feeding are often associated with women and suggest their voracious devouring of a man's spirit. Only the relationship with his sister Olive is slightly different in that it calls to mind soothing memories of the past. By burning Olive's cake – another reminder of past and stability – Margaret threatens those memories, symbolically destroying his special appreciation of the past and forcing him to recognize the present. Similarly, Gwen disrupts Mr Stone's relationship with Olive, and he maliciously encourages her passion for chocolate in order to keep her as unattractive as possible.

Nearly half of this novel is devoted to portraying Mr Stone's transition from calm living in the past to fear of the future. Unlike Mr Biswas and Ralph Singh who apprehend chaos from early in their lives, Mr Stone, in an established and structured society, has a concept of order which breaks down only as his own physical vulnerability becomes evident. The second half of the book concerns his attempt to foil the passing of time and his subsequent disillusionment when his scheme is corrupted by those who fail to appreciate the anguish which prompted its conception. Briefly, though, the act of writing brings joy, release and calm as it does to many of Naipaul's protagonists. Once again the mere appearance of words on a page is a source of pleasure: "He wrote, he corrected, he re-wrote and fatigue never came to him. His handwriting changed. Losing its neatness, becoming cramped and crabbed, some of its loops wilfully inelegant, it yet acquired a more pleasant, more authoritative appearance, even a symmetry. The lines were straight; the margins made themselves. The steady patterning of each page was a joy, the scratch of soft pencil on receiving paper, the crossings out, the corrections in balloons in the margin" (SKC 73). When the process of creation is finished, exhaustion, sadness and emptiness return, warnings of disillusionment still to come despite apparent success and harmony. In the midst of savouring his triumph, Mr Stone is momentarily aware of betraying his scheme himself, of straining his relationship with Olive, of alarm at the story of the Prisoner, of growing discomfort at the intimacy with Whymper. Significantly, as the pilot scheme is concluded, the leaves on the schoolyard tree fade and fall. After the final triumph of the Christmas season, everything abruptly turns to dust and the novel is dominated by death. Ironically, while the tree heralds the approach of another spring, the cat is destroyed and Mr Stone feels only emptiness, a sense of his own futility, anxiety and anger. Although the passages expressing Mr Stone's disillusioned belief that true emotion is betrayed by its expression occur at this stage, they do not strike the note on which the novel concludes. As he walks home through long, dull city streets, Mr Stone hopes to numb the pain of disillusionment with exhaustion.

> And as he walked through the long, dull streets, as with each step he felt his hips and thighs and calves and toes working, his mood changed, and he had a vision of the city such as he had had once before, at the first dinner party he and Margaret had given. . . . He stripped the city of all that was enduring and saw that all that was not flesh was of no importance to man. All that mattered was man's own frailty and corruptibility. The order of the universe, to which he had sought to ally himself, was not his order. So much he had seen before. But now he saw, too, that it was not by creation that man demonstrated his power and defied his hostile order, but by destruction. By damming the river, by destroying the mountain, by so scarring the face of the earth that Nature's attempt to reassert herself became a mockery. (SKC 158–59)

V. S. Pritchett (1963, 832) has suggested that "Anyone with will and vigour left in him would say the very opposite: construction. In a way that weakens his work. Naipaul's observation inclines him to weariness and is at odds with his imagination. His mistrust of the continuous constructing will may be something he gets from his Hindu upbringing". If will and vigour are already deserting Naipaul at this relatively early stage of his career and weariness is weakening his work, the implications for his later work are serious, and need to be kept in mind in consideration of his subsequent writing. My own opinion is that the conflict between imagination and mistrust of creativity invigorates Naipaul's work; it is the source of much of the tension which makes his fiction and nonfiction alike stimulating and exciting.

Returning to the Indianness of this English novel, the statement of the futility, the meaninglessness of human endeavour with which the novel closes is remarkably similar in tone, though not in specific content, to a passage from R. K. Narayan's *The Printer of Malgudi* (1957, 261) to which Naipaul refers years later in *India: A Wounded Civilization* (24–25). As a mad artist, Ravi, undergoes a violent exorcism, Srinivas, the printer, has a vision of the sweep of Indian history from the creation of the Sarayu by Sri Rama to the arrival of Christian missionaries followed by soldiers and merchants. "The recent vision had given him a view in which it seemed to him all the same whether they thwacked Ravi with a cane or whether they left him alone, whether he was mad or sane – all that seemed unimportant and not worth bothering about. The whole of eternity stretched ahead of one; there was plenty of time to shake off all follies. Madness or sanity, suffering or happiness seemed all the same. . . . It didn't make the slightest difference in the long run – in the rush of eternity nothing mattered." Nearing home Mr Stone feels that he may possess that power of destruction; however, at home he finds the house empty but for the young black cat. His flash of fear at finding the cat recalls the opening incident of the book before it dissolves into guilt and a gesture from which the cat flees. Mr Stone's final perception is that "He was no destroyer. Once before the world had collapsed about him. But he had survived. And he had no doubt that in time calm would come to him again" (SKC 160). Srinivas and Mr Stone both arrive at inactivity but Mr Stone, Westerner, still centres his thoughts on the individual while Srinivas, Easterner, loses individuality in the sweep of eternity. Mr Stone perceives that huge tide, but he cannot quite abandon the dream of stemming its flow. He gives up his own attempt, realizing that he is no destroyer, but he still believes that some other can affect Nature's cycles. Mr Stone's world view seems to blend Hindu elements into a Western conception of the importance of the individual. Like many of his characters who seek order through the act of writing, Naipaul himself appears to create the fictional character, Mr Stone, in an attempt to resolve his own difficulties of perspective. Probably much of this process was unconscious; *An Area of Darkness* indicates that the threat of India to Naipaul's stability was so powerfully felt at the time he retreated to Srinagar that anything written then must have been coloured by his disturbance. Perhaps Naipaul tried to escape India by writing an "English" novel which came to be dominated by the philosophical preoccupations of this period of his life.

Among the elements in this novel which remind one that
it was written while Naipaul was engaged in the search for
his Indian roots are the emphasis in both structure and imagery – particularly the imagery of the tree – on the cyclical nature of life; Mr Stone's painful perception of personal
transience; the use of illusion to bring about a clearer
understanding of experience; and the concluding paradox
in which destruction and not creation is stated to be the only way to make one's mark on the universe. At first in *An
Area of Darkness* he claims he was ignorant of Hinduism
(AD 35), but within a few pages he comes close to reversing
his statement (AD 38); later he identifies in himself the
very quality that disturbs him most in Indians: "To preserve
this conception of India as a country still whole, historical
facts had not been suppressed. They had been acknowledged and ignored; and it was only in India that I was able to
see this as part of the Indian ability to retreat, the ability
genuinely not to see what was obvious: with others a foundation of neurosis, but with Indians only part of a greater
philosophy of despair, leading to passivity, detachment,
acceptance. It is only now, as the impatience of the observer is dissipated in the process of writing and self-inquiry,
that I see how much this philosophy had also been mine"
(AD 198).

The many varieties of Hinduism practised in India place
differing interpretations on human experience, yet share a
common base from which they examine life. Life is a "sea
of change" – *samsāra*; the emphasis here is on transience,
the inability of an individual to effect a permanent change
or to master the flow in any way. He will continue to be re-
born in fulfilment of his *karma* until he achieves release
through the transcendent state, *moksa*. Life is also frequently seen as illusion, *Maya,* a concept Naipaul refers to
several times in *An Area of Darkness.* Questions about the
nature of reality seem to prompt lines like these in *Mr
Stone*: "Of these familiar things, however, he could no
longer feel himself a part. They had the heightened reality,
which is like unreality, that a fever gives to everyday hap-

penings" (SKC 30–31). More important is Mr Stone's repeated vision of a city stripped of all its physical accoutrements, emptied of everything but its citizens. Physical objects lose their reassuring reality and Mr Stone perceives that "all that was solid and immutable and enduring about the world, all to which man linked himself . . . flattered only to deceive" (SKC 53). The illusion of being divorced from reality at Chysauster stays with Mr Stone and seems more real than rationality, than reality itself. Even Miss Millington's whispered (but overheard) conversation reminds one that there are many versions of "reality". The difficulty of knowing what is real or true is expressed in Hinduism by the duality of a goddess like Kali who is both creator, life force, and destroyer.

Accepting his own mortality, the transience of things of this world, their illusory quality and his own frailty and corruptibility, at the end of the novel Mr Stone has relinquished the illusion of power symbolized by his fantasy of flying in armchair or train seat over the heads of others, and he has given up the hope that he will effect any changes through a great action of creation or of destruction. The narrator/protagonist of Naipaul's most recent novel, *A Bend in the River*, similarly grapples with doubts about the reality of anything other than awareness of one's own physical existence and also concludes that all one can do is carry on with the business of living. Both Mr Stone and the Muslim Salim simply accept and survive which is the course prescribed by Hinduism. The religion offers the reward of transcendence, *moksa*, salvation from the endless cycle, in which the pilgrim discovers the Reality beyond self and beyond the word of *saṃsāra*. Naipaul offers nothing but survival and calm.

At the conclusion of *An Area of Darkness* Naipaul studies a piece of Indian cloth, the gift of a new friend on his departure and believes that it contains the clues which would unravel the mysteries of experience if he could only make the right cut. But he knows that he cannot. Finally he states his awareness of India's effect on him. "The world is illusion, the Hindus say. We talk of despair, but true despair lies too deep for formulation. It is only now, as my experience of India defined itself more properly against my own homelessness, that I saw how close in the past year I had been to the total Indian negation, how much it had become the basis of thought and feeling. And already, with this awareness, in a world where illusion could only be a concept and not something felt in the bones, it was slipping away from me. I felt it as something true which I could never adequately express and never seize again" (AD 280). This paragraph seems to offer at least a partial explanation of the unique role filled by *Mr Stone and the Knights Companion* in the body of Naipaul's work. The novel, despite the setting in which Naipaul wrote it, does not deal with the aftermath of colonialism; despite Naipaul's mood and objectives at the time of its writing, his protagonist is not a man without roots seeking a home and identity; despite Naipaul's growing interest in social and political analysis, it is not in any way political. The relationship of reality and fantasy is treated metaphysically, illusion is deeply felt, not "only a concept" as it is in the material, literal West. Naipaul's other works deal with questions of what is real and what is fantasy, and of the extent to which fiction captures truth in a way fact cannot, but only in *Mr Stone and the Knights Companion* is the treatment so abstract. The novel is a statement of Naipaul's view of man's place in his world which may be applied to any man, anywhere. It is a bleak vision, lacking in optimism and gaiety, in which man struggles against enormous odds to make his mark. In the end he may hope only for the calm of resignation as he accepts his own futility. A novelist who declares that true emotion is betrayed by its expression, and that creation is powerless to sustain might seem to be painting himself into a corner. One of the most fascinating ambivalences in Naipaul's writing lies in the contrast of these themes with his practice. In interviews he explicitly enunciates a belief in the writer's obligation to order experience for his readers and a conviction that in our society the writer must take the place of the tribal wise man. Much of the tension in Naipaul's writing and its energy are the result of conflict between a sense of man's helplessness and futility and his powerful impulse to create.

Response to India: *An Area of Darkness*

An Area of Darkness, like *The Middle Passage*, explores a myth in an attempt to discover the reality behind it. This time the myth is Naipaul's own creation, wrought from his family's portrayal of India. India became a snow-capped Himalayan peak in the background of a picture of a deity he could not worship. It existed in a few artefacts but, in spite of study of maps and books, it never assumed a concrete reality for him, any more than it does for Ralph Singh in *The Mimic Men*. In a *Times Literary Supplement* article (reprinted in *The Overcrowded Barracoon*), as he toys with the many meanings and variations of the word "Indian" and engages in self-satire, Naipaul reveals the ultimate loneliness of the colonial. His personal experience in India of seeming to glimpse a past life and experience as he half comprehends a few words of Hindi leads to the conclusion that "for the colonial there can be no true return" (OB 38). Because of the erosion of Indian culture (earlier portrayed in *A House for Mr Biswas*), a myth of India was all that was possible in Trinidad. Others — George Lamming, Edward Brathwaite — portray such cultural loss as a process of confrontation and conflict, and question Naipaul's concentration on the Indian community in isolation. He explains that " . . . to see the attenuation of the culture of my childhood as the result of a dramatic confrontation of opposed worlds would be to distort the reality. To me the worlds were juxtaposed and mutually exclusive. One gradually contracted. It had to; it fed only memories and its completeness was only apparent. It was yielding not to attack but to a type of seepage from the other" (AD 37).

Exploring myths, searching for roots may start with "safe"

attempts to describe, analyse and explain, but Naipaul discovers, as have many others before him and later, that the real subject of study is himself, his response to the "homeland" which is no home to him. While he recognizes in himself ways of thinking that he identifies as Indian (witness, *Mr Stone and the Knights Companion*), he feels that he can never remain in that world of the interior where Indians barricade themselves from the perception of the unpleasant. "But I had learned to see; I could not deny what I saw" (AD 225). The result is that, at times, he literally does not know where to place himself in his writing.

> They tell the story of the Sikh who, returning to India after many years, sat down among his suitcases on the Bombay docks and wept. He had forgotten what Indian poverty was like. It is an Indian story, in its arrangement of figure and properties, its melodrama, its pathos. It is Indian above all in its attitude to poverty as something which, thought about from time to time in the midst of other preoccupations, releases the sweetest of emotions. This is poverty, our especial poverty, and how sad it is! Poverty not as an urge to anger or improving action, but poverty as an inexhaustible source of tears, an exercise of the purest sensibility. "They became so poor that year," the beloved Hindi Novelist Premchand writes, "that even beggars left their door empty-handed." That, indeed, is our poverty: not the fact of beggary, but that beggars should have to go from our doors empty-handed. This is our poverty, which in a hundred Indian short stories in all the Indian languages drives the pretty girl to prostitution to pay the family's medical bills.
>
> India is the poorest country in the world. Therefore, to see its poverty is to make an observation of no value; a thousand newcomers to the country before you have seen and said as you. And not only newcomers. Our own sons and daughters, when they return from Europe and America, have spoken in your very words. Do not think that your anger and contempt are marks of your sensitivity. You might have seen more: the smiles on the faces of the begging children, that domestic group among the pavement sleepers waking in the cool Bombay morning, father, mother and baby in a trinity of love, so self-contained that

they are as private as if walls had separated them from you: it is your gaze that violates them, your sense of outrage that outrages them. You might have seen the boy sweeping his area of pavement, spreading his mat, lying down; exhaustion and undernourishment are in his tiny body and shrunken face, but lying flat on his back, oblivious of you and the thousands who walk past in the lane between the sleepers' mats and house walls bright with advertisements and election slogans, oblivious of the warm, over-breathed air, he plays with fatigued concentration with a tiny pistol in blue plastic. It is your surprise, your anger that denies him humanity. But wait. Stay six months. The winter will bring fresh visitors. Their talk will also be of poverty; they too will show their anger. You will agree; but deep down there will be annoyance; it will seem to you then, too, that they are seeing only the obvious; and it will not please you to find your sensibility so accurately parodied. (AD 47–48)

I have quoted at length because of the extraordinary shifts in perspective in this passage. The story of the Sikh, the comment on its Indianness is presented by a detached observer but the shift to the first person plural – "our especial poverty" – introduces a new note. At first this seems a parody of the Indian voice, and the next statement from a less detached and more critical observer seems to confirm that conclusion. But the next shift to the first person plural is sustained long enough for one to remember that the observer is himself an Indian and may share in the tradition of those stories. In the new paragraph the opening statement is made as if indisputable fact, but suddenly there is another shift in perspective. Someone is being addressed, but who? And by whom? It seems to be the observer, Naipaul, the speaking voice behind the book talking directly to the reader until the voice refers to "Our own sons and daughters." Now the voice seems to be that of India accusing Naipaul himself of being no more sensitive than hundreds before him in spite of his carefully cultivated powers of observation. Shortly one recognizes that Naipaul has adopted a voice with which to condemn himself and all who follow him in expressions of anger and sensibility. This remarkably complex manipulation of point of view expresses brilliantly Naipaul's own inner turmoil – his sense of belonging and not belonging. Following as it does his declaration of his need to feel different, to be recognized as distinctive, not just one of the Indian mass, it is especially telling.

Other incidents in this book reveal Naipaul's confusion about his cultural identity: he is pleased to be recognized as "brahmin" in his science class; he wishes to pay tribute to his dead countryman Ramon in England only because the old rites will save them both from the nonentity of having abandoned the culture that stamped them as different. But none is more revealing nor more honestly recounted than the visit to his grandfather's village, which has a fascinating precursor – another example of truth being less than absolute – in a *Sunday Times* (VSN, 1963b) article. In the article the events of several days are condensed to one brief visit to the village. The extreme reactions of the book version are, in the article, only mild withdrawal and disappointment. The stronger and darker figurative language achieved by changing such phrases as "crowded with peasants" to "infested with peasants" and "one village after another was obliterated by our dust" to "village after village died in our dust" indicates the direction the chapter will take. Naipaul adds his personal responses to the first description of the village (the parentheses enclose words that appear in both versions; they state fact without the personal responses of the new material):

> In spite of myself I was held. For us this land had ceased to exist. Now it was so ordinary. I did not really want to see more. I was afraid of what I might find, and I had witnesses
> . . .
>
> I knew about those spires and was glad to see them. My grandfather (had sought to re-establish the family he had left behind in India. He had recovered their land; he had given money for the building of a temple.) No temple had been built, only three shrines. Poverty, fecklessness, we had thought in Trinidad. But now, from the road, how reassuring those spires were! (AD 267)

Immediately his fears of reality replacing the childhood myth and of letting down his personal guard are apparent. Another major addition to the book's version is the romantic and sentimental story of Naipaul's grandfather told by old Jussodra. The first chapter of *An Area of Darkness* recalls the special Trinidadian Indian version of India; this concluding chapter reveals the development of a similar mythology in India about the emigrant's new life. In the book, Naipaul draws readers into events rather than leaving them as observers: the article's "Then our guide pointed out the village of the Dubes" becomes "Presently he pointed: there, on our right, was the village of the Dubes". Similarly, Naipaul uses direct quotation of the IAS (Indian Administrative Service) man's translations and his own replies to Ramachandra rather than the briefer reported conversation of the article. Naipaul's replies are also much more personally revealing of his increasing tension, especially after the circular repetitions of the confrontations with Ramachandra at Naipaul's hotel which are omitted from the article. To the limited and unemotional description in the article Naipaul adds an attractive detail such as "A man, clad in loincloth and sacred thread, was bathing, standing and pouring water over himself with a brass jar. How elegant his posture, how fine his slender body!" (AD 268). He makes his own rejection of these people that much more unsympathetic, but he is not trying to spare himself — "The ugliness was all mine" (AD 271).

Perhaps because he ends the book as well as the visit "in futility and impatience, a gratuitous act of cruelty, self-reproach and flight" (AD 277), Naipaul has been reproached for callousness and inhumanity in his response to India. It has not, perhaps, been sufficiently understood that he has gone beyond pity to a much more difficult understanding of the way in which the usual responses to India fail: Naipaul believes that pity is too easy and that it separates observer from object, denigrating the object; if he were able to accept what he sees, he could move on toward sustained action (see AD 263). He does show admiration and appreciation as well as rejection: "Nowhere were people so heightened, rounded and individualistic; nowhere did they offer themselves so fully and with such assurance. To know Indians was to take a delight in people as people; every encounter was an adventure. I did not want India to sink; the mere thought was painful" (AD 257). Nevertheless, he fails in his attempt to counteract the Sikh's rage and contempt for the people they pass on the road: "Love insensibly turned into a self-lacerating hysteria in which I was longing for greater and greater decay, more rags and filth, more bones, men more starved and grotesque, more spectacularly deformed. I wished to extend myself, to see the limits of human degradation, to take it all in at that moment. For me this was the end, my private failure; even as I wished I knew I would carry the taint of that moment" (AD 242–43). Naipaul's confession becomes an act of atonement or exorcism.

Part II of *An Area of Darkness*, describing Naipaul's lengthy stay at the Hotel Liward on the Dal Lake, seems to explain the reasons for his failure more calmly and objectively than the briefer episodes. His attempts to analyse the character of Aziz and their complex and finally incomplete relationship only partially succeed. Again Naipaul's confession of his failure is almost self-lacerating. He confesses that he sulks if Aziz seems inattentive, that he could be infuriated and suspicious that Aziz may be profiting unfairly from his employment. However, he comes to an understanding of the restrictions on Aziz's life – "he was only obeying an instinct. He could not read or write. People were his only material, his profession and no doubt his diversion; his world was made up of these encounters and managed relationships" (AD 161). And Naipaul penetrates the relationship of servant to master, discovering that the servant exercises power by the skill of service, which aids in the creation of another fictional character, Santosh (*In a Free State*). The complete ambivalence of his relationship with all at the Liward Hotel is captured in Mr Butt's letter which is reproduced without comment from Naipaul. The

awkwardness of language, the mixture of personal senti-
ment and business promotion, the self-conscious formality
of the letter which must have been translated and transcri-
bed by a third party all serve to obscure the true emotions
or motives behind the missive. Naipaul seems unable to
transcend the barriers of language and custom to interpret
the words and behaviour of people culturally so far removed from him. Part II of *An Area of Darkness* dramatizes the
traveller's sense of insecurity and the instinct to protect
himself and his dignity which lead to many failures to
achieve communication. On a broader plane, in much of
his writing Naipaul seems to portray these instincts at
work in human relationships, separating people even
when their backgrounds are similar.

In his attempts to portray the society, Naipaul is as specific and personal as he is in the exercise of self-revelation.
Speaking of *India: A Wounded Civilization,* he describes his
nonfiction technique: "The book was very exhausting to
write, this analysis, this shaping of chapters. I was unwilling always to describe simply; I always try to make description part of an argument" (to Wheeler 1977, 536).
Never content with the simple depiction of persons or
places, he constantly seeks to discover the causes of their
being as (or where) they are and to draw conclusions from
their existence. So the portraits of Ramnath, Malhotra, and
Malik, of Jivan and Vasant, and of the Brahmin brothers
engaged in the manufacture of leather goods are all used to
communicate Naipaul's understanding of the Indian sense
of degree. The first three have difficulties adjusting to the
pressures of the new society in which they move, because
each has a sense of his place in the social order which is not
accepted by their society. The others are successful but
unable to function outside what they believe to be their
sphere — to the extent of sleeping on the street or not
employing their own children for fear of caste contamination. Those who reject the sense of degree are themselves
rejected; those who accept it are unable to transcend it.
Similarly contributing to an argument, Naipaul's portrait of

Bunty demonstrates that no matter what the pretensions to
modernity, no matter how complete and polished the imitation of Western, especially English styles, the sense of
degree still operates and there is still a retreat deep inside
into which the imitators can withdraw in Indian negation.
Consequently, the outer trappings – buildings, railways,
government and civil service, economics and science – remain for Naipaul only

> simple mimicry, incongruous and absurd; . . . In the Indian
> setting this Indian English mimicry is like fantasy. It is an
> undiminishing absurdity; and it is only slowly that one for-
> mulates what was sensed from the first day: this is a mimi-
> cry not of England a real country, but of the fairytale land
> of Anglo-India, of clubs and sahibs and syces and bearers.
> It is as if an entire society has fallen for a casual confidence
> trickster. Casual because the trickster has gone away, los-
> ing interest in his joke, but leaving the Anglo-Indians flock-
> ing to the churches of Calcutta on a Sunday morning to
> assert the alien faith more or less abandoned in its country
> of origin; leaving Freddy crying, "Just bung your coat down
> there, Andy"; leaving the officer exclaiming, "I say, by Jove!
> I feel rather bushed." Leaving "civil lines", "cantonments",
> leaving people "going off to the hills": magic words now ful-
> ly possessed, now spoken as of right, in what is now at last
> Indian Anglo-India, where smartness can be found in the
> cosy proletarian triviliaties of *Womans Own* and the *Daily
> Mirror* and where Mrs Hauksbee, a Millamant of the sub-
> urbs, is still the arbiter of elegance. (AD 61)

The increasing tempo of the passage, the use of keywords
in Naipaul's vocabulary – "mimicry", "absurdity",
"fantasy", and the abandonment of formal sentence structure attest his deep conviction and frustration at Indian
imitation of England. Mimicry in Trinidad – and the double mimicry of Indians trying to imitate Creole styles –
were different, for West Indians were aware of other countries besides England, especially of America. In India the
England of the Raj still lingers on.

In the writing of fiction and nonfiction alike, Naipaul frequently uses architecture to make an abstraction tangible.

In *The Middle Passage* one remembers the varied architectural styles of Maraval Road which illustrate Trinidad's cosmopolitanism. In Naipaul's fiction many houses reflect and reveal the character of the resident: foremost among them are the successful Ganesh's two-storied concrete block mansion with red roses painted on the bright blue drawing-room wall (*The Mystic Masseur*); Mr Biswas's series of half-built houses which collapse as he does until he achieves a limited success in an imperfect but stable house; Ralph Singh's retreat behind the blank walls of his Roman-style house (*The Mimic Men*); Jimmy Ahmed's attempts to import English "style" to the Trinidad bush (*Guerrillas*); and Salim's "borrowed" flat which reflects his unsettled borrowed lifestyle (*A Bend in the River*). In India he finds the architecture of the Raj "a little too grand for their purpose, too grand for the puniness, poverty and defeat in which they were set. They were appropriate to a conception of endeavour rather than to endeavour" (AD 201). The buildings seem to participate in the spiral that turns the ice lingam at Amarnath into a "symbol of a symbol" when it fails to appear; "'The spirit of the thing'" (AD 179) is what matters not the achievement. Naipaul compares the architecture of nationalist India with that of the Raj in that "they are both the work of people consciously seeking to express ideas of themselves" (AD 218). Modern India attempts to preserve its glorious past through poor imitation of the architectural features of its ancient culture. The difficulty is that the ideas of themselves entertained by both the Raj and by modern India are essentially fantasies.

Just as architecture may manifest a way of thinking so may literature reveal a society's understanding of itself. Naipaul demands of the novel that it be fiction without being fantasy, a story not a fairytale because fiction can be used to reveal the truth, to portray reality – or as much of it as one author can discover, but fantasy obscures reality. Out of the myth of Englishness, whose evolution he traces from Jane Austen to Kipling and Forster (see AD 206–7), grew the double-edged fantasy at the heart of the Raj: there was simultaneously racial arrogance and a spirit of service – the old "white man's burden". In Indian literature, Malgonkar's novel *The Princes* (1963) provides for Naipaul corroboration of Bunty's "withdrawal, denial, confusion of values" (AD 66). He believes the book's narrator personifies the distortion of English values, for while the phrases of democracy seem to receive approval in Abhayraj's story of his princely father's loss of his state, according to Naipaul's reading, Abhayraj rejects revolution against the unequal distribution of wealth. Naipaul interprets Abhayraj's ambivalent treatment of Kanakchand as evidence that the prince's son embraces the medieval concept of degree, which permeates Indian consciousness through the Gita, the classic of Indian literature and moral handbook. Although Naipaul discusses the narrator's distortion of English values, he seems to imply that Malgonkar may share in the confusion. The author's own comments suggest otherwise: he seems to be well aware of the confusion of values in his characters, but he seems to tolerate that confusion better than the young Naipaul (see Dayananda, 1975). To Naipaul the majority of contemporary Indian novelists, with their concern for the unseen, for spirituality, for the symbol rather than the reality fail the genre which "is part of that Western concern with the condition of men, a response to the here and now" (AD 226). "The sweetness and sadness which can be found in Indian writing and Indian films are a turning away from a too overwhelming reality; they reduce the horror to a warm, virtuous emotion. Indian sentimentality is the opposite of concern" (AD 227). For Naipaul only Narayan and Jhabvala succeed as novelists of India; honesty, humour and irony save them from the unquestioning acceptance of conditions and attitudes Naipaul finds overwhelming.

Through his journalism Naipaul reveals himself as an uncompromising realist who will not allow humanitarian impulses or sympathy to cover up the unpleasant truths that he discovers as he collects material from various corners of the globe. Naipaul's plea on Trollope's behalf might equally well apply to his own writing:

. . . what he saw as the idleness of the West Indian Negro is the subject of some of his warmest vituperation. This should not be suppressed, not only because it is so much part of the book, but also for another reason. Many humanitarians continue in their faith by ignoring the unpleasant; Trollope arrived at his humanitarianism almost, it seems, through a contemplation of the unpleasant. His anger at this refusal to work is grounded not in racial feelings, but in his religious sense of duty and in his Civil Servant's sense of what helps to balance a budget. (VSN 1962b, 461)

Naipaul's *Saturday Evening Post* article "What's Wrong with being a Snob?" (reprinted in Hamner 1977) elaborates on this theme. He believes that mindless egalitarianism – embodied in the meaningless statement "A man is a man" – leads to a reduction of man to mere "flesh capable only of pleasure and pain". The recognition of difference is the necessary first step toward the improvement of the condition of any oppressed group, be it the Indian sweeper caste or a primitive African tribe. Naipaul believes the instinct which says "I do not want to be like them" is precious even though it is the cry of the snob: "In those fantasies about the future, when man has been reduced to a unit and Big Brother rules all, it is the cry of the hero, the man who revolts, the man with a cause" (CP 35). Of course his choice of the word "snob", the "dirty little word" suggesting "insecurity and meanness" is a deliberate provocation, challenging readers to disagree and be proved unthinking.

Naipaul believes that the failure of British rule in India was the result of the acceptance in England of the myth of Englishness. Attracted to the Old British sensibility, Indians were misled into mimicry of the new Englishness, itself an imitation, and into a nationalism of their own. But nationalism forces a people to regard themselves from the perspective of others, and in India this brought to the consciousness an awareness of spirituality and ancient culture as attributes to be cultivated. The result is the confusion and schizophrenia Naipaul discovers in architecture and literature, and in the failure of creativity.

The Indo-British encounter was abortive; it ended in a
double fantasy. Their new self-awareness makes it impossible for Indians to go back; their cherishing of Indianness
makes it difficult for them to go ahead. It is possible to find
the India that appears not to have changed since Mogul
times but has, profoundly; it is possible to find the India
whose mimicry of the West is convincing until, sometimes
with dismay, sometimes with impatience, one realises that
complete communication is not possible, that a gift of vision
cannot be shared, that there still survive inaccessible areas
of Indian retreat. Both the negative and the positive principles have been diluted; one balances the other. The pene-
tration was not complete; the attempt at conversion was
abandoned. India's strength, her ability to endure, came
from the negative principle, her unexamined sense of continuity. It is the principle which, once diluted, loses its virtue. In the concept of Indianness the sense of continuity
was bound to be lost. The creative urge failed. Instead of
continuity we have the static. (AD 228–29)

So in Naipaul's view, Indians have their own fantasies with
which they protect themselves from the painful awareness
of present distress and past degradation.

Despite Naipaul's insistence on the need to observe and
record the world as it is and not as one might wish it to be,
reality appears to be very ephemeral. Legends may replace
history: even the college-educated, English-literate Bashir
turns Kashmiri history into legend and ignores the British
influence entirely, just as West Indians protectively erase
memories of slavery from their history of the Caribbean.
The fantasy concept of Englishness seems likely to outlast
the reality of England. In this way living out a fantasy may
make the fantasy seem real, dangerously obscuring reality.
But the revelation of reality seems to need the ordering imagination of an artist: of Simla, he says, "No city or landscape is truly real until it has been given the quality of
myth by writer, painter or by its association with great
events" (AD 205). We have noted before that Hinduism
teaches that life is illusion, *maya*, and that Naipaul's whole
concept of the close link between fantasy and reality may

have roots in his father's interest in Hindu metaphysics. Amusingly, he tells Charles Wheeler (1977, 537), "I regard it as part of my bad blood coming to the surface when I start playing with ideas of time and space."

Rejecting the Metropolitan Model: "A Flag on the Island"

Dated August 1965, "A Flag on the Island" was probably written while Naipaul was also working on *The Mimic Men*. Seeming almost a joke at the expense of a film company which requested a comic musical with an American character and explicit sex (FI 7) — not Naipaul's usual *métier* — the story takes up themes concerning the nature of reality, postwar development of colonies, and the influence of metropolitan powers which have already appeared in the widening perspective of *Mr Stone and the Knights Companion* and *An Area of Darkness*. In addition, Anthony Boxill (1976) points out many links between "A Flag on the Island" and *The Mimic Men* despite the metropolitan origin of the narrator of the story. Besides structural similarities in the organization of the works, he discerns similarities between the narrators in that they are self-searching and self-accusing, aware of the shortcomings of society and of their own complicity in creating them. Boxill recognizes, however, the fundamental difference that Frankie suffers guilt for the American role in the world and sees no solution but annihilation, while Ralph Singh, also yearning for extinction, seeks order and is finally able to achieve a degree of reconciliation as an individual. Interesting mostly in that it takes up the question of the influence of metropolitan powers even after colonial ties are severed, "A Flag on the Island" is rather more polemical than the rest of Naipaul's fiction, and shows him experimenting with a more impressionistic style.

In a phrase that recalls *An Area of Darkness* as well as the experience of Mr Stone, Frankie states, " . . . I felt again

that the reality of landscape and perhaps of all relationships lay only in the imagination" (FI 157). Frankie's personality seems to make him susceptible to the sense of colonial dislocation which characterizes the island sensibility.
In one passage, as he attempts to define reality, Frankie
seizes on objects labelled with the name "Hilton" which
recall the artificiality of tourism as the new colonialism.
Earlier, ascetic withdrawal had failed when "Moore-
McCormack" seems to take over his identity, denying him
the joy of extinction. In addition, Blackwhite expresses the
sense Ralph Singh has that a colony can cease to exist
when it is forgotten by the rest of the world. Blackwhite
both articulates and personifies the colonial dilemma of
the loss of identity; his name and its change, his struggle to
choose a language and themes for his novels, his pursuit of
foreign money and his knowledge that it is destroying the
very culture it claims to support, his awareness that the
"old days" recreated by his cultural revival were days of
degradation for his people – all of these are treated comically, satirically. However, now as Naipaul moves outward
from the circle of light which circumscribed his early
satires, the objects of satire also include metropolitans.

Frank is a well-intentioned expatriate, whose attempts to
improve the lot of a colonial people are mainly subconscious efforts to hide his own weakness and only in small
part responses to a genuine altruism. On his return to the
island, he remembers the result of his interference with
the lives of the people he had genuinely wanted to help:
Mano, dead because he could not accept success as a walk-
er when he lacked courage to become a runner; Mr Lam-
bert, dead (along with his house) when financial success
destroys the balance of power in his marriage. As dialogue,
it is more preachy than usual for Naipaul, but the following outburst from Blackwhite sums up Frankie's fraudu-
lence:

> "This is just an interlude for you, Frankie. This is your little
> Greenwich Village. I know, I can read. Bam, bam, bram,
> bram. Fun. Afterwards you leave us and go back. This

place, I tell you, is nowhere. It doesn't exist. People are just born here. They all want to go away, and for you it is only a holiday. I don't want to be any part of your Greenwich Village. You beachcomb, you buy sympathy. The big rich man always behind the love, the I-am-just-like-you. I have been listening to you talking to people in Henry's yard about the States; about the big cinemas with wide screens and refrigerators as big as houses and everybody becoming film stars and presidents. And you are damn frightened of the whole thing. Always ready for the injection of rum, always looking for the nice and simple natives to pick you up." (FI 187)

Apparently all Frankie and his society can offer are models for hollow mimicry. Carnival costumes reflect a society engaged in nothing but imitation of metropolitan figures and styles, and as Frankie discovers on his return, the imitation continues. Thus, at the conclusion of the story when all lives revert to sterility after the failure of the hurricane to bring drama and release, Frankie and the island itself are once again imprisoned by the labels of economic domination.

Frankie's affair with Selma symbolizes the relationship of colonized to colonizer as did Biswas's relationship to the Tulsis. Henry warns that Selma brings out the "vice" in people by making them long to reform her − "'And you know what reform is? Reform mean: keep off, for me alone'" (FI 179). Frankie should also be warned by his annoyance at Selma's direct admission of her poverty, a condition which is soon changed but without the addition of taste or values, just as Henry's floorshow and White's books are tasteless "improvements". Furthermore, the relationship fails to meet the colonizer's needs because the colonized refuses to be possessed completely. Frank interferes because the islanders' regard reinforces his idea of himself, both in the sense of a self-concept and in the existential sense. The colonial parallels are obvious, but failure and disillusionment are not restricted to former colonies and their residents.

A taxi driver criticizes the new flag: "'This look like something they make up'" (FI 156). The impersonal "they" suggests the former masters who took away the "real flag", the Union Jack, and sent this mockery of sun's rays on a wavy blue sea in an effort to "create the tropics" much as the Americans did on their army base. In seeking to impose a national personality, the former colonial power has created something even the locals recognize as false; the tragedy is that they are unable to redefine themselves and establish a true national identity, partly because of the ingrained habit of self-denigration Naipaul acutely records in the short stories of *Miguel Street* and *A Flag on the Island*, and partly because a new form of colonial domination has begun to assert itself through economics. The new flag may symbolize the island's claim to independent political existence, but it is not the only flag suggested by the title. Besides the Union Jack, there is also the Stars and Stripes, and should the national flags be gone, Moore-McCormack and Hilton remain, their banners flying.

Rejecting the Metropolitan Model:
The Mimic Men

While the *The Mimic Men* (1967) returns to the Caribbean setting and to the political protagonist of Naipaul's early novels, it continues and intensifies his investigation of the human individuality caught in conflict between reality and unreality, order and disorder. In this novel Naipaul also continues to widen the circle of his experience and understanding by investigating more deeply conditions in the metropolis as they affect the colonial who seeks there the solution to his disorientation. Unlike traditional political autobiographies with their dates, significant events and great names obscuring personal realities, Ralph Singh's memoirs record his attempt to explain the forces that have shaped his life, to find a pattern in what he perceives to be chaos and disorder. However, Naipaul warns readers to judge carefully Singh's rationalizations and self-justifications (about his marriage, for example) with defensive signals such as: "I have gone over this moment more than once in my mind, I do not think my recollection of it is wrong (MimM 55), or "my mood must be born in mind" (MimM 56). Despite this distancing, there appear to be moments when author and narrator merge into one. Kenneth Ramchand (1973, 30) considers that "where it matters we can find Naipaul standing critically outside of Singh", and Landeg White (1975, 160) believes that "The crucial point of this merging of identity between Naipaul and Kripalsingh is that it is obviously intentional". Both critics catalogue items in Singh's personal history which are drawn directly from Naipaul's experiences, Ramchand stressing passages in *An Area of Darkness* which describe Naipaul's expectations and experiences in London and which seem direct precursors of Singh's reactions to the city. In a larger sense, this most introspective novel seems almost a necessary outcome of the period of intense self-contemplation which produced *An Area of Darkness*. Accepting Naipaul's assertion that as a novelist he works toward conclusions in a way he cannot as a nonfiction writer, and remembering the unhappy ending of *An Area of Darkness*, further consideration of his antecedents through a different mode seems inevitable. In one respect, however, Naipaul and Singh differ considerably: Singh claims to record fact, which according to Naipaul, means he must "analyse and decide" before writing rather than allowing the conclusions to emerge gradually; after engaging in this process, Singh abandons his ambition to write history, whereas Naipaul the novelist immediately becomes historian, publishing *The Loss of El Dorado* only two years after *The Mimic Men*. This duality — fiction purporting to be fact, facts (of Naipaul's own background and perceptions) turning into fiction — yields the most subtle investigation of the relation between fiction and nonfiction in Naipaul's writing.

Perceiving the chaos in a postcolonial society, Singh seems to articulate the fears about reality Naipaul himself struggles to suppress: "Far away on the beach I could see the stripped remains of a great tree, washed up, I had been told, months before, coming from heaven knows what island or continent, drifting on the ocean night and day for weeks, for months, for a year, until stranded on our island, on this desolate beach. I had thoughts, too alarming to pursue, about things existing only when seen" (MimM 128). Even as he indicates the metaphysical difficulty, Naipaul's Singh reminds us of the voyages of the Middle Passage, and suggests that for much of the "Old" World, the Third world ceases to exist when it is not forced to mind. On two occasions, feeling that his interpretation is too absurd to be true, Singh asks himself whether events are what they seem to be: anticipating that he will become the political scapegoat for his Negro-dominated party, he recalls his fears of execution when his affair with his cousin Sally was discovered. All along Singh believes that he could halt the rush of violent events, "But control, the prospect of power, and its corollary, the prospect of keeping power in a situation which could always turn to air in my hands, the prospect wearied me" (MimM 263). Singh enters exile because he cannot summon up the strength to affirm the reality of the threat. The same fear of losing hold of reality, of extinction overwhelms Mr Biswas and is Seepersad Naipaul's legacy to his son; many novels later Salim articulates it and links it to the fantasies which replace clear-sighted evaluation of experience. These fantasies possess the narrator of "Tell Me Who to Kill" and Jimmy Ahmed (and his real life prototype, Michael de Freitas).

Naming becomes, for Singh, a charm which can ward off the demons of doubt when reality is threatened. In trying to find the god of the city of London, the god who would unite individuals in a common order, Singh "would play with famous names as I walked empty streets and stood on bridges. But the magic of names soon faded. Here was the river, here the bridge, there that famous building. But the god was veiled. My incantation of names remained unanswered" (MimM 23). The reality of his political career is also reinforced by a private game of naming buildings, roads, documents, and schemes. Thus, Singh's decision to change his name is not as simple as wishing to compete with the young Deschampneufs in quantity of names, or wishing to dissociate himself from his family heritage and his insignificant father. In re-naming himself, Singh is attempting to reinforce his reality in his own eyes and possibly to redefine that reality.

Through Singh's quest for reality, *The Mimic Men* dramatizes a seminal theme in Naipaul's work: the difficulties faced by the colonials torn between their past which lies in India or Africa or wherever they think their roots to be, their present in a place which they cannot believe matters in the scheme of things, and their future which they long to associate with a metropolis that does seem to matter and to be going somewhere. In the specific case of Ralph Singh, this conflict gives rise to some splendid ironies. He simultaneously romanticizes the Aryan past, fantasising himself as a Rajput warrior galloping across plains dominated by snow-capped mountains, and anglicizes his name. And when he is able physically to escape the confining island of Isabella, he flees not to the sweeping plains of India but to the small rooms and narrow streets of London. Yearning to assert the importance of the individual, he retains a Hindu view of the enormous sweep of existence in which the individual dwindles into insignificance. His Hindu background tells him all human existence is a ceaseless sea of change, and all progress only an illusion, but Ralph Singh turns to study and writing of history for relief from his vision of chaos, and he enters into a political movement whose goal is the correction of colonial abuses. Naipaul presents Ralph Singh as the archetypal colonial person, uncommitted and uninvolved, believing all decisions to be in the hands of the masters. Though completely isolated and unable to identify with anyone, Singh is the champion chosen to fight the son of the master in the name of slaves and coolies. Guilt at his failure to commit himself drives him to uncharacteristic behaviour, but at the same time he withdraws to a house which offers a blank face to the world and turns inward.

These are some of the ironies of existence contributing to the chaos out of which Singh tries to extract some sense or philosophy of order.

One of the key words of *The Mimic Men*, "order", is used by Singh in a variety of ways reinforcing his perception of a disordered universe. Order may be simply the regularity of life in the hotel, reassuring and anaesthetizing, or it may have existential implications as "when [one] feels strongly there is some connection between the earth on which he walks and himself" (MimM 248). But another irony operates in that Singh cannot discover the links between events in his life until he writes them out of chronological order; this novel differs from much of Naipaul's work in the complex movement backwards and forwards in time which suggests Singh's internal disorder as he struggles to exorcize his vision of chaos. In terms of the structure of the novel, Naipaul is elaborating on the technique of *A House for Mr Biswas* in which the Prologue reveals the end of the story; the purpose of telling it is not to let readers know what happened but how and why. The emphasis in these books, and in *Miguel Street* and *In a Free State*, is on growing understanding which develops as the parts gradually come together and reveal the whole. Singh's method for ordering the parts is symbolized by the preparation to eat by the diner he calls Garbage: as the novel ends, Singh has separated the "garbage" – childhood, study, marriage, business and political activity – from the real business of living, "the work of a minute" (MimM 295). Not for him the technique of other diners who bring chaos to the apparent order of their dinner plates immediately to surrender them.

Singh's movement toward self-expression is captured by his response to the nursery rhyme "Who comes here?": on beer mats it at first suggests the false chumminess and hilarity of the pub from which he flees, but later the slogan is part of the unchanging order of life he has created and discovered through his writing. Additionally, that nursery rhyme, read in Lady Stella's *Oxford Nursery Rhyme Book*, calls up a past of which colonials are deprived, and in which they cannot participate, for they lack the common experiences of sharing the same children's book.

Dominating his memoir, the image of shipwreck conjures up all Singh's fears of the "haphazard, disordered and mixed society" (MimM 66) of his island; sounding very much like his creator in *The Middle Passage*, Singh writes, "To be born on an island like Isabella, an obscure New World transplantation, second-hand and barbarous, was to be born to disorder" (MimM 141). The arrival by sea of successive waves of misfits after Columbus's accidental discovery of the island seems the trick of frivolous and perverse fate. Shipwreck becomes a metaphor for colonial history and there seems no hope of rescue. Further, shipwreck suggests the experience of being stranded without the necessities of life. Naipaul's own contention has always been that Caribbean communities are culturally starved. The "innocence" of a group that can expose its son to ridicule by having them sing "coon songs" and the cruel "simplicity" of a society that looks anxiously week after week in the newspaper society pages for the satire of the rising man have been created by the whole colonial experience which Singh (or Naipaul) keeps before the reader's eyes throughout the book. On a Sunday family outing, the Singhs drive through a mulatto village; the residents are called Spaniards and had lived apart even in slave days. They then pass through a Carib area in which the people are more Negro than Carib: " . . . it was like being in an area of legend. The scale was small in time, numbers and area; and here, just for a moment, the rise and fall and extinction of peoples, a concept so big and alarming, was concrete and close. Slaves and runaways, hunters and hunted, rulers and ruled: they had no romance for me. Their message was only that nothing was secure" (MimM 136).

Always aware that the history of empire has created this world, and aware that his island lacks a history of its own, Singh has been enticed by the study of history and, more important, by the writing of history which promise a means to the discovery – or imposition – of order. History, as

Naipaul writes it in *The Loss of El Dorado*, imposes a pattern on events that are themselves unplanned, chaotic, unrelated in most people's minds. The following passage, written when the El Dorado project may well have been taking shape in Naipaul's plans, seems to reveal his motives and his doubts about carrying it through:

> It was my hope to give expression to the restlessness, the deep disorder, which the great explorations, the overthrow in three continents of established social organizations, the unnatural bringing together of peoples who could achieve fulfilment only within the security of their own societies and the landscapes hymned by their ancestors, it was my hope to give partial expression to the restlessness which this great upheaval has brought about. The empires of our time were short-lived, but they have altered the world forever; their passing away is their least significant feature. It was my hope to sketch a subject which, fifty years hence, a great historian might pursue. For there is no such thing as history nowadays; there are only manifestos and antiquarian research; and on the subject of empire there is only the pamphleteering of churls. But this work will not now be written by me; I am too much a victim of that restlessness which was to have been my subject. And it must also be confessed that in that dream of writing I was attracted less by the act and the labour than by the calm and the order which the act would have implied. (MimM 38–39)

At times of great stress, such as the collapse of his marriage and the failure of his political career, "safe" subjects – the precision of a dead language, the puzzle of Pompey's behaviour – occupy Singh's mind. Instead of seeing history in the Hindu way as an endless repetition, an ebb and flow, Singh tries to freeze events in their time slot and deny them contemporary relevance. This is the error of the antiquarian research which he says replaces history in modern times and which he finally rejects.

The awareness that colonials have no history of their own is an important theme in many postcolonial writers – George Lamming, Derek Walcott, and Orlando Patterson to name a few. Ngugi wa Thiong'o (1972) validly compares

Patterson's Alexander Blackman with Singh, but while recognizing the limitations of *An Absence of Ruins* (1967) as fiction, Ngugi fails to appreciate the essential difference between Blackman's and Singh's respective retreats to London. Blackman feels that history, culture and race are merely abstractions that offer only hollow rationalizations for his failure as a human being. His only recourse is total self-effacement, retreat into the London crowd. His self-pity tends, however, to alienate him from readers who may have felt sympathy for him earlier in the novel. When Blackman asserts, "'I have no past . . . I cannot say whether I am civilised or savage, standing as I do outside of race, outside of culture, outside of history, outside of any value . . . '" (Patterson 1967, 160), he seems to neglect the essential complexity of the relation of the past to the present and of both to the future, a complexity with which Singh wrestles and comes to terms. Hence, the tone of the ending of *The Mimic Men* is very different from that of *An Absence of Ruins*.

In *The Mimic Men* Naipaul depicts the failure of a shattered society to provide an individual with a coherent self-concept. Since the members of Singh's family are equally disoriented, they are unable to help him; finally his confusion forces him into relationships that cannot be satisfactory for they are built on the quicksand of an incomplete personality which responds to similar distress in others. Singh's longing for the support of his parents and simultaneous embarrassment at accepting it are summed up in his reaction to preparations for his school sports day. Oedipal longings and conflicts are apparent but such an explanation would grossly oversimplify the social pressures that complicate Singh's relations with his parents. His mother does not belong to his creole world, and his father's failure to accommodate himself successfully to its pressures make him an inappropriate model. With youth's intolerance of eccentricity, especially in those close to them, Singh feels betrayed by his father's fits of irrational violence and his final withdrawal into the character of Gurudeva, which make his son a target first for ridicule and later for devotion. " . . . I would say that the episode gave me a sensation of rawness and violation. It was as though I was chewing rubbery raw flesh and being made to swallow tainted oil" (MimM 158). The sacrifice of the racehorse Tamango makes obscene Singh's reverence for the Aryan past, his dream of escape. The ancient ritual *Asvamedha* had seemed to him an act of beauty, power and bravery, especially because of its association with the expulsion of the Greeks from Aryan lands. But instead of becoming a grand challenge to the colonial masters, it betrays him and subjects him to ridicule. His father's attack on his taste in reading material has become an attack on his soul. (Readers familiar with *Finding the Centre* will wonder about the parallels of this story with the sacrifice of a goat to Kali which was forced on Seepersad Naipaul; V. S. Naipaul says he was unaware of this incident until 1970.) Nevertheless, Singh reveals his sympathy for his father in his reactions to Dalip's demand for repayment of his debt and in his memories of isolated moments of closeness; Lord Stockwell's recollections of Gurudeva emphasize the adult Singh's sense of solitude so strongly that he feels physically ill.

As are so many of Naipaul's protagonists, Singh seems to be propelled into action by forces outside his control. His father's movement forces him to accept a role, fighting Deschampneufs and joining Browne in politics, but his association with these representatives of historically opposed forces on the island is characterized by an ever-present discomfort at his difference from them, as "picturesque Asiatic" and late arrival. As Singh puts together the pieces of his experience, he remembers a tea party at the home of the Deschampneufs and his sense of shame at not having made clear his rejection of what they represent, but the full incident and its significance are not revealed until another hundred pages have chronicled the boys' association. At the crucial tea party Singh is forced to react to the family's "idea of itself" which includes their being French in spite of the island's English affiliation, masters of slaves in spite of abolition, and owners of racehorses despite the humiliation of Tamango's sacrifice. The horse's name itself, associated with the slave period, suggests their arrogance in recalling the past. At the same time they take pains to assert their essentially Isabellan heritage: Mrs Deschampneufs uses the Negro street term "whitey-pokey" in warning Singh against bringing back a white bride and Mr Deschampneufs remarks, "'But where you are born is a funny thing. My great-grandfather and even my grandfather, they always talked about going back for good. They went. But they came back. You know, you are born in a place and you grow up there. You get to know the trees and the plants. You will never know any other trees and plants like that'" (MimM 204). Naipaul's irony is that those plants have all been imported, many of them, as Browne points out, in the intestines of slaves.

Singh's response to Mr Deschampneufs's story of Stendhal shows the reverence for the past and the historical sense (shared by his creator) which is present in so much of his narrative, and explains his ambivalence toward the tradition represented by the old French family. "I was deeply impressed. I felt that Mr Deschampneufs's story had brought the past close. It was possible to believe in the link between our island and the great world. My own dreams were rendered absurd. The outside world was stripped of its quality of legend and reduced to the comprehensible. Grand figures came near. A writer accounted great had been turned into a simple man, fat and middle-aged and ironic. And nearness exalted; it did not diminish" (MimM 208). Understanding Julien's human need to search (in *Le Rouge et le Noir*) for melodrama and style, Singh appreciates, as he could not when a student, Stendhal's device of making Julien identify water on the church floor as blood. Mr Deschampneufs's story and his insult in refusing to shake hands combine to make Singh see blood in the red sky at sunset and to think, "Why, recognizing the enemy, did you not kill him swiftly?" (MimM 209). The same historical sense makes Singh aware of the essential injustice of the island's past and of his weakness in not taking up the cause of the blacks and coolies, and forces him into political action. But when he proclaims his father's name in *The Socialist*, his response is as ambivalent as that of Patterson's Alexander Blackman to his wife: " 'I share the same ambivalence to you that I share to the island: the grief, the aimlessness, the guilt and the commitment . . . well, not commitment, I should say, the desire for commitment. A desire which I couldn't help admitting was false, the result and the cause of my guilt' " (Patterson, 42).

In portraying Singh's attempt to define himself through political activity, Naipaul gives politics in a postcolonial society a more extended and penetrating investigation than he does elsewhere in his fiction. When Singh admits that "satire creeps in" (MimM 251) despite his wish to avoid it, the presence of his creator is very evident; satire is the only response to increasing numbers of white expatriate civil servants, Czechs who get government support to produce stinking plastics, and treating the colony's delegates to the metropolis as troublesome schoolboys. Singh's view of the postcolonial situation moves from satire toward tragedy, however, just as Naipaul's did as he wrote of Mr Biswas. The situation of the colonial politician, writes Singh, "satirizes itself, turns satire inside out, takes satire to a point where it touches pathos if not tragedy. Out of his immense violation words come easily to him, too easily. He must go back on his words. In success he must lay aside violation. He must betray himself and in the end he has no cause save his own survival. The support he has attracted, not ideal to ideal, but bitterness to bitterness, he betrays and mangles: emancipation is not possible for all" (MimM 250). Driven by a sense of incompleteness and of separateness from those they lead, colonial politicians soon abandon their missions and are imprisoned in the role, caring only to preserve the trappings of personal power. Soon after Singh and Browne attempt to replace illiterate and crooked politicians with a new order, Singh recognizes "the flesh

swelling on the backs of their necks" (MimM 228) and
realizes that "Each attempt at the establishing of a personal
security prepared the way for further disorder" (MimM
246). Naipaul's growing awareness of political realities is
apparent in that he can now see that such reinfection is not
simply the result of human failing or of following corrupt
colonial models, Singh felt outrage at seeing estate labourers wading in the mud, but he was forced to face the economic realities of agriculture as an issue and eventually he
must forget his outrage (see MimM 249).

A number of the political articles collected in *The Overcrowded Barracoon* were written in the same period of developing political understanding and awareness of historical influences as *The Mimic Men* and *The Loss of El Dorado*.
A failure to define and deal with the real problems of their
countries is the failure of one politician after another.
Mauritius is being choked to death by overpopulation but
the government coalition parties espouse Black Power and
talk of conspiracy by the holders of economic power
against those in political power; as conditions in the country degenerate, " . . . politics absorbs all their frenzy.
Speech and elections are free; real power is unobtainable;
and politics is the opium of the people" (OB 264). But the
opposing parties do not really differ in their analyses of the
problems.

> They both recognize the efficiency of the economy, and its
> brutality. They both speak of the need to diversify agri-
> culture and selectively to industrialize. They would both
> like to separate the sugar factories from the sugar estates, to
> separate, that is, management and money from the land.
> And they both seem to recognize that, at the end of the day,
> they will be left with what they started with: an agricultural
> colony, created by empire in an empty island and always
> meant to be part of something larger, now given a thing
> called independence and set adrift, an abandoned imperial
> barracoon, incapable of economic or cultural autonomy.
> (OB 270)

To keep alive, the parties must deal in the politics of race.

The New Left MMM is inter-racial and is answered by a new Indian party, the Jan Sangh, and by Duval's Black Power — "fantasy responding to fantasy" (OB 275), comments Naipaul. "'They all deal in fantasies. And it's rooted in the colonial situation'" (OB 284). The words are Berenger's, the young leader of the MMM, not Naipaul's, but as if he were Naipaul's student, he talks at length of the myth-making capacity of his people, in Naipaul's eyes a stranded people with a powerful need for drama to sustain them. In this they are just like the Isabellans of *The Mimic Men*.

Berenger and Duval in Mauritius, Papa Bradshaw in St Kitts personify the "style" that Naipaul sees as the basis of political power in former colonies. Bradshaw, a man of the people, a folk leader who organized the sugar workers' thirteen-week strike in 1948, adopted a gold swizzle stick for his champagne, a gold moustache brush, and formal English court dress as component parts of his early style. Through the figure before them, the people can participate imaginatively in the glamour or drama of the metropolis. Increasingly, however, the mixed races of former colonies turn to the imported and anachronous message of American Black Power to find personal dignity; Bradshaw's gold brush is now the clenched fist. But Naipaul's view in "Power?" (OB) is that this is only an attempt to realize the black millenarian dream and has nothing to do with the reality of political programs. Obviously, Black Power can have no sensible interpretation in the racially chaotic "Ultimate Colony" (OB), British Honduras, where two-thirds of the population are descendants of Negro log-cutters, the rest are indigenous Maya Indians, Black Caribs (from St Vincent), Spanish and mestizo refugees from Yucatan, and German-American Mennonites, and the Premier is a white-appearing Maya Indian-European with some Negro antecedents. Independence is held up by the Guatemalan claim for the colony, but Guatemala does not want and fears the large Negro population. In British Honduras, the Opposition claim the Premier will turn the country over to Guatemala because he is Catholic and not

Negro, but in Guatemala, he is considered black and un-
trustworthy. British Honduras is the "ultimate colony", the
embodiment of colonial chaos. And the world, America
with its message of Black Power intrudes.

Two years after publishing *The Mimic Men*, Naipaul describes Norman Mailer as he gradually ceases to be a
writer and becomes a politician during his campaign for
mayor of New York City; the subject himself chooses the
key word — "dull": "'I've become duller. Steady, serious,
duller'" (OB 180). Throughout the article Naipaul explores
the differences between the response of a writer who
observes, stores impressions, and orders experience and
that of a politician who is, in Mailer's words again, "'aware
of people only as eyes, a type of response. It's more like being an actor'" (OB 180). Because Naipaul chose to place
himself in the action — that is, to show himself following
Mailer, interviewing his associates, collecting the material
for the article — we become doubly aware of him as a
writer, in contrast to Mailer who cannot remember detail
or assess the value of the campaign when it is over. Again
the conclusions reached through writing fiction seem to be
relevant to subsequent nonfiction, as Naipaul's coverage of
the campaign also demonstrates the modifying effect a
society has on its politicians. Over the period of his campaign Mailer becomes increasingly conservative and adopts
the style expected of an American politician. His flamboy-
ance gives way to dark suits and ties; a haircut is decreed
not only for himself but also for the hirsute young cam-
paigners around him; the rowdy Greenwich Village meeting is replaced by handshaking on the pavement outside
Macy's. The quality of intellectual and social rebellion
infusing the campaign is modulated by the security of
American life; such rebellion is glamorous rather than
threatening as it might be in a less settled community.

Realizing that "in a society like ours, fragmented, in-
organic, no link between men and landscape, a society not
held together by common interests, there was no true internal source of power, and that no power was real which

did not come from the outside" (MimM 246), Singh chooses
not to defend his position, for the stability and definition
he seeks are totally lacking. Further, he becomes aware of
the threat posed by police and military in such a situation.
Not only do writers of fiction — Achebe (*A Man of the People*, 1966) Awoonor (*This Earth My Brother . . .* , 1971),
Ngugi (*A Grain of Wheat*, 1967) — support Naipaul's view
of colonial politicians, but also his perceptions are validated by trained political observers. A. W. Singham's study of
the crises in Grenadan political life in 1951 and in 1962,
The Hero and the Crowd in a Colonial Polity (1968), expands
into generalizations about the course of events in many
Third World countries. More than providing absorbing
background to Naipaul's journalistic account of the American invasion of Grenada in 1983 (VSN, 1984a) it seems almost to predict the rise and fall of Bishop, Coare and the
men of their ultimately divided party. Singham contends
throughout his book that the particular type of society
created by colonial rule fosters individuals whose personality patterns are authoritarian (as opposed to "creative"). Expecting control to be exercised over themselves, they turn
heroes into political leaders, but because of the political
unreadiness of the leader as well as of the mass, genuine
political socialization does not take place and the movement develops no ideological content. Compare the following two passages, the first Singham's, the second Naipaul's:

> Unlike his African and Asian counterparts, the West Indian
> colonial has no traditional culture to escape into. One consequence of this type of political socialization is that the
> individual finds it very difficult to develop a political value
> system that differentiates between rational and irrational
> demands for change. Such an individual does not readily
> respond to ideologies or ideological values but rather to
> leaders who can articulate his hostility. The object of his
> rebelliousness is not clearly focused: the individual is
> against the state, or the economic conditions he suffers
> under, or just against "them". Electoral politicians, and particularly the hero, exploit this hostility and provide tempor-

ary relief for the mass through crowd catharsis. (Singham, 193)

> We spoke as honest men. But we used borrowed phrases which were part of the escape from thought, from that reality we wanted people to see but could ourselves now scarcely face. We enthroned indignity and distress. We went no further. (MimM 237)

A key word in Singh's description of the group around him and Browne is "awe"; it is not a real political party machine that is being formed, but a cult. In *The Overcrowded Barracoon*, Naipaul analyses this aspect of Mauritian politics (see especially OB 261), and in *A Bend in the River* it explains the popular appeal of the President.

In Singham's analysis of Grenada, Singh's of Isabella, and Naipaul's of Grenada after the invasion, aggression is inward-turning, as Frantz Fanon has predicted. In Grenada the initial violence in 1951 set striker against non-striker; only after the trade union leader had been arrested was violence directed at the planters and colonial government. In 1983, the revolutionaries observed only the forms and mimicked the language of socialism, accusing each other of being *petit bourgeois,* and finally left nothing but "a murder story" (VSN 1984a, 31). In Isabella violence is racially oriented, setting elements of the lower classes against each other, despite the fact that the issue is supposed to be the nationalization of the sugar estates. Kenneth Ramchand (1973, 27) argues that Naipaul skilfully weaves into Singh's personal account references to the complexities of international finance and agriculture. On the other hand, Karl Miller (1967, 686) (who compares the "integrated" party of Browne and Singh to that of Burnham and the Jagans in Guyana) believes that "*The Mimic Men* does not really do justice to the intricate difficulties inherited by those in the Jagans' position, to the causes of those upheavals which the new states invariably undergo". Naipaul may very well omit or neglect, in the novel *The Mimic Men*, important elements of many crises — the role of the trade unions or of the entrenched colonial bureaucracy, for instance. But

these omissions are required by his thematic objectives as
a writer of fiction and need not be interpreted as ignorance
of the importance of these forces in many well-document-
ed crises, which he deals with in his nonfiction. Naipaul
presents Singh's political movement as the product, not of
reason but of emotion, particularly the negative emotion of
bitterness. Blessings conferred upon it by organized groups,
such as the trade unions, would suggest that it exercised an
ideological appeal and diminish the effect of chaos Singh
stresses constantly. Singh does, in fact, note passingly the
number of expatriates in the civil service and that the trade
unions did not support his party, but the characterization
requires that Naipaul reveal the limitations of his understanding and the confused state of his mind and emotions
at the time of crisis. Later as Singh analyses his experiences, he sees the parallels between Isabella and the other
colonial dependencies, a realization that directs his quest
for order towards the view of colonialism as a tragedy and
of himself as a victim. In *The Middle Passage* Naipaul
begins to analyse the effects of the World War II presence
of American troops in Trinidad; their influence on individuals had already been noted in early fiction. In *The Mimic
Men* Singh continues the investigation, arguing that "the
pace of post war political change . . . is not the pace of creation. Nor is it the pace of destruction, as some think. Both
these things require time. The pace of events, as I see it, is
no more than the pace of a chaos on which strict limits
have been imposed. I speak of course of territories like Isabella, set adrift yet not altogether abandoned, where this
controlled chaos approximates in the end, after the heady
speeches and token deportations, to a continuing order.
The chaos lies all within" (MimM 230). Close to Naipaul's
own statements in nonfiction and at the thematic centre of
"A Flag on the Island", this is offered in this novel not as a
complete analysis of the colonial situation but as part of a
fictional portrait of a disturbed man looking for peace.

The same pattern of fragmentation that drove Singh into
politics compels him to seek identity and self-definition in

personal relationships, which are almost certain to fail. As Singh begins his memoir, he establishes both his sense of sex as a mutual violation and his avoidance of intimacy. Ideally an extension of the self, a moving out of the self, sex should discover "the larger erotic dream, the god", but the ideal is never realized in the seductions and visits to prostitutes of his student days which bring him close to breakdown. Blinded by his own aimlessness to Sandra's vulnerability and despair, he attributes to her the qualities of strength and maturity, firmness and precision which he most needs himself. Singh's crippling self-awareness and his inability to act to avert a crisis destroy the marriage. Structurally, the novel peels away the layers of Singh's experiences as from an onion; when his memoir moves back in time to his youth, he reveals the one nearly perfect sexual relationship of his life: he had known his cousin Sally so closely that her flesh was "almost my own" (MimM 186). Although intercourse with Sally reinforces his failing sense of himself, his own identity and reality, it cannot aid his search for order, since it only insulates him from disorder and drives him deeper into himself instead of releasing him.

Finally, release from the tyranny of his own flesh is achieved during an encounter with a prostitute at the time of the political crisis. At last he is carried beyond distaste for things of the flesh which has often sounded like Brahmin fastidiousness, and beyond the images of vulnerable flesh which have haunted him (and so many of Naipaul's other creations – Biswas, Stone, Bobby, Roche, Salim). Refusing himself the right to judge or disdain the distorted body of the woman releases him from condemnation of his own, from the fears of flesh's demands and the threats against which flesh must be defended.

> The self dropped away, layer by layer; what remained dwindled to a cell of perception, finer and finer, having validity, existing only because of that probing which, growing fainter, yet had to be apprehended, because it was the only proof of life: fine perception reacting minutely only to time, which was also the universe. It was a moment that

was extended and extended and extended. There could be
no issue; it was a moment which, when release without
fruition came and perception widened again, defined itself
as an extended moment of horror. It is a moment that has
remained with me. After three years I can call it back at
will: that moment of timelessness, horror, solace. (MimM
282–83)

The experience seems to be similar to Mr Stone's in the mist
at Chysauster, but loss of self is not only terrifying to
Singh, it is also comforting. Thus, he can draw on the experience to solace Indian victims of racial violence; recall
the enormity of time, and the insignificance of momentary
glory or suffering is obvious. All that happens can be viewed impersonally: "Do not tell me how people died. Say instead 'Race riots occurred'. Say, 'There was loss of life'"
(MimM 289). But Singh realized that something other than
withdrawal, avoidance of disturbing fact, is required if the
discovery is to prove beneficial, and again the character
and the author seem to merge in their perceptions of their
failings. Singh is aware of his ability to transmit his own
vision of the world as, certainly, is Naipaul, but neither
author (at this stage of his career) nor narrator is able to
issue a "call to action and self-fulfilment" and without it the
"gift of comfort" is useless and destructive (MimM 289).
That call requires "an assurance of imminent order" in
which neither can believe.

The issue of active involvement with others is central to
In a Free State also and to other later fiction. It seems that
there is only one counter to this impulse towards destruction rather than construction: the creative imagination.
The development of Singh's understanding as he writes his
memoir and his willingness to re-engage life are achieved
by his creation of patterns of imagery which order experience; his technique is also Naipaul's. Singh's sense that he
has not been responsible for the events of his life — "my
belief in my star [that] . . . would take me to my appointed
place" (MimM 248) — cannot be the source of strength that
it is for Narayan's characters with their conviction that the

universe is ordered. Writing is the necessary therapy, but only with time does Singh learn what he must write and how it will release him from visions of disorder. The recurrence of the image of the child outside the hut which Naipaul has used to symbolize himself and major characters of his fiction indicates the strength of his identification with Ralph Singh. One-third of the way through his narrative, Singh is tormented by the vision of disorder, by his longing to enter the past, and by his recognition of the impossibility of doing so' " . . . in the middle of an assessment of my situation that is so practical and realistic, I am like that child outside a hut at dusk, to whom the world is so big and unknown and time so limitless; and I have visions of Central Asian horsemen, among whom I am one, riding below a sky threatening snow to the very end of an empty world" (Mim 97–98).

However, he has already begun to impose the order on events that will make them manageable. The difficulty of beginning to write was surmounted when Singh's memory of his first snowfall led to the discovery that "Certain emotions bridge the years and link unlikely places" (MimM 184) and the related discovery of the house as one of the central images of his writing, again one to which Naipaul himself constantly returns. The view of red brick houses from his hotel window, the girl's house in the photograph which his imagination tried to enter and order, the ugly houses in the snow viewed from the Kensington attic, and the houses of tropical Isabella all become linked in Singh's imagination. "Sometimes by this linking the sense of place is destroyed, and we are ourselves alone: the young man, the boy, the child. The physical world, which we yet continue to prove, is then like a private fabrication we have always known" (MimM 185). In the complex imagery of *The Mimic Men* the house expresses the owner's personality, but it is only a fabricated personality he creates for his public. The interior of Browne's house is cluttered with fussy knick-knacks, a lacy table cover, a palm in a crepe paper covered tin, and framed pictures of Joe Louis, Jesse Owens, Haile Selassie,

Jesus, and the Browne family before a photographer's backdrop of Grecian ruins. It conveys the family's self-concept and its ideas both of heroism and gracious living, just as the Deschampneufs's portraits of family ancestors, old prints of Isabellan scenes, pictures of the French countryside, and photographs of racehorses convey their public posture. Singh reacts to these interiors with discomfort. The pictures on his grandfather's back veranda, although hung with the same instinctive need for self-definition, have a significantly different effect on Singh, who sees the religious pictures and photographs of Indian film stars selected by the old man as "an act of piety towards his past, a reverencing of the land of his ancestors. Details like this had gone towards the making of my picture of him" (MimM 119). However, when the calm old man is reduced to frenzy by the insults of two field labourers, Singh discovers that he is as vulnerable as others. Singh is obsessed in youth with the belief that his father's house, which represents both a family tradition and the society about him, is about to collapse; though he fears the catastrophe, he is disappointed when the house survives a heavy tropical storm. Singh's Roman house, with its logical plan, its climatic suitability, and its unrevealing facade offers him a haven from external chaos. Its "outward austerity" and its "inner, private magnificence" (MimM 84), express Singh's self-concept as completely as the other houses express those of their owners even though he seeks to hide himself within its historical connotations. Only when Singh withdraws to the anonymity of a hotel room can he discover himself and express that self with any semblance of truth. Such a pattern of imagery orders the experience of the writer as it unifies the work.

Running through the novel in counterpoint to the theme of fragmentation is Singh's growing awareness, arrived at as he reflects on his past in isolation, that the human personality is indivisible although it may be distorted by attempts to assume the roles devised for it by others. In analysing the London dandy pose (chosen for him by Lieni),

Singh writes, " . . . at the time I thought I was simply playing, that in the keeping of trophies and writing-up of experience I was expressing a non-existent side of myself. As
though we ever play. As though the personality, for all its
byways and wilful deviations, all its seeming inconsisten-
cies, does not hang together" (MimM 31). The pattern is repeated. The pose, adopted in stress, becomes a distortion
and must finally be cast off, but it is not long before new
stress brings a new pose or the resumption of an old one.
The important recognition is that ultimately the personality does "hang together". This discovery is part of Singh's
achievement in writing his memoir. That he can state it for
the first time early in his book may be an indication that
Singh is analysing and deciding prior to writing as Naipaul
says one must in writing nonfiction; that his understanding
seems to deepen as he continues may be an indication of
Naipaul's role as novelist working toward conclusions.

> As I write, my own view of my actions alters. I have said
> that my marriage and the political career which succeeded
> it and seemed to flow from it, all that active part of my life
> occurred in a sort of parenthesis. I used to feel that they
> were aberrations, whimsical, arbitrary acts which in some
> way got out of control. But now, with a feeling of waste and
> regret for opportunities missed, I begin to question this. I
> doubt whether any action, above a certain level, is ever
> wholly arbitrary or whimsical or dishonest. I question now
> whether the personality is manufactured by the vision of
> others. The personality hangs together. It is one and indi-
> visible. (MimM 219)

He comes to see that even in moments of acting out a role
for his own benefit only, there is some truth. Touching
Sandra's abandoned possessions or holding the photograph
in the London attic might seem empty gestures, but they
express one part of an individual's essence. Singh might
feel that his political career has been merely another
gesture, but after chronicling his youth and early manhood, he realizes that they have inexorably led him to his
career and, equally inexorably to his withdrawal from it.

In his affirmation there is also an affirmation of an independent reality, one that does not depend on the perceptions of someone external to it. The vision of extinction should the world forget one's existence has been banished.

Another forceful image expresses the unity and reciprocal relationship of those elements which constitute the modern political universe, the old world and the new, the colony and the empire: "The Niger is a tributary of that Seine." The phrase and the perception it expresses echo and re-echo in Isabella and call up memories of Conrad's *Heart of Darkness*. Singh calls it the "cry of the defeated in the war between master and slave" (MimM 95), and the suggestive power of the phrase brings to mind the whole experience of colonial corruption. Civilization's representatives bring with them the corruption of venality, inhumanity and power but soon become the prey of raw primitive instincts. The Niger may pay tribute to the Seine, but as a tributary it also contributes to the composition of its water. The complex of word associations suggested by the word "tributary" richly expresses Singh's ultimate view (which coincides with Naipaul's) of the mutual degeneration brought about by colonialism. Finally *The Niger and the Seine* becomes the title of a satirical pamphlet which chronicles the racial changes in two families who liberally allow inter-marriage until the once-black family becomes white and the once-white family black. The reversal of roles is complete when the white-skinned daughter of the Negro family is refused permission to marry the black son of the French family.

At one time in his active life, Singh had thought of writers "as incomplete people, to whom writing was a substitute for what it then pleased me to call life" (MimM 292). He discovers that "writing, for all its initial distortion, clarifies, and even becomes a process of life" (MimM 301). Writing clarifies, wards off the fear of extinction; it seems to be one of the rare sources of fulfilment for Naipaul and his characters. However, Parrinder (1979, 6) notes that "If he shows literacy as civilised man's most powerful instrument of self-assertion, it is at the price of revealing its subjection to all the defeats, distortions and violations imposed on the self by the modern world". He believes Singh's memoirs are a distortion of his initial impulse to write history, that they are merely a lengthy apology for his own futility. Again Naipaul and his creation must be separated. Writing is the key which gives Singh access to understanding and peace, but Naipaul does not suggest Singh approaches perfect self-understanding; though moving forward Singh remains humanly fallible, and one type of failure is the failure to act. Though he manages to sound disconcertingly confident at times, Naipaul himself shows, in Neill's words (1982, 55) "an unexpected and surprising humility, a disarming self-doubt expressed in the rigour with which his scepticism is extended to the very act of writing itself. For Ralph Singh, we might remember, the process of writing 'cleared the decks . . . for *action*'; yet the novelist can never entirely rid himself of the suspicion that writing is less a preparative for action than a corrupt substitute . . . " Withdrawal – from the world and into writing, for which Singh had yearned as an escape from the torment of his vision of disorder – finally provides the simplicity which enables him to free himself from one cycle of events. In fulfilling the fourth stage of Hindu life, Singh recognizes that to be without a past is to be as totally desolate as he had once felt himself to be on a country railway platform, waiting for a train to London on a public holiday. By imposing order on his past he has made events historical and manageable and freed himself from disturbance. Like Garbage he is now ready to bring the two-pronged knife down on the struggling cheese. Unlike Mr Stone, whose attempt to engage life leads only to a negative withdrawal and the promise of returned calm, Singh is ready to face what remains of his life, but we do not know whether he will do anything or whether the feast has ended.

Robert Morris (1975, 66–67) finds the conclusion to *The Mimic Men* unsatisfactory: "Singh falls from power in the literal and figurative senses with all substance (moral and material) dissipated. And having given over, at forty, the complexities demanded by life, he can only drift away from 'responsibility and attachment' toward the 'final emptiness', retreat into shadowy simplicity, and — the paradox is Naipaul's, not mine — become a slave to the total and useless freedom he has so long courted". Hena Maes-Jelinek (1967, 513) has taken the opposite view, remarking that Naipaul's "restrained and sensitive style records dispassionately Singh's progress towards maturity. Singh achieves detachment, what he calls 'the final emptiness'; then, as a free man, the first among Naipaul's characters, he prepares for fresh action confidently". The truth is probably somewhere between these contradictory views. Having completed his task — discovering how he came to be where he is, Singh frees himself from the vision of chaos by learning that events and conditions lead onward in inevitable and eternal progression. Western in his perception of discernible cause and effect relationships, Singh does not succumb to the Hindu vision of change as non-progressive and of existence as illusion, but he retains a Hindu sense of the enormous sweep of time. The use to which Singh will put the freedom he has won for himself from his earlier sense of chaos is not disclosed, but even the resolution to act should be recognized as an advance from Mr Stone's stoical expectation of returned calm. As disoriented by his experiences in the metropolis as he was in the colony, Singh demonstrates the failure of the metropolitan model for the postcolonial who has come to terms with neither recent past in the colony nor ancestral past. In addition, Naipaul demonstrates through Singh the experiences of a writer who discovers what he believes to be the truth about reality through the ordering experience of writing. While *The Mimic Men* purports to be Singh's autobiography, it is Naipaul's fiction, and Naipaul has written that it is in fiction that a writer truly reveals himself (see VSN 1964b, 76), in this case possibly to have some doubts about the process of writing itself.

Vision of History: *The Loss of El Dorado*

Naipaul's "Foreword" to *The Loss of El Dorado* (1969) expresses his sense that in Trinidad there is no past, only a discontinuous and anomalous present. His alienation from the West Indies in general and Trinidad in particular and his failure to achieve any identification with his Indian heritage — which together result in the major themes of his fiction — are chronicled in *The Middle Passage* and *An Area of Darkness*. In Naipaul's attempt to achieve a personal perspective and to discover where and how the bus began its journey, the investigation of history is the next logical step. He writes,

> Port of Spain was a place where things had happened and nothing showed. Only people remained, and their past had dropped out of all the history books. Picton was the name of a street; no one knew more. History was a fairytale about Columbus and a fairytale about the strange customs of the aboriginal Caribs and Arawaks; it was impossible now to set them in the landscape. History was the Trinidad five-cent stamp: Ralegh discovering the Pitch Lake. History was also a fairytale not so much about slavery as about its abolition, the good defeating the bad. It was the only way the tale could be told. Any other version would have ended in ambiguity and alarm. (LED 375)

The Loss of El Dorado attempts to put the past back into a book, but not into a school history text book; rather, from the scholarly research into archives, from the author's own translations emerges a novelist's interest in character, and the history that is written is that of individuals who are moved by (and take part in) events that are now nearly legendary. This is passionate history of the kind one expects only when memory can recall actual events, and passionate history, history which captures people and effects of events on them, is the only kind which reveals the truth. Naipaul's *A Congo Diary* (VSN 1980b) remarks again and again that where history is known only through Belgian textbooks, it has disappeared (see below, p. 204). In deflating romantic legends which have become "history", Naipaul suggests that the distinction between fact and fiction, history and fantasy is frequently vague. In the writing of this book, Naipaul seems to discover the roots of the futility and sterility which in his view characterize life in Trinidad, but in concluding the "Epilogue" with the mystery of the slave Jacquet's death – did the self-confessed poisoner of other slaves and the master's infant son poison himself or was he poisoned by another? – he reminds us that historical fact cannot provide the answers to all the aberrations of human behaviour it reveals. The picture of Trinidad that gradually unfolds is indeed that of a place "where ignorant armies clash by night".

Naipaul's detailed history ends in 1813; by that time he believes certain patterns to have been established, and in demonstration the book abounds in historical repetitions. To those readers who see *The Loss of El Dorado* as Naipaul's personal attempt to define his own past, in the same way that Ralph Singh longs to define his, it need not be surprising that he does not actually write of the indentured Indians in Trinidad as part of this history. He is concerned with the conditions and events that created a situation which he knew as a child, preoccupation with which provides a major theme in his fiction. In discovering the patterns, he finds some of the answers to the questions that haunt him. At this stage of his career, he turns to history through which the circle of light can be enlarged and the mystery of the bus hurtling through the darkness be partially solved. Thus, it is enough for Naipaul to allude to his own people only in passing: "To keep the estate productive, contract labour – some Chinese, some Portuguese, but mainly Indians from the ancient, distressed Indo-Gangetic plain – replaced the Negroes on the estates. It was a new human dereliction, in the pattern of what had gone before. The Indians were people to whom authority had always been remote; they had little sense of history, were governed and protected by rituals which were like privacy; and in the Trinidad countryside they created a simple, rural India.

They were an aspect of the colony" (LED 374). The pattern
of what had gone before is summed up in an earlier statement: "So much was written about Negroes. But the Negroes of 1800 remain as anonymous as the Indians of Las
Casas three centuries before. It is the silence of all serfdom"
(LED 291). This is Naipaul's view of the destiny of his people – to become an anonymous aspect of a colony whose
history abounds in lies, delusions, failures, corruption,
brutality, absurdity and futility.

Half-truths, wishful thinking and outright lies first
brought Trinidad to the attention of the European world.
After the discovery of the riches of Peru and Mexico, the
Spaniards were prepared to believe anything – and the Indians had learned the wisdom of sending the hungry con-
quistadores on over the next mountain to find fabulous
wealth. Spanish soldiers, too, discovered a way to prefer-
ment in claims to have seen the lost city of El Dorado, the
gilded chief. Antonio de Berrio, founder of the first European settlement in Trinidad, found it prudent to perpetu-
ate some of these stories when he was captured by Sir
Walter Ralegh, and Ralegh's man, Keymis, also fed his
expectations. But none could deliver: "And then, like every
Indian guide to El Dorado, Keymis knew nothing. Nothing
about gold, nothing about the mine" (LED 102). These
deceptions, conscious and unconscious, have a parallel in
the second major episode which Naipaul believes to constitute the history of Trinidad – that is, around the beginning
of the nineteenth century, "the British-sponsored attempt,
from the newly captured island of Trinidad, to set going a
revolution of high principles in the Spanish Empire" (LED
17). The first British governor of Trinidad, Picton, seeking
personal military glory and to occupy the Spanish troops in
Venezuela, encouraged revolution across the Gulf of Paria
until he became uneasy about the revolution backfiring on
Trinidad. From then on Picton, like the Indians two hundred years earlier, said what was desired of him. Agents of
the revolutionary leader, Francisco Miranda who was in
exile in London similarly "fabricated a few encourage-

ments" (LED 167). Governor Hislop, who replaced Picton, also became a supporter of the revolutionaries, particularly when the celebrity Miranda arrived in Trinidad with the glamour of metropolitan connections – very much like the appeal of Jimmy Ahmed when he returns to his island from London in *Guerrillas*. But, just as none could deliver riches to Ralegh, no one could deliver Venezuela to Miranda.

Naipaul draws another parallel between Ralegh's story and Miranda's. According to him, both men needed the security of being restrained from action. As Helen Tiffin (1972, 101) remarks:

> The idea of action being a betrayal of feeling and truth, that detachment and contemplation are better than activity, is a very Indian one, and it is an idea to which Naipaul in his works frequently returns. Sometimes, as in *The Mimic Men* it is treated ironically, as an easy way of opting out. In *The Loss of El Dorado* it is however seen to be at the root of the tragic gulf between ideal and reality in the historical situation.

In his London exile Miranda was, like Ralegh in the Tower, seething with plans and full of hope for glory, but both men discovered that the reality was far different. For Ralegh, there was no El Dorado and no glory, only his execution as a traitor; for Miranda, the revolution ended in his betrayal and death in a Spanish prison. Further parallels may be drawn to Naipaul's fictional creations: Ralegh may be a prototype for Ralph Singh, writing in his hotel room and readying himself for new activity. Certainly Jimmy Ahmed's revolutionary plottings are very similar to Miranda's, but for Ahmed's case Naipaul had a contemporary model as well, lending further support to his theory of historical repetition.

The admiration for the successful rogue, which Naipaul, in *The Middle Passage*, says characterizes Trinidadian morality, and which he dramatizes in his early fiction, has an historical antecedent as far back as the 1590s. A contemporary and rival of Berrio governed Cumaná and dealt in Indian slaves, an illegal practice because the Indians were deemed to be subjects of the Spanish king with all personal rights. Berrio was jumping the governor's claim when he took possession of Trinidad, but Berrio could not use the slave-trading against him: "He could be handled only in the way of the Indies, where the law was to be obeyed but not always followed. This was possible because each official had a separate contract with the King; legality could be measured by achievement and every man was therefore as strong as he made himself" (LED 36). Under Spanish rule and under the English, Trinidad was not supposed to trade with the enemy, but "it was permitted by both sides. From Trinidad the launches took British goods and Picton's propaganda; from Venezuela they brought cattle, mules, tobacco, salt, dried meat, all contraband, and Spanish government spies. The spies were useful to Picton" (LED 169). The sardonic humour of these two statements is typical of Naipaul's treatment of the abuses of law in Trinidad's past, but the cumulative effect of his narrative is much darker than this would suggest.

Another pattern which is repeated is that of the governor being recalled to stand trial in the metropolis for his failure. Chacon, the last Spanish governor, was tried by a Council of War for turning over the island to the English without firing a shot. He was acquitted but three years later the Spanish king reversed the decision after the issue was revived by the French residents of Trinidad, who were not pleased about being consigned to the English and who wanted to sound loyal to Spain in case the island was restored. Similarly, Picton was brought to trial over his approval of the torture of a Spanish mulatto girl, Luisa Calderon. He was found guilty, but acquitted in a retrial two years later, again after a shift in public opinion in Trinidad. "In the next three years there had been a change. Picton no longer had enemies among the English; he was no longer a despot, an opponent of English laws; he was only a British governor being persecuted on behalf of some mulattoes and Negroes" (LED 309).

Thus, Naipaul reports a series of historical repetitions

but the most obvious – and continuing – cycle is of brutality. In his "Postscript" to *The Loss of El Dorado* (which does
not appear in the original Deutsch edition), Naipaul connects the beating or "blessing" of children, such as the
punishment administered by Baksh in *The Suffrage of Elvira*,
to the severe whippings of the slave era when slave actually outdid the master in the correction of slave children. In
Naipaul's history, the first brutality results in the disappearance of thirty-five to forty thousand aboriginal Indians from Trinidad alone, victims of battle and new dis-
eases. Next came the tit-for-tat ambushes and massacres by
Ralegh and Berrio. These are the roots from which springs
the savage brutality of the slave period. At first, the
Spanish Negro Code emphasized the care and protection of
slaves rather than their punishment; in fact the practice
was probably even milder than the code until after French
immigrants from racially disturbed islands brought their
slaves to Trinidad in response to Spanish invitations to
populate their islands. Under Picton, encouragement of
immigration continued, "and in Trinidad the principles of
their aristocracy, which had set the Caribbean ablaze,
were revived" (LED 183). Rewriting the code in answer to
their fears and their need to define themselves by the
expression of their superiority, Picton restricted the movement of Negroes, increased punishments and working
hours, and provided no protection against moral dangers
or against the abuses of owners. "The severest punishment
was for witchcraft and sorcery. Negro sorcery, leading to a
Negro underground, was the especial French terror. Subor-
dination, the suppression of competition, the suppression
of anything that might lead to conspiracy and riot: the code
marked the dangers of the slave island. There was no longer a threat of Venezuelan invasion; the Spaniards on the
island were negligible. The French free people of colour
were bitter but subdued. The danger lay in the Negroes
themselves, by whose numbers the prosperity of every
slave island was measured" (LED 184). In *Guerrillas* Naipaul contends that the fear remains when he presents the

story of Mrs Grandlieu's father-in-law, who died by poisoning in 1938 and spent his last hours "thinking about Negroes and the police and punishment. As though on the last day of his life he went back a hundred and fifty years" (G 132).

Naipaul's history of brutality becomes painfully detailed at the stage when French immigrant planters under Martiniquan Hilaire St Begorrat take over the investigation of an outbreak of poisonings of slaves in 1801. Counterpointed with the story of the poisoning commission's deliberations is the story of Luisa Calderon's torture which was intended to extract a confession from the girl to a robbery which never happened. Naipaul describes the jail in some detail – and especially "the punishment cells known as *cachots brûlants*. The temperature in these dark windowless rooms was never less than 100 degrees; prisoners there, chained flat on boards, quickly wasted away and became demented" LED 189). He also describes the accused prisoners – "foolish and derelict", "ruptured and swelling". And if the point is not already clear, Naipaul offers as an aside, the story of the death of a runaway slave as the torturer's knife sliced into his ear. While English and Spanish could massacre each other without mention of blood-letting, now Naipaul enters into detail. Perhaps his growing compassion for victims should be related to his discovery of Biswas's agony as Naipaul tried to tell the story of a man like his father. Later the easy brutality of the slave period is transmuted into the physical violence of *Guerrillas*: "The first cut: the rest would follow" (G 243). Naipaul's awareness of this brutality and his study of the victims of torture develops further his awareness of the vulnerability of the flesh, a theme already stated in his fiction but of increasing importance in later novels. As Naipaul finishes the stories of the accused poisoners and Luisa Calderon, he emphasizes the accuracy of his facts – brandings, hangings, burnings alive, spiking of heads – by reporting dates, even times of day and the day of the week. Mentioning that Luisa's second torture took place on Christmas Eve only intensifies the impression of total inhumanity, which is not much relieved when he recounts what happened to the slaves of any master who dared to oppose the events, for Picton could quiet obstreperous masters by trumping up charges against their people.

The chapter "Apply the Torture" ends with the assertion that the pattern was firmly established. A new outbreak of poisonings, new trials and sentences occurred at the end of 1802. Naipaul feels no need to detail these events. Nor is the reader surprised to learn that even after the drama of charges of brutality against Picton, another suspected poisoner was tortured under Hislop, the new governor who was "inexperienced" and "anxious to conciliate" (LED 271). Although the story of Luisa Calderon's torture and Picton's disgrace is, according to Naipaul, only an expression of a complication in the second sequence of events he records (LED 17), this is the section of the book with the greatest impact. Looking back to *The Middle Passage*. it is clear that he feels the slave era defined the racial sense which ultimately corrupted the whole society; he rejects Martinique almost totally in that book and in *El Dorado* Martiniquan immigrants are blamed most heavily for racial abuse. In *The Mimic Men* Ralph Singh's narrative recognizes as a legacy of the slave era the social fragmentation which remains under the veneer of racial integration. *A Bend in the River* is permeated with imagery drawn from the period of slave trading in Africa; this imagery reminds readers not only of the many forms of enslavement but also of the violence and cruelty Naipaul records more frequently in recent work. The contamination of the slave era is not restricted to the West Indies.

The slave poisonings have their parallel in the affairs of Europeans in Trinidad. Miranda's agent Manuel Gual was poisoned by a former revolutionary friend. Ten years later Simón Bolívar prevailed upon Governor Hislop to return Gual's bones to his native land, but the bones that arrived were apparently those of a small horse (LED 349–50). Even this absurdity has its parallel: the Spanish admiral Aristi-

zabel was supposed to remove Columbus's remains from
strife-torn Santo Domingo to Havana late in the eighteenth
century but he, too, took the wrong box (LED 138).

"Absurdity" is one of the key words of *The Loss of El
Dorado*. The history that Naipaul writes is of one absurdity
after another, from the search for a golden city no one has
seen but everyone believes in, to the English administration
of unknown Spanish laws to a French population. Governor Hislop finally had to send to Caracas for lawyers to try
to plug loopholes that allowed offenders in Trinidad to
claim, taking Picton's case as precedent, that they could
not be tried in England for an offence against Spanish laws.
The legal chaos of the situation after Picton's retrial led to
the appointment of George Smith to help with the administration of law in the colony. The trouble was that Smith
"didn't come out as an English-style Chief Justice. He came
out as a Spanish-style Royal Audience, a one-man Audience; and bizarrely, he came from London laden with
Spanish titles, all granted under the Sign Manual of the
King of England. Smith was a friend of Miranda's; he had
borrowed Miranda's Spanish law-books and carefully, after
many drafts, had written out his own comissions, including his title of address' (LED 334). Smith was a fanatic; his
"cause was the chastisement of English colonial society"
(LED 335). Governor Hislop called in a Venezuelan lawyer,
Level de Goda, to advise him on ways to curb Smith's
authority. Smith also engaged Venezuelan advisors. The
ultimate absurdity was that Level, a conservative planning
a counterrevolution in favour of Spanish authority on the
mainland, wound up unseating the representative of Spanish authority in Trinidad, while Smith's lawyers, revolutionaries in Caracas, tried to defend the authoritarianism they
fought at home.

In Trinidad alliances were often (and according to Naipaul, still are) based on expediency rather than on a strong
ideal or on loyalty to a political cause important in Europe.
At the time when French royalist settlers were arriving in
Spanish-governed Trinidad (fleeing the republicans who

had gained control of Martinique), Spain and France were
at war, and England was Spain's ally. England captured
Martinique and the republicans fled to Trinidad, adding a
new faction to Governor Chacon's problems. It was probably a relief to him when England, no longer an ally, attacked Trinidad. At any rate Chacon did not waste any
blood on its defence. The complications to national antagonisms were completed by racial differences. The colonial
Spanish feared French republicans because of their alliances in the islands with Negroes, but in France Napoleon
was plotting to destroy the Negro Revolution of Toussaint
L'Ouverture by inciting the British in Jamaica to attack
Santo Domingo for raids on Jamaican slave-holdings. Naipaul demonstrates his gift for wry understatement: "there
was generated just that degree of confusion in which a man
would sometimes find it hard to say where he stood" (LED
152). So Hislop found out when, with Spain and France
allied in Europe against England, he tried to govern under
Spanish law in England's name an island with a population
composed of French royalists and republicans, Spanish
Americans, English merchants and planters, mulattoes,
free Negroes and slaves. In presenting these shifting alle-
giances and the various betrayals of individuals and ideals,
Naipaul reveals the beginnings of the fractured purposes
and ideals he records as typical of Trinidad in *The Middle
Passage* and which make the introduction of universal suffrage a subject for satire in *The Suffrage of Elvira*.

Naipaul's vision of history at this stage of his career resembles Hindu philosophy in stressing the recurrence and
repetition of cycles of events, and finding the roots of present conditions in the past. Even the Spanish American
revolution has its precedent. Ralegh and Miranda were not
just temperamentally similar; Ralegh, too, dreamed of a
revolution – his would have freed the Indians from the
Spanish and restored the perfect, unviolated, and complete
world which was already being destroyed. Naipaul responds to the romance and lyricism of Ralegh's *The Discovery of the Large, Rich, and Beautiful Empire of Guiana*, while

at the same time recognizing that it was imprecise and written to try to regain favour in the court. When the British Empire finally arrives in Trinidad, it is with all the tools of torture, far from Ralegh's ideal. Returning to the "complete" world before the period of discovery and exploration is an unattainable dream to Naipaul, with his vision of a world fragmented and without roots. In the "Epilogue" of *In a Free State*, he tries to share the artist's sense of completeness (again, it is Naipaul's word) recorded on the walls of tombs at Luxor, but finally asks whether even the completeness might have been just a vision. Naipaul believes that the Spanish frenzy in the search for El Dorado resulted from their discovery of the value of what they had destroyed and their desire to find Shangri-La for the second time. Even the French had a pastoral dream which they tried to bring to life in the West Indies by naming their slaves "Thisbe" and "Priam" and "Icare". The modern tourist literature, condemned as a confidence trick on Trinidadian as well as tourist by Naipaul in *The Middle Passage*, tries to enliven the dream of Paradise yet again. It would seem that the whole story of Trinidad is, in Naipaul's view, based on the conflict of ideal with reality.

This conflict results in the intellectual confusion of the new arrival in the West Indies which Naipaul points out again and again. It is the same sort of confusion which defeats Peter Roche, former anti-apartheid terrorist in *Guerrillas* when he finds that he cannot say the right thing in a radio interview. His historical precursors are men like Dr Sanderson, abuser of slaves who campaigned for a British constitution defining personal rights for Trinidad; Fullarton who sought to be a "balanced administrator" in a colony that, by its very nature, made his goal impossible; McCallum who objected to slavery not on humanitarian grounds but because it reinforced class divisions among whites and because he feared the presence of Negroes; and Smith who defended the "illiberalism" of the Spanish code in the name of a liberal cause, protecting the franchise of the free people of colour. "At the heart of the difficulty was slavery":

The Loss of El Dorado as a whole is Naipaul's attempt to show how the varied and complex forces created by the imposition of slavery on Trinidad finally resulted in the fragmented and cynical society of which he writes. Both Naipaul and George Lamming (*In the Castle of My Skin* 1970, *Water with Berries* 1971, *Natives of My Person* 1974) demonstrate in their fiction the necessity of undertaking this task on behalf of a society which has protectively erased its slave past from its memory. These confused men – Smith, Sanderson, Fullarton, McCallum – illustrate what is, to Naipaul, the process of becoming colonial. Immigrants bring with them the "liveliness" of the metropolis, the "complex drives of their culture" which are soon reduced to the "simplicities of money and race" (LED 315). "In the slave society, where self-fulfilment came so easily, this liveliness began to be perverted and then to fade, and the English saw their pre-eminence, more simply, as a type of racial magic. The shifting of the Empire to the east, the emigration of the ambitious, was a further intellectual depletion. The English in Trinidad became like the French. The quality of controversy declined, and the stature of men. What was left was a colony" (LED 372–73).

The words "simplicity" and "simple" recur constantly in Naipaul's discussion of Trinidad's colonial history. They are used most commonly to indicate the egoism of colonial aims and aspirations. Thus, Naipaul writes of " . . . the high doctrine of borrowed constitutions disappearing in the simple factions of race, colour, region, the imperfectly constituted society decaying into minute egoisms" (LED 351). Race could hardly be called a "simple" issue in a society where 128 degrees of colour are separately and minutely defined and labelled except in the sense that everyone can be classed as being like oneself or not; only an egocentric evaluation can be simple. The degeneration to this simplicity is Naipaul's idea of what it means to become colonial. It must be a frustrating restriction on Naipaul who is so aware of individual complexity that in writing of Trinidadians he is forced to reduce humanity to outward appearances. In comparing Ruth Prawer Jhabvala's avoidance of racial issues while she concentrates on cultural differences, Yasmine Gooneratne remarked to me, "Naipaul, writing about Trinidad, has no option but to report life at its level of 'simple' racism, where the loss of cultural roots has made people dependent on the simplifications and impoverishments in human relations that come with colour awareness of this kind." After Picton's departure "'The issues in Trinidad had been simplified. . . . the confusion of philanthropy and Jacobinism among the English settlers, London talk from London people had disappeared" (LED 299). What is left is a "colonial society, that could refer only to race and money whose stored wisdom was only about cacao, tobacco, sugar and the management of Negroes, [and that] was as deformed as Governor Hislop had sensed in Trinidad and Miranda in his early life in Caracas and during his recent adventure at Coro. It wasn't only that the wines, the manners and the graces, the books and the art and the ideas of a living culture came from outside, the simple society bred simple people" (LED 332–33). And this society is incapable of supporting an ideal. "The imperfectly made society had disintegrated; it was too simple for lasting causes. The only cause was the self and survival: the tragedy of the simple . . . " (LED 365). Again Naipaul reveals the original in the historical past. He points out the egoism in a Spaniard's appeal to his King against threats from the governor of Margarita to build a city wall excluding his properties. Naipaul comments, "The egoism is another side of the Spanish simplicity" (LED 120). Also the Venezuelans Manuel de España who was won over to the revolution by the promise that he would be one of the first generals and Jose España who planned to start a Negro revolution with the Negroes of his own estate illustrate Naipaul's contention that the Venezuelan revolutionaries were "as simple as their words" (LED 175), both in the sense of placing their personal advantage first and in the sense of not understanding fully the implications of what they did. The "simple vocabulary of revolution" (LED 139) is the vocabulary of the French Revolution, of the Paris streets, which emphasizes the advantage to each individual of fighting. Such selfishness, the seeking of personal advantage before espousing any cause, is typical of the motivation of characters in Naipaul's fiction, even of characters for whom readers feel great sympathy. One of Ralph Singh's self-imposed tasks in *The Mimic Men* is to reveal the basic egoism of his political activity in spite of his party's expressed idealism.

Another aspect of colonial simplicity which persists to the present, according to Naipaul, is the reduction of every man's value to an estimation of his lineage, particularly as defined by his race, his degree of blackness, and of his wealth. Francisco Miranda was never taken seriously by a majority of Venezuelans because he was merely the son of a Canary islander, a shopkeeper who had, embarrassingly, been successful in Caracas. Picton, learning of Miranda's background, had warned London against consulting him or entrusting him with information about British plans for an invasion of Venezuela. "Picton . . . had become a colonial. Shaking himself free of the revolution, the revolutionaries and the Spaniards, he had made Trinidad his opportunity. He had become a planter; he owned Negroes. He had become a defender of slavery, vehement, like a convert to the cause. He had the vocabulary and could make the private jokes; he could describe the system as 'the assistance of Africans from the Coast'" (LED 182). Miranda exhibited in Europe the "insecurity of an outsider in a setting which he yet felt to be his own" (LED 164). He was aware of the elements of the metropolis which were missing from his colonial background – the culture, good food, wine, a genuine aristocracy, ideals – and he self-consciously sought to replace them in his life, accumulating and shuffling books and papers, giving himself the title of Count, romanticizing the revolution until (like Ralegh) he talked of freeing the noble Indians and managed to ignore the Negro presence in South America. Jimmy Ahmed's attempts to create a gracious home for himself and to write a romantic version of his life spring from the same needs.

Naipaul seems to delight in putting in perspective the events that have been romanticized by history. Seeing himself, perhaps, as a victim of the criminal acts which deprived his people, the Africans and other minority groups in the Caribbean of their cultures, it is possible that his technique satisfies a personal need to take the romance out of the events that led to the "shipwreck" (his own image in *The Mimic Men*). The growth of the Spanish Empire with its wealth and power is reduced to Fernando Berrio's lieutenant's salary for governing Trinidad – sixteen and a half pesos. "It gives a scale," writes Naipaul (LED 77). Ralegh's great discovery of Guiana is reduced to a "nervous six-day journey of exploration" (LED 107). One of Bolivar's close associates was on George Smith's payroll in Trinidad. "Again, it gives a scale" (LED 346). A republican reinvasion of Venezuela after one of many reverses was successful with ninety-four men, five muskets, a barrel of powder and no cannon. "It was the smaller South American scale" (LED 360). Colonialism created an environment in the West Indies that denied humanity or heroism to the people it settled there; it is as a result of colonialism that Naipaul's own fictional heroes, whether West Indian or of some other area, must either be anti-heroes or possess only a limited heroism. In puncturing the romantic myths of history, Naipaul deliberately – and ironically – sets the record straight.

In a similar way Naipaul strips Francisco Miranda's history of romance. Miranda's career was, by anyone standards, extraordinary. The son of a Caracas shopkeeper became, among others things, a favourite of Catherine the Great, a general in the French revolutionary army, a pawn used by Pitt to gain intelligence of the Spanish Empire in South America, a leading member of the Congress of Venezuela with Simón Bolívar, and finally the general who surrendered Caracas to counter-revolutionary forces and was turned over to the Spaniards by Bolívar. In telling his story Naipaul makes him seem an ineffectual dreamer obsessed with his papers, with his self-endowed title, a man out of his depth. In part, at least, all this is probably true. However, Salvador de Madariaga's (1947) portrait suggests the magnetism and personal charm, the flair for recording the age in which he lived, the eagerness to educate himself which also characterize the man. Naipaul does not tell the whole story of Miranda's final downfall, skipping over the events of nearly eighteen months in Venezuela during which Miranda and Bolívar nearly succeeded with the revolution. Most importantly, he does not tell of Miranda's capitulation to an inferior force which was, according to J. B. Trend (1946), to Bolívar simple treason for which he had to be punished. Naipaul writes of "Miranda's appalling discovery at the end of his long political life, which was like Level de Goda's at the beginning of his, that the society was wrong, the cause was wrong, that the good words didn't fit. An appalling discovery – those agents of his who had given up the cause and suffered – but it must also have been like reconciliation, because Miranda had lived out this truth in his own life. Defeated but still free to act, he began to think of Spain in a new way. He began to think of partnership. Then he was betrayed" (LED 351). Naipaul's view of Miranda seems to be very much based on the conclusions about politicians and their motives, and their relationship to colonial societies, that he worked toward fictionally in *The Mimic Men*. "Defeated but still free to act" after living out the truth in his own life, achieving reconciliation – is this not Ralph Singh?

Naipaul's omission of the usual style of historical documentation shows that his version of Trinidad's history is best treated as one coloured by his personal experience and his perception of reality. For example, on many key points regarding Ralegh's second voyage to Guiana, historians have disagreed dramatically for generations. Regarding Keymis's attack on San Thome – which was the action for which Ralegh was beheaded – Naipaul states, "The Spanish garrison and the Spanish settlers were prepared to surrender without a fight. They wanted to be rid of Palomeque: . . . What is certain is that the garrison deserted; and that the English night attack was on an abandoned settlement guarded by no more than three men . . . " (LED 101). But Edward Thompson's (1935) version of the story is that "A Spanish patrol of less than a dozen men attacked in the darkness . . . " and that although the Spanish deserted the settlement, it was certainly manned when the English attacked. Martin A. S. Hume (1906) quotes a letter from one of Ralegh's captains which claims there was no Spanish attack before the English action and says the Spanish fled. Here, perhaps we find seeds of the doubts about history Naipaul expresses in *A Bend in the River*, but it seems he suppresses the instincts of "bad blood" that might result in metaphysical questions. Each of Ralegh's biographers seems to tell the story with slightly different details. However, Naipaul does not even acknowledge the controversy nor does he document his statements with anything more than a bibliography at the end of his text; rarely are the sources of quotations given and if there is a citation it is often merely something like "an English witness wrote" (LED 102) or "an Indian witness . . . told his story to a Spanish official, who repeated it at the Spanish inquiry six months later" (LED 100). I do not wish to suggest that Naipaul's research was less than thorough; on the contrary, it seems most impressive. On the other hand, I do believe that *The Loss of El Dorado* must be considered as a rather personal version of Trinidad's history, closer perhaps to Naipaul's journalism than to conventional scholarly texts or perhaps comparable to Shakespeare's manipulation of historical facts to prove the divine rule of kings. For Naipaul, reality is what he knows and has experienced: this fosters an attitude towards Trinidad which many find cynical and pessimistic, but which he believes realistic and justified. This attitude is the basis for his structuring of plot and character just as Ruth Prawer Jhabvala's theory of a cycle of emotional variations in Europeans who travel East becomes a base for her novels and as Yeats's theory of cyclic changes in the world's history provides the base for "The Second Coming" and most of his later poetry. But conversely, Naipaul's understanding of reality is to some extent, at least, arrived at as he creates his fiction — "the novelist works toward conclusions . . . "

So when Naipaul, writing nonfiction, reaches conclusions on the basis of his studies — in his terms analysing and deciding before writing — the conclusions may well be those the novelist worked toward at some prior stage. For instance, "as soon as [Ralegh] was released his conviction weakened. The will to action dropped away. He threw all the responsibility for finding the mine to Keymis, his old friend, who claimed to have seen the mine" (LED 92): Naipaul attributes to Ralegh the same mistrust of action that afflicted Mr Stone and Ralph Singh. Another example: Ralegh's humane treatment of the Indians resulted in a legend which endured for over a century about the white man who would deliver them from the Spanish. In Ralegh's dream of releasing the Indians from Spanish domination, Naipaul sees neither humanity nor patriotism, only futility and empty romance. Is this not the novelist's conclusion about the inevitable loss of ideals by those engaged in political action? This idea suggests another: noting that Naipaul does not discuss the controversies about Ralegh or the slightly differing versions of events in Venezuela, possibly he is not yet prepared to question the efficacy of history in providing explanations for the origins of that bus that hurtles mysteriously out of the darkness. Years after turning historian, the novelist of *A Bend in the River* expresses some grave doubts about history.

At this stage of his career, Naipaul sees fact and fiction, history and fantasy as very closely connected, sometimes indistinguishable, but the implication he is willing to draw seems to be that reality may be discovered just as correctly or truthfully through fiction as through fact or history. The other outcome of such thinking — that reality may never be apprehended, the full existential dilemma, or that there may be a far less tangible reality (like that uncovered in *Finding the Centre*) — is the result of that "bad blood" he says he fights. And yet in writing *The Loss of El Dorado*,

Naipaul seems to come perilously close to the conclusions of *A Bend in the River.* "The legend of El Dorado, narrative within narrative, witness within witness, had become like the finest fiction, indistinguishable from truth" (LED 38). In telling Ralegh's or Miranda's story or in recounting the events of Picton's governorship as contrasted with the war heroism for which his name is known, Naipaul shows how closely the art of history approaches the art of fiction. Which facts are recorded and remembered are selected by some unspecified process, not unlike that of the writer of fiction, and very rarely represent the whole story. In writing *The Loss of El Dorado*, Naipaul himself seems to be consciously selecting the other facts.

"Steinbeck in Monterey" (OB) is also about making myths and about Janus-faced reality. Visiting the Monterey Peninsula in California, Naipaul sees it as the place where America with all its tensions, past and present, ends and fairytale begins. Steinbeck wrote of the tough and vicious world of the Depression and of exploitation but his sentimentality sowed the seeds of a myth. Now the dreadful reality of the canneries is transmuted into a tourist attraction full of businesses trying to capitalize on the myth and very few can remember, as Don Westlake or Wesley Dodge can, the truth. Dodge is still angry – angry at the Okies whom he blames for compounding Californians' problems and taking his job, and angry with Steinbeck for romanticizing the Okies and turning Californians into villains. "Westlake talks less with anger than with distress. He talks like a man who will never exorcise a personal hurt"; he realizes that living in pipes and boilers was neither romantic nor "funny" (OB 164). Naipaul's sketches of these men are selective and economical but give a strong impression of the individuals and their values; even speech patterns are reproduced, reinforcing physical description and the few bits of background information. The fascinating and relevant aspect of these two portraits to consideration of *The Loss of El Dorado* is that Naipaul shows that their truths about that period are different and that they differ also from Steinbeck's, which is considered the truth by readers of his fiction.

Not only the recording of fact but also the facts themselves, the events as they happen are a sort of make-believe. Naipaul repeats the phrase, "the New World as make-believe", in discussing both the pamphleteer McCallum's book *Travels in Trinidad* and the hidden Negro night life of playing out fantasies of white royalty. Finally he writes of the slave Scipio: "When Scipio joined the Carenage regiment he was offered the title of 'My Lord St John'. He said no; he just wanted to be 'Secretary'; and at gatherings he 'made a show of scribbling'. He belonged in real life to the Attorney-General, who was not really an attorney-general: one make-believe mingling with another" (LED 296). No wonder "fantasy" becomes another key word in Naipaul's history, used as it is in "Fact and fiction meet: Berrio links the two fantasies of the new world" (LED 41). Time and again Naipaul shows that the dream of a Sir Robert Dudley or Level de Goda or Miranda became the fact, the reality for them in the way that the Negro slave lived for his fantasy night-life which replaced the day-time reality. Dudley's expedition to Trinidad and El Dorado was, according to Naipaul, in the nature of an exercise to give a young man experience in leadership and adventure. Naipaul's estimation of the achievement of the voyage is made very clear by his parenthetical comments, such as " . . . he had sent to Berrio (or pretended to send) a message of disdain . . . " (LED 45), or "They marched through the thick woods over 'high and unpleasing mountains' – which do not exist – . . . " (LED 55). But to Dudley and to his Captain Wyatt, whose manuscript record became the fullest account of the expedition, "That time in Trinidad had been a time of fantasy and knight-errantry, of brave deeds poetically witnessed, of challenges, of seeking out an ordained enemy – and how well the Spaniards filled that role – in a strange glittering forest full of dangers and wild folk. . . . Wyatt saw Dudley as the greatest hero of chivalry and himself as Dudley's squire. He aimed at a style that matched the

adventure and his role" (LED 45). Thus, the fantasy becomes part of the historical record. An article "Columbus
and Crusoe" (OB) takes up this theme — that legend may
replace historical fact. But the emphasis of the article is on
the avarice and brutality of the period of exploration. Naipaul's word for Columbus is "banal"; what is most appalling
to Naipaul is Columbus's failure to respond to the romance
of the great adventure.

Naipaul's sensitivity to and awareness of the interplay
between fact and fiction is demonstrated by his treatment
of Defoe's *Robinson Crusoe* in both the article and *The Loss
of El Dorado*. Besides responding to Defoe's method of
creating fiction from fact — although in mentioning sources for *Crusoe*, Naipaul does not name Alexander Selkirk
whom, according to Pitt's introduction to the 1963 Airmont
edition, Defoe met in Bristol after Selkirk's rescue from the
island of Juan Fernandez — Naipaul is particularly interested in two aspects of the story. First, Crusoe personifies the
dream of a Berrio or a Ralegh "to be the first man on the
earth, to see the first shoots of the first crop, to let off 'the
first gun that had been fired there since the creation of the
world': it is an aspect of what the El Dorado quest had become" (LED 41). In the second half of "Columbus and
Crusoe", Naipaul outlines the relation between the myth of
Robinson Crusoe and the Spanish fantasy of rediscovering
Shangri-la in El Dorado; both express the double dream of
innocence and of exercising total power over it. Secondly,
Crusoe is in crisis when he runs short of writing materials.
The need to record, to work out the significance of events
through writing them down, is one Naipaul and his characters share with Crusoe. Naipaul also notes that, as Crusoe
wished of the Spaniards he was to rescue, Berrio actually
asked his soldiers to make a written declaration of loyalty
— " . . . fact again answering Defoe's imagination . . . " (LED
43). Crusoe's Spaniards had neither pen nor ink, and that
was nearly the case in the province of El Dorado also. The
governor of Trinidad lost his silver inkhorns to buccaneers
and there was a shortage of paper on Margarita; survival

was the only concern, and the paperwork of the Spanish Empire, the volume of which was once a serious liability, was abandoned.

For Naipaul, the dilemma of the Spanish settlers without paper and ink becomes a metaphor for a life without the solace, the opportunity for investigation and consolidation offered by writing. Such a life is reduced to survival in a void, cut off from the sources of one's heritage, whatever they may be. Naipaul is using his art partly in an attempt to discover what his own mixed heritage is. In noting that the only piece of literature produced by the Spaniards in Trinidad was a poor poem about the martyrdom of some monks on an Indian mission, Naipaul is virtually stating the reason that Trinidad cannot offer him a source of intellectual or emotional strength. Other pieces of writing he mentions, Ralegh's book about his Guiana journey and McCallum's pamphlets, do not offer what he needs.

The province of El Dorado was lost by the Spanish when their empire disintegrated. The portion which most concerns Naipaul, Trinidad, was lost again when it passed into English hands before finally becoming independent. Naipaul's history of Trinidad concentrates on the period during which patterns of colonial behaviour were established. In both his journalism and his fiction, he shows the origins of the sterility, the lack of creativity, the racial stratification, the roguery and the self-denigration he has recorded in *The Middle Passage*. The El Dorado that was lost was not just a province; it was a golden dream, an untouched, unspoiled wilderness, a chance of establishing a Utopia. The tragedy of modern history, as Naipaul sees it, is that the Utopian dream is mere fantasy, turning into the nightmare of colonialism and imperialism that robbed human nature of its dignity and human societies of their complexity.

Part Three

The Destination

Deracination: *In a Free State*

"Writing must be pursued as a very special, private activity" (Naipaul to Drodziak 1978, 21). Perhaps his habitual withdrawal has led to Naipaul's vision of the human condition as one of isolation in a cocoon of self-awareness. At least two other authors who share Naipaul's experience of expatriation have made similar declarations: "The classic definition for me of the writer's life is that laid down by James Joyce: 'Silence, exile and cunning'. This I interpret for myself to mean that I must keep my mouth shut, stay aloof from the world around me and carry on my business like a thief in the night, pillaging what I need and hoarding it in the secret recesses of my imagination to make of it what I can" (Jhabvala 1971, 25). Jhabvala's pillaging and hoarding also sound much like Naipaul's technique. He describes "the method of the novelist, [as] making art of egotism, creating a private impenetrable whole out of fragments which from a distance might appear unrelated" (OB 192). As Naipaul sees it, the trick seems to lie in translating experience into an idea and then infusing life and authority into the idea itself. And this requires luck as well as skill and vision. Of all his books, *In a Free State* (1971) seems, more than any other, to exemplify the technique of creating a whole out of fragments. When it was published, Naipaul told an interviewer: "The promptings for a book are so manifold, and to find a kind of framework which will carry all the promptings and express them fully requires luck. . . . Just to settle down and convert an idea into words on a page, and to let that have authority and life − I think that too requires an awful lot of luck" (to Henry 1971, 721).

Not a traditional novel, the carefully constructed individual parts of *In a Free State* are welded together by powerful and unifying themes: materialism, imperialism, cruelty and violence, the rootlessness and paradoxically, the confinement of modern life. Each of the five sections of the book presents individuals struggling unsuccessfully to find a place for themselves, release from their sense of dislocation in a world through which people seem to move at random. Prologue and Epilogue, containing parallel incidents in the life of a journal writer (with whom Naipaul seems to identify himself by not specifying a different persona as he usually does in first person narratives), respectively introduce and reinforce the major themes, and emphasize both the heartlessness of individuals and the futility of compassion.

The sections are linked by recurring motifs. Clothing, particularly business suits, associated with materialism and imperialism forms one such group. Viewed from afar, an English tramp appears to be neatly and jauntily dressed in lovat tweed and grey flannels, but on closer examination, his clothes, like his Empire, are seen to be in ruins and his neck scarf seems more like a noose. The Indian emigrant Santosh purchases a green suit in Washington with the proceeds of the sale of his "weed", but, like American culture, the suit will never fit him. The wedding suits in "Tell Me Who to Kill" are a mark of the West Indian Dayo's capitulation to the second-rate in English culture, and in the same story Frank's tweeds are admired by the narrator who can not imagine himself so elegantly dressed. The Africans of "In a Free State" replace tribal dress with English-style suits, and when they can not afford to pay for them, deport the Indian tailors. The Chinese circus performers are impeccably dressed in business suits, as neat in the heat of the desert as in the cold rain of Milan. The failure to put elements of another's culture to their proper use is illustrated by Bobby's dancing "native" shirt of fabric "designed and woven in Holland" (FS 112) and the Edwardian dresses worn by women of the African king's tribe. In a contrasting image, the naked men/boys chalked with white (the colour of the spirit-world) whose wraith-like appearance beside the road contributes to Bobby's sense of nightmare, are identified with the rocks, "the knotted, scaly lower half of the tall cactus plants", and "The dead branches of trees whose roots were loose in the crumbling soil" (FS 218). Their roots, too, are weakening and the white paint suggests also, in a concentrated image, the mimicry of white civilization which their city cousins have already begun. Other image-clusters occur, supporting and illuminating the themes of *In a Free State*.

The quest or journey has perhaps never been as central a metaphor to man's thought as in the mid-twentieth century, and in each section of *In a Free State* characters are on the move. Typical of our age, they invariably fail to find the freedom they seek, nor is that freedom adequately defined. The title embodies the irony of their dilemma. Where is the "free state"? Each of the former colonial states is now nominally free, but continues to be dominated by its colonial past and by stronger nations. Residents in the metropolitan countries, native or immigrant, find no greater freedom there, not even in the "Land of the Free" (the USA). The title also suggests the scientific state of freedom, unbound particles moving at random. However, Naipaul's characters are shown to be restricted and bound not only by laws and the demands of others but also in a deterministic sense by personal past and an historical past, a theme John Thieme (1975, 13) recognizes throughout Naipaul's work.

> . . . his whole *oeuvre* is bound up with the familiar twentieth century theme of the conflict between determinism and existentialism.
>
> Naipaul gives the theme an original twist by considering it within the framework of the colonial experience and its aftermath. For him colonialism and determinism go hand-in-glove; the essence of the colonial mentality is the abnegation of free choice:
>
> " . . . to be colonial is, in a way, to know a total kind of security. It is to have all decisions about major issues taken out of one's hands. It is to feel that one's political status has been settled so finally that there is very little one can do in the world."

(Thieme quotes Naipaul to Hamilton [1971])

"The Tramp at Piraeus"

The Prologue establishes with remarkable economy the themes of sordidness, cruelty and materialism, and the experiences of isolation and restless wandering through a harsh and overcrowded world. The "dingy little Greek steamer" (possibly recalling Hellenic roots of Western democracy) with its cupboard-sized bar, tiny public rooms and shared cabins confines tourists, businessmen and refugees in unbearably close quarters. It is a dirty vessel with a slovenly bad-tempered crew; "Greek civility was something we had left on shore; it belonged perhaps to idleness, unemployment and pastoral despair" (FS 9). The gloom and cynicism of such a comment is typical of the tone of other stories.

In its mixture of passengers – American youths, Lebanese businessmen, Egyptian students, Egyptian Greek refugees, Germans, the Austrian, the lonely Yugoslav and the English tramp – the ship becomes a microcosm of the crowded modern world on the move. The Egyptian Greeks epitomize the dilemma of postcolonial peoples of many lands who have lost their sense of personal and national identity. "They were Egyptian Greeks. They were travelling to Egypt, but Egypt was no longer their home. They had been expelled; they were refugees. The invaders had left Egypt; after many humiliations Egypt was free; Greeks, the poor ones, who by simple skills had made themselves only just less poor than Egyptians, were the casualties of that freedom. Dingy Greek ships like ours had taken them out of Egypt. Now, briefly, they were going back . . . " (FS 9–10). Alienation and deracination are not, however, exclusive to colonials, a discovery Naipaul made in writing *Mr Stone and the Knights Companion* and "A Flag on the Island". The English tramp speaks only of the places which he has visited, the number of journeys he has made, and the years he has spent on the move. "It was as though, over the years, he had developed this way of swiftly explaining himself to himself, reducing his life to names and numbers. When the names and numbers had been recited he had no more to say" (FS 10–11). Frail, elderly, isolated in his eccentricity, the tramp is vulnerable both physically and emotionally, but he arouses the anger, latent cruelty and the fear of other passengers. The journal-writer fears to become involved with him, and when the Lebanese and Hans humiliate the old man, neither he nor anyone else moves to help him. It is as if the by-standers are conscious of a world growing more and more overcrowded in which only the strong and the wealthy will survive, and they must choose the winning side. The tramp has his minor victory of cunning, but having proved their superiority, the others are no longer interested in him. In fact, even his tormentors are not really interested in the tramp; they look on the baiting of the old man as a game, "a tiger-hunt, where bait is laid out and the hunter and spectators watch from the security of a platform" (FS 17). This description would apply equally well to the whipping game played in the Epilogue, to the tormenting of a roti shop owner by London toughs, to Africans' goading Bobby, or to the attack on Santosh by an airline stewardess. Not really mattering to the perpetrators, when the game ends, simply "that passion was over" (FS 22).

"One Out of Many"

In this section Naipaul treats imaginatively and sympathetically the loss of that Hindu perspective which he characterizes as the curse of India in his nonfiction. The title combines a play on the motto of the United States of America, "E pluribus unum", with reminders not only of Santosh's destination, but also – ironically – of Western emphasis on the individual distinct from the crowd, as opposed to the Hindu view of the individual as part of a system. The domestic servant, Santosh, knows security as part of the crowd on his Bombay street, sleeping with them in the open, chatting and smoking with them in the evening, and enjoying the respect accorded him because his employer is an important man and because he has the use of "facilities". He refers in the first person plural both to himself and his friends, and to himself and his employer. Lacking personal identity as an individual, he neither yearns for individuality nor ascribes it to others. "Once my employer had been to me only a presence. I used to tell him then that beside him I was as dirt. It was only a way of talking, one of the courtesies of our language, but it had something of the truth. I meant that he was the man who adventured in the world for me, that I experienced the world through him, that I was content to be a small part of his presence" (FS 40). Here is personified the philosophy attacked by Naipaul a few years later in *India: A Wounded Civilization*: "Men had retreated to their last, impregnable defences: their knowledge of who they were, their caste, their *karma*, their unshakeable place in the scheme of things . . . " (IWC 32) The nonfiction strongly states Naipaul's sense of danger and loss in the acceptance of such limiting self-concepts: "Hinduism hasn't been good for the millions. It has exposed us to a thousand years of defeat and stagnation. It has given men no idea of a contract with other men, no idea of the state. It has enslaved one quarter of the population and always left the whole fragmented and vulnerable. Its philosophy of withdrawal has diminished men intellectually and not equipped them to respond to challenge; it has stifled growth. So that again and again in India history has repeated itself: vulnerability, defeat, withdrawal" (IWC 52-53). As it did in *An Area of Darkness*, that first person plural almost inadvertently creeps into the passage which otherwise is written from the perspective of an external observer/ analyst. Using his observations of Aziz as raw material but concentrating, in "One Out of Many", on the tragedy that befalls a man who loses the vision which has insensibly ordered his life, Naipaul seems again to be working toward a conclusion which will be presented analytically in his nonfiction. His abhorrence of the caste system has already been stated in *An Area of Darkness*, but in that book there is less understanding of the security it may offer to individuals who need never question their role.

Even after Santosh has been in Washington for some time, he still tries to apply the simple formulae supplied by Hinduism's rigid structure to the things he sees around him, so that he may judge what to like and dislike, what to approach and what to avoid. When Santosh discovers that the appearance and pronunciation of the hippie devotees of Krishna are wrong, he tries to explain their presence in terms of what he knew in India: " . . . perhaps once upon a time they had been like me. Perhaps, as in some story, they had been brought here among the *hubshi* as captives a long time ago and had become a lost people, like our own wandering gypsy folk and had forgotten who they were. When I thought that, I lost my pleasure in the dancing and I felt for the dancers the sort of distaste we feel when we are faced with something that should be kin but turns out not to be, turns out to be degraded, like a deformed man, or like a leper, who from a distance looks whole" (FS 30). Naipaul thus suggests, as he did in the case of the tramp, that the vigorous and sound appearance of individuals in an apparently free state cannot always withstand close inspection.

The complexities of American race relations are similarly beyond Santosh. "I know that this might seem strange to people over here, who have permitted the *hubshi* to settle among them in such large numbers and must therefore esteem them in certain ways. But in our country we frankly do not care for the *hubshi*. It is written in our books, both holy and not so holy, that it is indecent and wrong for a man of our blood to embrace the *hubshi* woman. To be dishonoured in this life, to be born a cat or a monkey or a *hubshi* in the next!" (FS 38). Marrying a Negress, Santosh loses not only his cultural ties with India and a way of orienting himself in the world, but his soul and his hope of final salvation and release from worldly existence. Large enough to engulf the small man, she is to him the incarnation of Kali, the black Hindu goddess of destruction. Ironically, Kali's other aspect is of creation, and a new Santosh is born as a result of their union. Santosh first realizes that he has reality as an individual when this woman takes an interest in him. Trying to discover why, he looks into a mirror and discovers that he is handsome; his features no longer serve "as identification alone" (FS 39). The woman brings to Santosh an Adam-like shame at his appearance, which he tries to cover by clothing himself in a green suit. The apartment becomes a sanctuary in which he hides his shame rather than a prison, and he no longer yearns for Bombay.

However, Santosh discovers his own confusion as he tries to work out a relationship with Priya. The humour in Naipaul's portrait of Priya mingles with pathos born of an awareness that both men are losing the safety of instinctively understanding others, and being understood. Santosh understands:

> "But I have enemies, you know, Santosh. The Indian restaurant people are not going to appreciate me. All mine, you know, Santosh. Cash paid. No mortgage or anything like that. I don't believe in mortgages. Cash or nothing."
> I understood him to mean that he had tried to get a mortgage and failed, and was anxious about money. (FS 46)

But Bob does not:

> "But, Bab, how can *you* ask *me* for money? Anybody hearing you would believe that this restaurant is mine. But this restaurant isn't mine, Bab. This restaurant is yours."
> It was only one of our courtesies, but it puzzled Bab and he allowed himself to be led to other matters. (FS 49)

In America, the relationship Santosh and Priya would have enjoyed in India is differently defined. Unable to "easily become part of someone else's presence" (FS 45), Santosh never calls Priya "sahib" until, under stress and in fear, Santosh seeks his protection.

> I had used the wrong word. Once I had used the word a hundred times a day. But then I had considered myself a small part of my employer's presence, and the word was not servile; it was more like a name, like a reassuring sound, part of my employer's dignity and therefore part of

mine. But Priya's dignity could never be mine; that was not our relationship. Priya I had always called Priya; it was his wish, the American way, man to man. With Priya the word was servile. And he responded to the word. He did as I asked; he drove me back to the restaurant. I never called him by his name again. (FS 52)

No longer satisfied by such a relationship, in his act of self-assertion over his salary, Santosh enjoys a victory over Priya, but his triumph soon gives way to fears and sickness of mind: " . . . sorrow lasts and can make a man look forward to death but the mood of victory fills a moment and then is over. . . . the victory I had had was not something I had worked for, but luck; and that luck was only fate's cheating, giving an illusion of power" (FS 55–56). Priya's advice that Santosh marry the *hubshi* to protect himself from deportation is, in a way, a form of betrayal – for Priya admits "I joined them. They are still beating me" – but it acknowledges the impossibility of Santosh's ever reverting to his former life.

Culturally unprepared for the concepts forced on him in the city which considers itself the capitol of the world's democracies, Santosh discovers in freedom not fulfilment but a sense of having been abandoned and left alone. Santosh chooses to find his strength in remaining a stranger to the world he entered with his marriage; he does not "want to understand or learn any more" (FS 61). All that is left to him of his Hinduism is the calm of renunciation and withdrawal. There is a suggestion that such loneliness – the sense that "all that my freedom has brought me is the knowledge that I have a face and have a body, that I must feed this body and clothe this body for a certain number of years. Then it will be over" (FS 61) – is common to all in the free state Santosh has entered. When Santosh says that he feels everyone in the park shares his sense of "the waste and futility that was our world" (FS 56), there is no technical hint that the author wishes readers to reject Santosh's perception. On the contrary, in terms of technique the story suggests as it develops that Santosh is moving steadily toward greater awareness and perception. Short sentences, a simple vocabulary, and statements of objective fact and direct observation are gradually replaced by longer more intricately constructed sentences and a vocabulary of greater complexity and abstraction as Santosh seeks to explain and analyse rather than merely report on the world about him. There have been objections to this story on the grounds that the sophistication of language is beyond the reach of an uneducated peasant. It should be noted that when Santosh reports his proposal of marriage, "I said to her *in English*, 'Will you marry me?'" (FS 60, emphasis mine), Naipaul implies that he still thinks in Hindi, and it is for the most part thoughts that the story records. We have already noted that Naipaul uses formal English similarly to suggest Hindi speech in *A House for Mr Biswas*.

The effect of this story is to record the process by which a "primitive" is "civilized", and one culture is imposed upon another. By moving the colonial to the metropolis, Naipaul is able to isolate his loss and loneliness more poignantly, but those who remain in a colony under the influence of another culture suffer similar loss. Santosh's friends in Bombay may not yet have suffered the conflict he knows, but those in higher places (represented by Santosh's master, a diplomat) would have been exposed to it. Ultimately, as Naipaul shows in *India: A Wounded Civilization* with the organizing of a Bombay slum into a cooperative or the changing relationship of landholder and peasant, all will be affected.

"Tell Me Who to Kill"

West Indians in Britain, having been twice removed from their own original culture, are even more exposed than Santosh to the onslaught of an incompletely comprehended culture. Since, in Naipaul's view, the colonial society is an inferior copy of the metropolitan, and the former slave or coolie can only mimic that copy, the narrator of "Tell Me

Who to Kill" will not succeed in living by the standards of his adopted home. Characteristically Naipaul uses the sordidness of the setting, both English and Trinidadian (the island is not named but Trinidad is suggested by the presence of Indians and the dialect employed by the narrator), to establish from the first lines the mood of his narrative. The narrator observes rubbish-filled, dirty milky-coloured streams and steaming, smelly people in England and recalls a similarly wet, but hot day at home, full of mud and nauseating smells. By the end of the tale it has become evident that neither place provides an acceptable life for the narrator or his brother. Incidentally, the almost Swiftian sensitivity to smells comprises another linking element between sections of the book: Santosh falls into sin because of the disturbing smell of the *hubshi* woman, the wet African unionists fill Bobby's car with their smell, and Linda's husband compares the president to a polecat.

The reader is offered early warning that the narrator may not be entirely reliable as a reporter. Anomalies in his description of Frank and of his relationship with him signal both confusion and tension, possibly paranoia. Frank is described, for instance, as being both "puffed up with pride" and "happy to make himself small" (FS 65); he treats the narrator better than anyone else does, and seems a good friend to him, but still makes the narrator feel diminished. A few pages later Frank appears to expose the narrator deliberately to a scene that will cause him pain, and to challenge him to become violent so that Frank may take on the role of comforter. Only after we learn the story of the narrator's failed business and his violence do we surmise Frank to be perhaps a psychiatric attendant, but we are never quite certain whether Frank is attempting to break down barriers or whether he is merely goading the narrator into making an interesting display. The narrator appears unable, too, to assess his brother's lies and manipulations accurately; the reasons seem to be partly his unquestioning love for the vulnerable child who nearly died before his eyes, and partly the narrator's inability to deal with their adopted culture.

From childhood the narrator's experiences have conspir-
ed to make him a totally disillusioned man. He is conscious
of the restrictions of his environment in the West Indies,
knowing "how ordinary the world was for me, with nothing
good in it, nothing to see except sugarcane and the pitch
road, and how from small I know I had no life" (FS 70).
Worshipping a man who appears rich and well-housed, the
narrator is surprised that there is no cinematic climax, no
drama when he is shot; without the owner's presence, the
grand house is revealed as a small, decaying repository of
useless objects subject to the rapidity of tropical rot. The
models from which the narrator deduces the standards of
the metropolitan culture are shallow and artificial Hollywood films. His basic misunderstanding as well as his illiteracy are conveyed by his failure to get the actors' names
right − "Fairly Granger", "Errol Flim", "Laurence Oliver",
etc. Even his subconscious is dominated by this world of
shadows; the central image of the story, the dream which
expresses the narrator's forebodings about his brother and
his sense that there is a threat lurking in hopeful expectations, is based on the films *Rebecca* and *Rope. The Middle
Passage* describes as incalculable the influence of the
American cinema in Trinidad and emphasizes that audien-
ces respond with especial enthusiasm to the "style" of
Bogart, to the humiliation of women, and to fight scenes.
Quantity − the duration of a fight, the number of reels in a
serial − provides the basic criterion of excellence. "The
Trinidad audience actively participates in the action on the
screen. 'Where do you come from?' Lauren Bacall is asked
in *To Have and Have Not*. 'Port of Spain, Trinidad,' she
replies, and the audience shouts delightedly, 'You lie! You
lie!'" (MP 58). Contrasting his humiliation within his own
family with these models, the narrator is filled with self-
disgust, convinced that neither he nor his culture have
anything to offer. Characteristically for a former colonial,
he directs his hatred at those most like himself, the witnes-
ses and reminders of his shame; "I am just waiting for all of
them to die, to bury my shame with them. I hate them" (FS

77). Even after his failure in London, for which he could reasonably blame and hate white people, he still directs his anger at his family. The old colonial attitude persists: " . . . like all poor people, they want to be the only ones to rise. It is the poor who always want to keep down the poor" (FS 78). This suggestion is repeated in each of the five sections of *In a Free State*: the Lebanese businessmen, the president's army, the Arab with the whip are not far removed from their victims.

Many try to free themselves from the degradation of life in the colony by "pursuing their studies abroad": the phrase recurs in newspaper reports of departures and returns as if an education were something elusive, always one step ahead and never to be caught. Like many others, the narrator's cousin is unable to cope with the pressures of life in Montreal despite having been to "good" schools. Dayo, with his back-street education, has no chance of succeeding, but the narrator, his own self-esteem at stake, will not release the dream. The narrator distinguishes himself from his family only in that "The world change around me when I was growing up. . . . I get the ambition and the shame for all of them. The ambition is like shame, and the shame is like a secret, and it is always hurting" (FS 71). Living vicariously through Dayo, the narrator hopes to erase this shame.

Expecting "everything nice" from life in London, from the moment he boards the ship, the narrator feels a prisoner, that he will "never be a free man again" (FS 85). Here is the central irony of the whole book. The colonials seek freedom outside their restricting colonies, only to discover the still greater restriction of being strangers in an incompletely understood environment. The Europeans suffer the same difficulty in Africa, their troubles being compounded by the illusion that they have created a culture which they do not understand. Even before leaving the ship, the narrator recognizes that "the mystery land is theirs, the stranger is you. None of those houses in the rain there belong to you. You can't see yourself walking down those streets set down so flat on that cliff" (FS 85). All he has learned of the new society's values is "Work hard and save your money"; he has not learned what to do next or how to do it. Completely unprepared for his new life, he cannot manage the regulations, the forms, or even the language of his "customers" in the roti shop. Trying to escape to the metropolis from a culture they believe to be inferior, these colonials discover a greater humiliation and closer imprisonment. Conditioned from childhood to take the apparently easy and attractive path of self-improvement in the metropolis, Dayo capitulates to the new environment and becomes the "ugly labourer", marrying the corpse-like girl with the "blank and broad and very white" face (FS 106). The narrator's repugnance at being in a church, his recollection of the elaborate Hindu wedding ritual, his refusal to eat meat only to be served raw and rotten fish all parallel Santosh's losses, foreshadow Bobby's retreat into the Collectorate as his self-assurance is stripped away, and remind the reader that with his marriage Dayo is entering the same abyss as Santosh whether or not he is conscious of it.

The narrator prefers violence to capitulation. Echoing *The Mimic Men*, he says, "When you find out who your enemy is, you must kill him before he kill you" (FS 83), but he finds himself incapable of violence at his uncle's house, and in England his attempt to strike back at the louts who plague him in his roti shop results only in his ultimate breakdown. Trying to leave the shop, trying to give up the effort to adapt to an alien environment, thoughts of his suffering dissipate his strength and new sense of freedom. The image of wires replacing the bones in his arms suggests tension, loss of strength and also that he is a puppet. His words to the youths — "I am taking one of you today. Two of us going today" (FS 102) — come straight from a Grade B Western move and support the impression that by this stage we are observing the actions of a conditioned subject rather than an independent man. The narrator's final detachment from his action, and his failure to comprehend what he is doing as he slips back into the dream which has conveyed his earlier fears underline the point that he has been the plaything of forces over which he has no control. Naipaul suggests that history does not answer the personal need of victims such as the narrator to affix blame and direct an attack. Any such attack would be like the one in the narrator's dream, directed against the son of parents who appear welcoming: the quarrel between friends, the friendly scuffle would result in a horrifying betrayal of hospitality. The immigrant is, in a sense, Britain's child and cannot strike back against the authority that has created his colonial culture and ordered his life. The scream of fear and horror is also a scream of rage and frustration and (like many cries of child against parent) it can never be voiced.

"In a Free State"

When Bobby tells Linda, "You've been reading too much Conrad. I hate that book, don't you?" (FS 170), Naipaul brings to readers' conscious attention many echoes that reverberate through the story "In A Free State". Like *Heart of Darkness*, this is the story of a journey through Africa in the course of which very dark discoveries are made about the nature of colonialism. Unlike Conrad's narrator, Marlow, however, Bobby and Linda do not come to a shattering self-discovery, but return unenlightened at the story's end to the same patterns they had followed before their journey began. Naipaul's fastidiously impersonal narrative tone – the third person narration contrasts strikingly with the very personal narration of other sections of the book – may indicate that as a writer he cannot engage himself as closely in the fates of these characters as he does with Santosh and the West Indian, both of whom do become aware of themselves as victims of forces beyond their control. (In fact, Frank ["A Flag on the Island"] is the only white character who narrates his own story and he differs from others in his involvement with nonwhite characters and in recognizing the encroachment of his own culture on theirs.)

Bobby and and Linda are like the colonials in this book,
however, in being victims of the postcolonial period in the
sense that the withdrawal of Empire has set them loose to
wander through the former empire never belonging to a
place, never at rest, and always regarding as "home" an
England that cannot fulfil their needs. Failing to appreciate
the incompleteness with which one culture has been graft-
ed onto another, Bobby and Linda suffer from the illusion
that they understand the culture in which they live. In
Conrad's *Heart of Darkness*, Kurtz must face the primitive
within his own soul, but Linda's morbid fascination with
unspeakable rites results only in a minor thrill of sexual
excitement, and Bobby insists that the ceremonies have
been emasculated. The Africans, with their English-style
hair and Daks suits who are in power in the "free state"
through which Bobby and Linda travel, seem to support
Bobby's conviction. The journey through Africa reveals a
modern version of colonial exploitation of the native, but it
also shows the corrupted victim becoming the new exploiter. Naipaul's description of naked prisoners lying in the
shade (FS 235) is significantly very reminiscent of Conrad's,
the difference being that in this case the guards are not
European but African.

"In a Free State" is powerful in its psychological analysis
of two characters and their complex interaction with each
other and the strange world they travel through, in its use
of changing scenery to complement and create event and
mood, and in the consistency of its thematic statements.
Linda resembles many of Naipaul's female European characters physically in her rather pinched slimness, and also
in her playing the role of dependent female. The description of Linda as a "man-eater" recalls the voracious feeding
of Mrs Springer (*Mr Stone and the Knights Companion*) and
foreshadows the image of Jane in *Guerrillas* as a sea
anemone. Linda's asssumption that Bobby will challenge
an intruder parallels Mrs Springer's assumption that Mr
Stone will play protector; Jane and Linda both appropriate
the attitudes of the men in their lives. Linda, her husband,

and their associates are the type of expatriates attracted to
a colony by opportunities for financial or professional profit, especially when they have not been successful "at
home". Their attitudes are epitomized by the owner of the
Hunting Lodge: "'The witchdoctor's all right. Oh no. No
trouble here. Tourism's going to be big business, and the
African knows he can't manage it by himself. Say what you
like, the African's no fool'" (FS 141). On one hand, Linda
adopts a mystical tone and speaks romantically of the land
and occasionally of the people in their primitive state,
usually placing the emphasis on their timelessness. Permanence and immutability would, of course, be appealing to a
European aware of shattering changes in a world made un-
stable by the retreat of Empire. On the other hand, Linda's
prejudice against Africans who attempt European style is
apparent from her first remarks about the painter, John
Mubende-Mbarara. A clear picture of Linda emerges from
her speech rather than through the narrative or description:

> "I like to think of my savages as lean. You wouldn't believe
> it now, but Sammy was as thin as a rake when he came back
> from England. Martin showed the president around the
> studios. Sammy, of course, doesn't know a microphone
> from a doorknob. Do you know the first thing Martin said
> afterwards? It's so embarrassing to say. Martin said, 'I'll say
> this for the witchdoctor. He smells like a polecat.' Martin!
> Well, you know, that sort of thing makes you feel ashamed
> for everybody, yourself included. But then." (FS 148)

Bobby's vicious personal attack forces the most direct statement of her hostility, one which compares with Kurtz's
"Exterminate the brutes": "'You should either stay away, or
you should go among them with the whip in your hand.
Anything in between is ridiculous'" (FS 226). Similarly Bobby speaks directly and truthfully in the heat of argument:
"'You came for the freedom'" (FS 225) and "'It's nobody's
fault if the people you find are just like yourself'" (FS 226).
Discovering reflections of their own inadequacies and
prejudices, Bobby and Linda are as imprisoned in the com-

pound – the name suggesting a prison camp rather than a residential area – as Santosh in Washington and the West Indian in London. Imprisonment is another linking image in these stories. The Greek steamer and the West Indian immigrant ship confine their passengers; Santosh's Washington apartment is both jail and refuge; the West Indian, hemmed in by surrounding cane fields on his island, enters an endless cycle of work and returning to his dungeon-like lodgings in London. The confinement of Bobby's car is heightened by the rain; the circumscription of the tombs at Luxor both comforts and disturbs the journal writer. The metaphor suggests that all characters are further entrapped by the past, which has shaped their lives and their societies directly and indirectly.

Bobby is, if possible, as confused and contradictory as Linda. Sounding idealistic and optimistic, he talks of serving the people and not interfering in their politics, and he condemns European corruption and profiteering. But he uses African boys, preferably young and unspoiled, for his homosexual needs, and he uses Africa as a refuge from the pressures which caused his breakdown in England. His proprietary interest, his paternal possessiveness reveals itself when he looks at a famous vista: "'I feel all this . . . belongs to me'" (FS 125). Bobby's reaction to the stares of the lorry-load of Africans shows his fear and his need to hide that fear. His assumption of a simple, friendly manner, and subtly modified language when he is dealing with an African assert his real sense of superiority. When he is incited to rage by the African who gouges his windscreen, he claims to have been humiliated, not (as Naipaul first leads the reader to believe) by the African's mistreatment of his property, but by his own attack on the man's dignity. But again truth emerges under stress: "'I'm a government officer! . . . How dare you turn your back on me while I'm addressing you?'" (FS 156). He requires that his position be recognized. For this reason, after Luke sees the result of the beating to which Bobby submits himself almost in an act of martyrdom, Bobby can no longer have him around.

Luke's laughter recalls an exchange between Bobby and Linda after the service station incident:

" . . . They've called in all their friends and they are killing themselves with laughter."

"We misinterpret their laughter," Bobby said, his hand playing with the gear lever.

"That may well be. It's embarrassment or disapproval or something like that. Sammy Kisenyi was telling me. And some European probably told him. But I feel that some of it is good old-fashioned laughter." (FS 159)

Wishing to leave, Bobby has no destination; unlike the others he cannot go South for he needs the self-esteem his liberalism brings him at the same time that he needs to feel superior to someone. While the colonel sustains himself by hating the African, Bobby must keep up his "selfless" sacrifice and love for his black brother.

Naipaul repeatedly emphasizes the failure of Europeans as role models for Africans. When he calls attention to the gross obesity of Europeanized Africans, he parallels it with the eating habits of the German and Belgian parties at the hotel. References to the dirtiness and smell of Africans are balanced by allusions to Linda's vaginal deodorant and Bobby's sexual activities. One recalls that in *Heart of Darkness* Marlow is astonished by the clean collar and careful grooming of the acccountant at the Middle Station because all the other company men are so dirty.

In much the same way that passengers on the steamer to Egypt wanted no association with a loser, the white men in this African state have decided to support the "gangster" president who controls the army rather than the king whom they personally prefer. The state's freedom is to be replaced by a military dictatorship bent on genocide of the king's people. In the past the king's people had been skilled builders of straight roads over difficult terrain; they had been a "clothed people" and "forest conquerors". Their roads, built only of the perishable products of the forest, earth and reeds, have lasted for centuries while more "durable" products introduced in more modern times have fallen into decay — the 1920s palace on the ancient site of the king's authority is "its first true ruin" (FS 242). This proud tradition has been lost by a people doubly imprisoned; before becoming the naked prisoners of the president's army with the burning of their villages, they had been "civilized" by the colonialists. Bobby's description of a typical member of the king's people is adroitly counterpointed by narrative comment:

> "I know the king's people," he said. "He's probably a Christian. He goes to church every Sunday. He keeps his clothes very clean. He washes and irons his own two shirts very carefully. His wife does a little teaching in their village in the Collectorate. He reads. He had that foolish little paperback in the back pocket of those dungarees." Bobby was thinking of his own houseboy, who was also small and fine-featured and of the king's tribe: a churchgoer and a reader of devout or educational primers in the second moneyless half of the month, a drinker in the first half, often tortured by hangovers, light and silent then, with an additional quality of delicacy. (FS 158–59)

One is first aware of Bobby's failure to recognize Luke's need to escape into alcohol from the idyllic life Bobby pictures for him; second, of Bobby's appreciation of his "delicacy" and the relationship between the two on which Luke's job probably depends; and third, of the abandonment of their own ways of life by the king's people for a shallow imitation of the white man's culture and the gratification of his wishes.

Attempting to perform incompletely understood roles in the new social structure, Africans vent their frustration in increasingly violent challenges to the white men around them. The petrol station attendant, provided with a broken tool, uses it to damage Bobby's windscreen. The trade unionist who cannot define or pronounce his job demands a ride and bullies Bobby into taking his friend into the car. African troops, being trained by a tough Israeli, fall into the "trance-like dance of the forest" (FS 181) rather than exercise away the fat deposited by an army diet, but they are effective enough in beating Bobby. The atmosphere of menace builds as these and other incidents reveal the anger of Africans; because preceding sections of the book deal with colonials from other areas, Naipaul seems to imply that the threats will be repeated and expanded throughout the world. So far, the attacks are not continued when the attackers are challenged: for instance, when Linda orders the unionists out of the car, they leave quickly and without argument, but they will not necessarily retreat in future confrontations. There is a ring of truth in the colonel's certainty that Peter is awaiting a chance to kill him; Peter is a real threat because he has learned to play the colonel's games so well. Like the dogs which have forgotten they were trained only to attack Africans, other weapons of the white man will be turned against him.

A related group of images involves road accidents and motor cars. The owner of the Hunting Lodge, an accident victim who constantly invokes memories of England, becomes an appropriate representative of the battered state of the Empire. In the hands of Africans, the motor car has become a weapon which leaves the compound looking like a ski resort (most residents in splints), a weapon which is used against Bobby, and a weapon which may have been used to kill the king. Africans have also adapted the motor car for "traditional" purposes. A mangled dog by the roadside recalls Wole Soyinka's *The Road* (1965) with its description of dogs that are run down deliberately as a sacrifice to Ogun, god of the road, who will himself take, as a substitute, the driver who fails to give him a dog. In failing to offer Ogun his meat, the Europeans court disaster by failing to take note of the primitive forces that lie just beneath the calm of Europeanized African culture.

Thus, the story gains a wider symbolic significance: the increasing violence of the attacks made on Bobby foreshadows attacks to be made in the future against all that he stands for, particularly the paternalism which the narrator of "Tell Me Who to Kill" could not counter; but by recalling the violent attacks on and by that narrator, the violence of

American blacks rioting in Washington, and the attack on the tramp, the attacks against Bobby become just a part of a pattern of violence resulting from the frustrations of the free state of the postcolonial world. The introduction of an Israeli army officer, American foundation money, Australian wine and Belgian cigarettes to "In a Free State" suggest the likely involvement of the rest of the world. Other sections of the book contribute more nationalities, and widen the implications of the book as a whole even further, to reach a climax in references to Chinese Communists in the Epilogue.

The conflicts of "In a Free State" are not the simplified hostilities of black against white. The story is, in the first place, a chronicle of Bobby and Linda's journey and of their changing relationship. One of the ironies of the title lies in the fact that, for all the physical confinement of their car, especially in the rain, Bobby and Linda are in that particular type of free state which consists of being cut off from the inhibiting and stabilizing influences of everyday life exerted by routine, and by personal and social relationships. Their relationship passes through stages of reserve, hatred, annoyance, friendship, communication, irritation, simple quarrelling, verbal attack, compassion, and finally separation. Although the impression is of mutual antipathy, there are times when out of loneliness, fear of pain, they draw together and offer comfort to each other: Bobby's kiss when Linda is stung is gentle and affectionate, and when Linda tries to help him after the beating, Bobby thinks, "With sudden passing sorrow for her, for whom so much had also gone wrong: but these are the hands of a nurse" (FS 241). Their real tragedy is that these humane feelings are so often stifled: "He wanted to say: I know why you're crying. But he decided to let her be, to do nothing that would feed her mood" (FS 215). Sympathy passes to be replaced by regret at having revealed a softer, inner self: "He had spoken too much; in the morning he would be full of regret; Linda would be another of those people from whom he would have to hide" (FS 170). In the end no lasting friendships develop among the Europeans in Africa, no relationships that do not end in backbiting and bitchy gossip; the compound is riddled with destructive stories, personal and professional jealousies. Despite the need for comfort and human warmth, everyone is at war – not just in this free state but everywhere.

"The Circus at Luxor"

The Epilogue reinforces the theme that even when people are moved to compassion and intervention on behalf of others, the act generally proves to be both futile and regrettable. Recording a second trip to Egypt by the journal writer of the Prologue, the Epilogue offers compensation for his refusal to become involved with the tragedies of others on the steamer. But his lonely protest against the violent "game" of whipping children who are lured into range by tourists leaves the writer "exposed" and the others unabashed, uncaring, or simply bewildered by his odd behaviour.

These events are not the only "circus" at Luxor. The first seeds of a new empire are being sown in the ancient land by a touring Red Chinese circus. In an old rest-house, the Chinese offer all the waiters gifts of money, medals bearing Mao's likeness, and postcards of Chinese peonies. "Peonies, China! So many empires had come here. Not far from where we were was the colossus on whose shin the Emperor Hadrian had caused to be carved verses in praise of himself, to commemorate his visit. On the other bank, not far from the Winter Palace, was a stone with a rougher Roman inscription marking the southern limit of the Empire, defining an area of retreat. Now another, more remote empire was announcing itself. A medal, a postcard; and all that was asked in return was anger and a sense of injustice" (FS 255). The Chinese empire is unlikely to be more permanent than any of the others recalled directly by the references in the passage or suggested indirectly by the presence of Greek and Lebanese businessmen, a Hilton hotel, and evidence of economic distress. Wisely making their appeal for "anger and a sense of injustice" in a more receptive quarter, the Chinese may possibly get more response than the writer did, but even that is doubtful. Naipaul compares the waiters with soldiers being decorated, and closes the Epilogue with a glance into the future when Arab soldiers, defeated in the Six Days War, are lost in the desert. The juxtaposition suggests that the army of revolution the Chinese are trying to form is unlikely to be any stronger than that army of peasants on the railway platform in Cairo whose fate is well-known. "Those men with shrunken faces were the guardians of the land and the revolution; but to Egyptians they were only common soldiers, peasants, objects of a disregard that was older and more rooted than the revolution" (FS 250).

Such cynicism causes the writer to doubt even the ancient vision of wholeness he had glimpsed in one of the tombs. "The ancient artist, recording the life of a lesser personage, sometimes recorded with a freer hand the pleasures of that life: the pleasures of the river, full of fish and birds, the pleasures of food and drink. The land had been studied, everything in it categorized, exalted into design. It was the special vision of men who knew no other land and saw what they had as rich and complete" (FS 251). All that the writer now sees and experiences in Egypt makes it "hard to believe that there had been such innocence. Perhaps that vision of the land, in which the Nile was only water, a blue-green chevron, had always been a fabrication, a cause for yearning, something for the tomb" (FS 255–56). In categorizing, exalting into design, the ancient artist is engaged in the same task as Naipaul sets himself. The novelist presents in a fastidiously ordered, carefully structured volume a vision of disorder. The fictional character recurrent in Naipaul's writing who needs to write in order to cope with his perception of chaos is replaced in this book by Naipaul himself; when he encloses the three stories between entries from what purports to be his own journal Naipaul seems to say, "I am here, this is my hand at work."

Closely linked by parallel situations and recurring images which develop themes, each section contributes to understanding of the others, but the cumulative effect is of increasing darkness, cruelty and futility. With the suggestion that the artist's vision of completeness had always been a fabrication, Naipaul seems momentarily to challenge his own stated goal as a writer – to impose order. Again in his fiction he seems to be working toward a conclusion which may be dangerous and from which he retreats. For the time being he will stand by the linked ordering images, the artistically unified structure that is one of his greatest achievements as a writer. The whip wielded by the Arab at Luxor or the (implied) cane-field overseer in "Tell Me Who to Kill" or advocated by Linda is an appropriate symbol of colonialism, but it is also basic equipment for the ringmaster of a circus; Naipaul thus suggests that the world's peoples are no more than a cosmic circus responding to the crack of fate's whip. Those who imagine themselves to be in a free state are in reality the prisoners of the colonial experience; each is a citizen of a world that offers neither security nor fulfilment. Through several fictional permutations of the basic elements of the postcolonial experience, Naipaul shows that each attempt to relocate leads to misunderstanding and further dislocation. But there is no escape, for all that has occurred is predestined by history and irreversible. Before publication of *In a Free State*, Naipaul had been exploring the origins of the bus that hurtles out of the darkness past the child stranded in his clearing. He discovered dislocation and despair in the metropolis as well as in the colony. With this work of genius, he views the road ahead and discovers only a bleak terminus for humanity's journey.

Disengagement and Violence: *Guerrillas*

Two words which recur frequently in Naipaul's works – "derelict" and "desolation" – dominate *Guerrillas* (1975).

Repeated description of the setting, which is recognizably
Trinidad though the island is unnamed, provides a background against which Naipaul portrays fragmented personalities in a postcolonial world. The personal histories of
the novel's three main characters identify them as part of
the human flotsam generated by the same forces which cast
adrift the characters of *In a Free State*, but this book focus-
ses on political issues as they dominate individual lives.
Naipaul's articles about Argentina and Uruguay, as well as
his study of Michael de Freitas, reveal just how closely the
two circles of interest intersect in Naipaul's mind; his ex-
tensive discussions of South American society, published
in the period when he was writing *Guerrillas*, also suggest a
direct cause of his extremely negative frame of mind.

> Commentators like Mariano Grondona, unravelling chaos,
> tying themselves up in *etapas* [stages], will try to make
> sense of irrational acts and inconsequential events by talk-
> ing of Argentina's French-style history. Others will offer
> political explanations and suggest political remedies. But
> politics have to do with the nature of human association,
> the contract of men with men. *The politics of a country can
> only be an extension of its ideas of human relationships.*
>
> Peron, in himself, as folk leader, expressed many of his
> country's weaknesses. And it is necessary to look where he,
> the greatest macho of them all (childless and reportedly im-
> potent), pointed: to the center of Buenos Aires and to those
> tall brothels, obscenely shuttered, that stand, suitably, be-
> hind the graveyard. (REP 156–57, my emphasis)

Sex becomes the ultimate weapon in personal power struggles in *Guerrillas*, as Naipaul observes it to be in Argentina,
a society he regards as having been subjected to the worst
phase of colonialism. Men exist in this materialist society
without ideals, without even ideas of human association;
all that remains is "machismo" achieved by the conquest
and humiliation of women. Naipaul has never before articulated so clearly the connection between politics and
human relationships, though on reflection, he has been
writing from this perspective throughout his maturity. In

The Loss of El Dorado the only way of making sense of the chaotic history of Trinidad was to focus on the individuals who made that history; then the ordering principles emerged from their stories, and Naipaul could discuss cycles and parallels – but the order could not be imposed artificially as Grondona's *etapas*. So in writing an intensely political novel – *Guerrillas* – Naipaul concentrates on the people rather than the politics. By this time in his career, compassion and personal anguish make satire no longer possible.

Each time Naipaul studies a postcolonial country, he discovers the confusion of mimicry as the colonials try to duplicate metropolitan sophistication in denial of their inferiority. They only become increasingly colonial, parasitic, inadequate and fraudulent. Uruguay's imitation of the Swiss welfare state has eaten up the country's great wealth and the country is "dying on its feet", while Argentina's economy also founders. With his sense of history, of past events directly conditioning the present, Naipaul points out the parallel events in the past of South America and Africa.

> It was the time of the great imperialist push in many continents. While President Roca was systematically exterminating the Indians, the Belgians were opening up their brandnew Congo. Joseph Conrad saw the Belgians at work, and in *Heart of Darkness* he catches their frenzy. "Their talk was the talk of sordid buccaneers: it was cruel without courage; there was not an atom of foresight or of serious intention in the whole batch of them, and they did not seem aware these things are wanted for the work of the world." The words fit the Argentine frenzy; they contain the mood and the moral nullity of that Argentine enterprise which have worked down through the generations to the failure of today. (REP 139)

Again Naipaul's word is "frenzy". Both Uruguay and Argentina seem merely resorts to their wealthy European-oriented residents, but when imprisoned by economic conditions, the holiday-makers are unable to discover the talents and resources necessary to rejuvenate the society.

The novel *Guerrillas* is the fictional counterpart of Naipaul's *Sunday Times Magazine* articles on the career of Trinidadian Michael de Freitas (Michael X, Michael Abdul Malik); these two substantial articles (REP) contain more than usual of the basic material which Naipaul's art transmutes into a chilling and depressing literary analysis of appalling world-wide corruption and fragmentation. Naipaul's portrait of Malik indicates his deep interest in the individual case, and without excusing or glamourizing the petty murderer, also reveals his compassion for a man who exercised as little control over his own fate as have many of Naipaul's fictional characters. One of Naipaul's additions to the raw material of Malik's story is the South African character Peter Roche whose presence broadens many of the implications of the novel. Also missing from the nonfiction is the detailed use of setting to create atmosphere.

Subtle variations to descriptions of the landscape modulate readers' emotional responses, preparing them for the increasing violence of the plot. Frequently repeated is the journey between the Ridge – haven for the privileged and expatriates – and the Grange – the name an ironic evocation of the order, restraint, and social status of the Grange in Bronte's novel as opposed to the violence and animalistic existence at Wuthering Heights. Details of the crowded city, backyard shacks, swarms of children, broken pavements, burning rubbish, carrion corbeaux, pink bauxite dust, abandoned factories, scarred countryside are descriptive constants to which are added figures like the disordered man Jane and Roche see running by the road as they return from the Grange the first time. When Jane travels through the city with Jimmy in his pretentious chauffeur-driven hired car, she has a "feeling of a sudden descent into the city itself, until then unknown, unexplored" (G 74). With alarm she notes new details – ragged beggars of vacant expression, "old women selling muddy-looking cakes", "diseased pariah dogs . . . one, dead-eyed with a growth like raw flesh protruding out of its mangy yellow fur" (G 75). Her dalliance with Ahmed is to expose her to new regions of debasement, terror and pain. After an abortive assignation, she conceives the thought, "I've been playing with fire", but her relief at reaching the safety of the city is undermined by the description which immediately follows.

> The rubbish dump was burning: unusually thick brown smoke, oily and acrid, which made her turn up her window: mounds of rubbish like confetti, lorries and men and women and children blurred in the smoke, lightening occasionally into yellow flame, the carrion corbeaux, nervous of men, restless and squawking near the wire fence. (G 84)

Smoke from fires in the drought-stricken hills and fields unites with smoke from the dump to foreshadow the arson of the riots and turn the setting into a hell. When Roche and Jane enter the city as the riots begin, its emptiness and quiet, in contrast to the unrelenting noise emphasized in earlier descriptions do more than any other detail to convince the reader of the danger. In contrast, the sheer normality of "all the stations of that familiar drive" (G 250) when Roche returns to the city from the Grange for the last time intensifies the nightmare quality of Jane's murder and his discovery of it.

In addition to presenting a detailed physical picture of the island, Naipaul suggests its colonial past which explains how a mixed society was thrown together to form a community without common standards or goals. The fictional characters seem more aware of this causality than real people described in Naipaul's nonfiction. Jimmy Ahmed tells the story of the foundation of the Sablich family fortune (the real-life original is in *The Loss of El Dorado*), and seems to recognize in its opportunism and exploitation the seeds of present corruption under the veneer of respectability. Harry de Tunja is similarly aware of his family heritage of impermanence: " . . . the surname I carry is really the name of a town in South America . . . When we were in Tunja we were called de Cordoba. And I suppose in Cordoba it was Ben-something-or-other. Always the last place you run from" (G 130). But contrast this awareness with Jorge

Borges's myth of Argentina: honouring the heroic deaths in
battle of military ancestors and the graciousness of Buenos
Aires, he ignores the reality of the extermination of pampas
Indians, just as he ignores the presence of Peron's police
terror squads. Borges says he could not use Peron's name
in a speech or in a poem: Naipaul comments

> It is the Argentine attitude: suppress, ignore. Many of the
> records of the Peronist era have been destroyed. If today
> the middle-class young are Peronists and students sing the
> old song of dictatorship –
>
> *Perón, Peón, qué grande sos!*
> *Mi general, cuánto valés!*
> (Peron, Peron, how great you are!
> How good and strong, my general!)
>
> – the dictatorship, even in its excesses, is respectable
> again, it isn't because the past has been investigated and the
> record modified. It is only that many people have revised
> their attitudes toward the established legend. They have
> changed their minds. (REP 114)

Despite Harry's and Jimmy's apparent understanding of
some of the historical forces operating on the island society,
the local attitude to the past is curiously ambiguous. Even
Jimmy, uncomfortable as he may be, delights in using the
Prince Albert Hotel, not because going there proves he is
no longer oppressed but because the name itself still suggests "privilege and splendour" (G 69). Because they know
where they stand with Mrs Grandlieu – who openly challenges the black men she must now invite to her parties –
and because of the habit of respect for her position, the islanders defer to her as a representative of the colonial past.
Despite their ability to circle the truth, the characters of
the novel seem unable to find the centre. Hemenway (1982,
191) tries to portray Naipaul's vision: "It is easier to describe than define. It is fiercely pessimistic, singularly un-
sentimental, somewhat lacking in charity and sympathy,
but also curiously idealistic. The idealism arises from the
author's confidence, some might say arrogance, in the ar-

tist's talent for seeing clearly, for puncturing illusions, for avoiding the temptation 'not to see what is obvious'. Naipaul wants his work to be judged by how well he devalues the rewards of self-deception."

Also ambiguous is the islanders' response to Roche, but as Naipaul draws him, he is such an ambiguous, fragmented character that this is hardly surprising. Because the islanders' values are based almost entirely on material possessions and social status, Roche's ideals are nearly incomprehensible to them, and they feel the need to challenge him to prove his liberalism, to make "some personal declaration of love" (G 52). In the end, however, their doubts are realized as Roche exposes himself as a refugee, someone who fled both South Africa and London because of fear and who will flee again. Roche is something of an enigma, because we never learn how he came to be involved in guerrilla activities in South Africa. The repeated statement, "'I have always accepted authority. It probably has to do with the kind of school I went to'" hardly suggests a terrorist in the making. Perhaps the vulnerability and fear, obscured when he takes on the role of Jane's comforter or Sablich's social worker, are the essentials of his character not simply the result of torture. Even the interview with Meredith which seems to strip away some of Roche's pretences is ambiguous in that Meredith's motives in conducting the interview are suspect, so we cannot be sure how much of what Roche says is genuine revelation and how much of it is falsely drawn out of him as Meredith, working for the government, seeks to discredit him, and with him, Jimmy. When Meredith induces Roche to admit that he never considered Jimmy's agricultural commune a viable project, though he publicly supported it, and that he never considered the Grange a cover for guerrillas because he did not believe in their existence, Roche reveals himself as something of a fraud and a fool. Jimmy's association with Roche in a scheme doomed from the start makes him a fraud, too, and Meredith is careful to remind everyone of Jimmy's English connections, his woman and the scandal

there. At best what is certain about Roche is that, in his disillusionment with the cause, he has become at least half
colonial, belonging to the Ridge, the Establishment, his
firm. He seems to personify Naipaul's assertions that a colony reduces its inhabitants to its own level of cynicism.
Roche will not express anger or bitterness about the islanders' dilemma or against colonial authority. Meredith comments, "'. . . I can see how that attitude can give you a kind
of personal peace. But it's a dead end. It doesn't do anything for the rest of us. It doesn't hold out hope for the rest
of us'" (G 211). In failing to condemn corrupt authority,
Roche indirectly sanctions its exercise of power, even when
that means torture. He admits his obsessions with pain and
human suffering but his attitude is not fear or a desire for
revenge, but shame "that the body I had could be treated in
that way" (G 212). Like Ralph Singh and Bobby, he seems
to feel embarrassed at his own physical vulnerability, a
weakness he hates to admit. Roche is characterized by the
image of a grinning skull: "Roche laughed, and the corners
of his mouth rode up over the receding gums on his molars,
which showed long, with black gaps between them. It was
like a glimpse of teeth in a skull, like a glimpse of a satyr;
and she felt it was like a glimpse of the inner man" (G 49-
50). Without his laugh, without his cheap sarcasm, Roche
might be seen as a saint, endlessly forgiving, thinks Jane,
but she decides that he is incapable of resentment or passion, that "he was a man with nothing to revenge, that
some part of his personality, some motor of action, had
been excised" (G 54). What is not clear is whether that part
of his personality ever existed.

Without ambiguity, Naipaul's nonfiction warns against
the Roches, the "doers of good works", against

" . . . all those who helped to make Malik, and . . . those
who continue to simplify the world and reduce other men
— not only the Negro — to a cause, the people who substitute doctrine for knowledge and irritation for concern, the
revolutionaries who visit centres of revolution with return
air tickets, the hippies, the people who wish themselves on

societies more fragile than their own, all those people who in the end do no more than celebrate their own security" (REP 71).

The islanders' own political efforts to bring about reform, revolutionary or constitutional, are no more efficacious. The callousness with which the government treats Meredith Herbert validates Jane's disillusionment with the local political situation:

> . . . the personalities were so many, the principles on which they acted so confusing, and the issues so evanescent, that she had soon lost interest, had closed her mind to talk of new political alliances, that so often seemed to come to nothing anyway, and to analyses of new political threats, that could also quickly disappear. Nothing that happened here could be important. The place was no more than what it looked. (G 51)

In tracing the failure of Roche's friendship with Meredith Herbert, the novel's representative politician, Naipaul exposes Meredith's strained efforts to appear whole. As Roche begins to penetrate the facade of calm, ordered domesticity, he realizes the "hysteria, . . . rages, deprivations and unappeased ambition" (G 136) behind it, and grows wary of Meredith. With Roche, readers are prepared to accept Meredith's insight into situations – for instance, when he warns that not enough allowance is made for the madness of the people in the streets, but we must continue to question his position – his own political hunger is revealed when he comments on that of others.

Meredith, presented as an intelligent and even reasonably sympathetic character, shows that little is to be hoped for from political orthodoxy on the island, but the people of the island have neither the political awareness nor the stamina to create a revolution based on genuine ideals. Naipaul's rejection of the philosophy of Black Power as a force for reform is first stated in his 1970 *New York Review of Books* analysis of the Carnival demonstrations in Trinidad. To him, speaking of Black Power on an island where political power is already in the hands of black people is an irrelevance.

> Black Power in these black islands is protest. But there is no enemy. The enemy is the past, of slavery, and colonial neglect and a society uneducated from top to bottom; the enemy is the smallness of the islands and the absence of resources. Opportunism or jargon may define phantom enemies: racial minorities, "elites", "white niggers". But at the end the problems will be the same, of dignity and identity. (OB 250)

Most disturbing is Naipaul's view that these problems will never be solved. Reiterating the main theme of *The Middle Passage*, he says that the islands will always be consumers of other peoples' goods and culture, never creators of their own. This seems to me to reduce to insignificance the considerable achievements of his contemporaries and of himself; as is the case quite often in Naipaul's work, the nonfiction seems more negative than the fiction, more willing to reject categorically while the fiction recognizes greater possibilities and expresses less certainty. Again I think of his own words: obviously, analysing and deciding in advance allows him less intellectual space than working towards a conclusion. The "Killings in Trinidad" articles stand somewhere between "Power?" and the fiction of *Guerrillas*. Naipaul's nonfiction usually takes up individual cases but few concentrate on a person in the way of these two features, and typically when Naipaul becomes interested in the individual case, his compassion grows, along with his appreciation of the shades of grey in human experience. Consequently, he writes of Malik: "A real torment was buried in the clowning of the racial entertainer. Black Power gave order and logic to the life; it provided Malik with a complete system" (REP 28). Naipaul analyses the forces that drove Malik toward Black Power — both white liberals in England who inflated his sense of his own importance, and his own society's rejection of him as a Trinidadian "red man" (half-caste), the son of a brothel-keeper. Simultaneously, Naipaul reveals the reasons for his growing apprehension and consciousness of violence close to the surface of human relations.

> Trinidad's urban north-west is a great parasitic suburb, through which money is yet magically cycled. Much of the population is superfluous, and they know it. Unemployment is high but labour is perennially short. The physical squalor, the sense of a land being pillaged rather than built up, generates great tensions; cynicism is like a disease. Race is an irrelevance; but the situation is well suited to the hysteria and evasions of racial politics. And racial politics – preaching oppression and easy redemption, offering only the theory of the enemy, white, brown, yellow, black – have brought the society close to collapse. (REP 55)

In these articles Naipaul moves from the easy rejection of Black Power as a ridiculous anomaly in the earlier journalism to recognition of it as a threat to the possibility of progress.

> The streets of Belmont are still full of Joe Skerritts. The walls are still scrawled with the easy threats and easy promises of Black Power. The streets are still full of "hustlers" and "scrunters", words which glamorise and seem to give dispensation to those who beg and steal. Another Malik is possible. At every stage he was supported by some kind of revolutionary ideal.
> Malik's career proves how much of Black Power – away from its United States source – is jargon, how much a sentimental hoax. In a place like Trinidad racial redemption is as irrelevant for the Negro as for everybody else. It obscures the problems of a small independent country with a lopsided economy, the problems of a fully "consumer" society that is yet technologically untrained and without the intellectual means to comprehend the deficiency. It perpetuates the negative, colonial politics of protest. It is, in the end, a deep corruption: a wish to be granted a dispensation from the pains of development, an almost religious conviction that oppression can be turned into an asset, race into money. While the dream of redemption lasts Negroes will continue to exist only that someone might be their leader. Redemption requires a redeemer, and a redeemer,

in those circumstances, cannot but end like the Emperor Jones: contemptuous of the people he heads, and no less a victim, seeking an illusory personal emancipation. (REP 70)

I have quoted at length from these articles because I wanted to let Naipaul's passion speak for itself and refute those who see him as aloof, patrician, uncaring, Establishment, nihilistic. On the contrary, I believe he writes to shatter the complacency which defeats reform before it begins, and although he is no optimist, he must believe reform is possible or there would be no reason to go on writing.

As a writer of fiction, however, he will not allow himself to reduce art to polemic. When he spoke of *In a Free State*, he said an author had to have an idea (see above, p. 147), but in "Conrad's Darkness", he criticises Conrad for coming between his story and his reader. If a piece of fiction is to be pure in Naipaul's terms, reality must fuse with fantasy, so that the story speaks for itself. The kind of explicitness Conrad adopted refines away the fantasy and makes involvement with the story impossible. The writer must seek the "scene . . . that takes us beyond what we witness and becomes a symbol for aspects of our own experience" (REP 223–24). One small example of how Naipaul achieves this in *Guerrillas*: Roche observes Meredith after his recall to power with the government and the narrative comments, "He had been confirmed in his power; he was a minister in a government that had survived. But Roche thought that Meredith was still uncertain . . . " (G 199). In the midst of specific description of Meredith's manner, the indefinite article "a" before "minister" and "government" implies the existence of many like him all over the world, but is much less obvious than Ralph Singh's "It has happened in twenty countries". In *Guerrillas* the effect of Black Power on the people is portrayed through Stephens's mother and Harry's comments on the rioters. Although she rejects Jimmy as corrupted by his sexual involvement with white women and the Grange as a reversion to plantation days, Mrs Stephens mouths the meaningless slogan "After Israel, Africa" with conviction and assurance that Scripture has promised that blacks will have their turn. Harry, the successful businessman is the Israelite who will be replaced. This naivety is not replaced by greater courage or acumen in the young rioters. Newspaper reports can offer no reasons for the riots until after they have been quelled, because the rioters had no logical motivation; "protests against unemployment and continued foreign domination of the economy" were not in the thoughts of the rioters. Harry's analysis is close to the truth: "'But in the end, you know, that is what those guys down there would believe they were doing. Because what they're doing is too crazy'" (G 192). Naipaul's 1970 article called the riots "A spontaneous, anarchic outburst: a human society divided between its wish for order and its various visions of redemption" (REP 41). The fiction portrays this perception but without intrusive comments.

Naipaul's portrait of Jimmy Ahmed reveals, in detail, the quicksand upon which revolutions are built on such an island. Like Malik, Jimmy is turned into a Black Power leader by pseudo-liberal white women who are more interested in getting him to bed than to a demonstration and by the attentions of the media in England. The novel does not explore Ahmed's British period in any great detail but the journalism investigates Malik's past thoroughly, elaborating themes to which the novel alludes. The newspapers created a playboy image for Jimmy, but he misuses the word when he wishes to say he was made a plaything. The two self-concepts are inextricably mixed in his own mind: he sees himself exercising power that is often expressed sexually, while he is aware at the same time that he is being used. Consciously or unconsciously, Malik and Jimmy both create a character for their British audience, "everybody's Negro, and not too Negroid" (REP 23). In the journalism Naipaul's most scathing comments are reserved for the secure middle class "for whom Malik's kind of Black Power was an exotic but safe brothel" (REP 29). Jane represents these people in the novel, but again Naipaul deals with the fictional character with greater compassion for her personal dislocation. Also in the journalism, Naipaul is scathing at press credulity about Malik. He refers to a major article in *The Observer* in July 1965 in which Colin McGlashan built up the image of Michael X, organizer of the Racial Adjustment Action Society (Naipaul points out the joke in the acronym which is a Jamaican obscenity), with an enormous membership and plenty of money. In a letter to the *Sunday Times Magazine* (26 May 1974), McGlashan defends himself by pointing out that he was not alone in having been taken in and that the game lasted a number of years: " . . . one may conclude either that journalists are a good deal sillier than I've always feared, or that Michael de Freitas was very much less of the pathetic, cretinous and unsupported con-man Mr Naipaul so stylishly portrays. Perhaps both?" One imagines that Naipaul might accept the final suggestion, since so often he writes of different interpretations of events and observations. But in his references to the media which support his contentions about Malik being created by the press and thrill-seeking women, Naipaul also refers to Jill Tweedie's interviews of two American Negroes in *The Guardian* (9 August 1971). The first interviewee is a female school counsellor, moderate and constructive in her views and work; the other is an outrageous militant con man who exudes sexual energy. He gets most of her attention.

Naipaul's characterization of Jimmy is rich in complexities. He is at once absurd, dangerous, and a victim. His absurdity is evident first in the Thrushcross Grange signboards: Roche is convinced that Jimmy sees no symbolism in the name, that he just picked it up in a writing course; the revolutionary signs all bear advertising for numerous, largely American-financed commercial ventures; Jimmy's pathetic pretension and deep-seated insecurity are revealed by his use of the title "Haji" — Roche says " 'to mean "mister" or "esquire". When he remembers, that is' " (G 12). Even more revealing and damaging are the times when Jimmy's mask slips and his own speech reveals his resentment at his background and his efforts to be someone important

in the white man's world (see, for instance, G 27–28).
Nevertheless, he is dangerous enough to be described repeatedly as a "succubus: demon that mates with a sleeping
man" (G 6]), and Jane's speculation on the meaning of the
word when she first hears it makes its hidden threat explicit: "'It sounds like a grub of some sort. Something you
have to carry. A kind of leech'" (G 31).

As do many of Naipaul's characters, Jimmy turns to writing for emotional release; he writes "out of disturbance, out
of wonder at himself, out of some sudden clear vision of an
aspect of himself, or out of panic" (G 38). Unlike the writing of Naipaul's other "authors" – Ganesh, Mr Stone, Ralph
Singh, Salim – Jimmy's writing does not provide him with
comfort or a purpose in life, define his role; or secure
material advantages for him. The story on which he works
is a cliche-ridden fantasy about the fatal attraction of an
Englishwoman to an arresting, powerful, intellectual
saviour of the people. In the three instalments Naipaul presents – each broken off when Jimmy wakes to the melan-
choly emptiness about him and then turns to Bryant for
comfort – Jimmy reveals his romanticizing of himself, his
bitterness at his background, and his violent hatred and
fear of the white world. Jimmy's habit of retreating into a
fantasy world of authorship is also borrowed from Jimmy's
prototype, Malik. Quotations from Malik's writings in the
articles show the same stylistic patterns and rhythms, failures in punctuation, and themes. Part of the persona created for Malik in England was that he was a writer and so,
dutifully, he tried to write. The importance of the real-life
and the fictional attempts to write fiction is stressed by
Naipaul in a statement that seems to declare open season
on his own character for readers of his fiction: "An autobiography can distort; facts can be realigned. But fiction never
lies: it reveals the writer totally. And Malik's primitive
novel is like a pattern-book, a guide to later events" (REP
63).

Jimmy's first essay into fiction is prompted by Jane's visit
to the Grange with Roche. Comparison of Jimmy's version

of the scene with Naipaul's illuminates the absurdity of Jimmy's pretensions. Throughout, the contrast between Naipaul's elegant, technically pleasing understatements and Jimmy's ungrammatical, poorly punctuated, and trite prose is extreme. No detail is more telling a revelation of Jimmy's distress than his emphasis on his golden, not black, body. Perceptive in his comments on Roche's confused liberalism, Jimmy fails to see that his own motives are very similar. The second attempt to write adopts Jane's point of view, and pathetically tries to turn his racial insecurity and confusion into lone grandeur. Here Jimmy's obsession with *Wuthering Heights* is explained – Roche was wrong, Jimmy does understand the symbolism. Jimmy prefers to see himself as Heathcliff of unknown, mixed and romantic origin – "Your mother was an Indian princess and your father was the Emperor of China" – rather than as a "Chinaman's lucky shot on a dark night" (G 62). Continuing the parallel, Jimmy, like Malik and Heathcliff, has been taken in by privileged English people only to be deprived by them before being rejected and thrown back on his own resources. Jimmy's violent revenge also parallels that of Heathcliff, but *Guerrillas* ends without the integration and resolution in a succeeding generation that concludes *Wuthering Heights*. The third passage, the product of Jimmy's sexual failure with Jane, warns of the violence building within him as he reconstructs the story of the pack rape of a white girl. His writing is interrupted by Bryant's hysteria over Jane's visit which causes Jimmy to promise, "'I'll give her to you'" (G 90).

At this stage, only just over one-third of the way through the novel, Jimmy is removed from the reader's sight, though the threat of his promise to Bryant hangs like a lowering cloud over the rest of the narrative. Not until his confessional letter to Marjorie are any details of his activities during the riots revealed; like Malik's letter to his mother, "it is the truest thing [he] ever wrote and the most moving. It explains so much . . . " (REP 28). The pathos of Jimmy's aspirations, of his unrealized dreams of escape and power, and of his desire to give in and cease struggling are indeed genuinely moving. Jimmy's anguish for Bryant, who is maddened by his grief for Stephens and for the end of Jimmy's dreams of a better world, mixes with his fear, love and hatred: " . . . last week I could have burned this place down to the ground, until that dead boy's mother refused to have me in her house and those crazy black people started shouting for Israel and Africa, and I was a lost man, but I was always lost, I knew that since I was a child, I knew I was fooling myself" (G 229). The inability of a man such as Jimmy to comprehend intellectually the political realities of the world he inhabits is dramatized by his tendency to express all emotions in sexual terms. Jane comes to symbolize for him the white women who "interested" themselves in his movement, and who not only failed to support him but tainted him with their own corruption. The sacrifice of Jane to Bryant fails to erase his guilt; his vision of a prostitute taunting him from her coffin brings back his total desolation after the momentary relief of disembodiment after the murder. Jimmy's other dream-vision – of an offer of water from cupped hands turning a victim's fear into love – shows his desire for a trusting, generous human relationship, but his dream is so distorted that the act of giving can only follow one of violation. He must do as he has been done to before he can forgive, and so forgiveness comes too late.

Like Jimmy, Jane tries to define herself through sexual relationships. Her failure to do so is graphically represented by the lack of a record of her existence on the island. Harry reports after her disappearance, " 'The immigration people have no record of her departure. But they don't know anything about her arrival either. Officially she's never been here. You and I and a few other people know she's been here. But officially she hasn't been' " (G 252). The last statement has existential implications. With no existence of her own, Jane assumes the ideas and adopts the phrases of the men she attracts, remaining unassailable in her inconsistency because "she was indifferent, perhaps blind, to the contradiction between what she said and what she was so secure of being" (G 25). The image Naipaul chooses to characterize Jane is the sea anemone "waving its strands at the bottom of the ocean. Rooted and secure, and indifferent to what it attracted" (G 22). Hemenway believes that Naipaul blames women for the failure of the sexual contract and points to the many unflattering portraits of females in his novels; I believe Hemenway makes the same error in this judgment as those who claim Naipaul must be a neo-colonialist because he writes of the limitations of post-colonial societies. His politics, sexual or other, blame both sides when humans fail to achieve his ideal. Jane's entire existence is based on contradictions and paradox. She disregards, even abuses, the body she cares for with apparent affection. The narrative dwells on the careful creaming of her skin, tanning, shaving her legs, yet she is often revealed in careless and unattractive poses – a leg drawn up and casually opened revealing her nakedness, or the extraordinary insertion of a tampon in Roche's presence. She lacks physical grace even at moments of sexual intimacy; her lack of sexual skill or delicacy despite her experience is indicative of her view of sex as a means of entrapping the man from whom she will take her identity and her comfort without yielding anything of herself – the self Naipaul suggests does not exist.

Thus, Jane embodies the thesis behind this novel, that personal relationships reveal the nature of a society, and she is as much a victim of Jimmy and Roche as she is an exploiter of them. However, in portraying a white woman from the metropolis as lacking in identity in the same way as the colonial half-caste, Naipaul suggests that impermanence is not a condition exclusive to the postcolonial island. "She lived in the midst of change, repetitive and sterile; it did not disguise the fact of the greater impermanence. But she was privileged: she told herself that once a day. Security was the basis of her privilege. . . . Out of this contradiction between what she did and said and what she felt, out of this knowledge of her own security and her vision of decay, of a world running down, she moved from one crisis to another" (G 56). Perhaps the island has "exhausted its possibilities" (G 50), but Naipaul insists that no migration to Canada or the United States will discover a promised land. The slogan daubed over the city — After Israel, Africa — sums up the historical inconstancy of power. Mrs Grandlieu, the last representative of colonial power, is the only character who seems fixed, but she lacks family to carry on the name and tradition. At the same time that her name recalls the temporary French presence on the island, it also carries the ironic assocation "instead of" grandeur. Having rejected the possibility that compassionate intervention will reform abuses in *In a Free State*, Naipaul seems unable to conceive human warmth, compassion or understanding in his characters' behaviour. Nor do the characters achieve the ideal of a creative imagination in control of the raw material of human experience; Peter Roche's memoir and Jimmy Ahmed's novel fail to resolve any issues. The threat suggested by Mr Stone's rejection of constructive activity seems to be realized in *Guerrillas* as it portrays a world in which cynicism and violence replace compassion on all levels of human interchange. Again Naipaul seems to be in danger of painting himself into a corner, but now he seems to be conscious of the danger. Both Hemenway (1982, 200–201) and Neill (1982, 57) call attention to Meredith's warning that "if you see too much, you can end up living by yourself in a house on a hill" (G 144), noting that here Naipaul acknowledges the risks he takes in trying to impose order, "darkly hoping that his imposed vision will make a difference, believing that it cannot" (Hemenway, 200). In the terms of the image I use to describe Naipaul's investigation of the postcolonial world, he has moved completely out of the circle of light and sees clearly in all directions into the darkness surrounding the hut; tragically, *Guerrillas* suggests that all he sees is more darkness. But paradoxically, his art offers the ray of hope. For this narrative is not ascribed to a character, it is Naipaul's, and the ordering intelligence is still apparent. And so is the compassion of the

author for even these unattractive characters whose dislocation, confusion, failure of identity result from the chaos
of failed imperialism. The fact that they are victims earns
them some measure of compassion but does not spare them
from Naipaul's scorn at their failure to see, to learn the
truth about themselves and their society. For this he rejects
even Jorge Borges. Willingness to remain comfortably
ignorant provokes the anger and frustration which is so
evident in the nonfictional writing of the same period.

India Revisited: *India — A Wounded Civilization*

In the eleven and a half years separating the completion of
An Area of Darkness and the beginning of *India: A Wounded
Civilization* (1977), Naipaul says he has "come to terms with
the strangeness of India, [and defined] what separates me
from the country" (IWC 9). The success of his endeavour is
demonstrated by the absence of the hysteria often so near
the surface of the earlier book and the presence of much
more dispassionate analysis of the fantasy at the centre of
India's postcolonial failure. India's failure, politically,
economically and socially, is similar to the failure of
Borges to recognize in his Argentine history the extermination of the pampas Indians; India reveres a past that did
not exist, a past characterized by simplicity and bountiful
harvests, and by the absorption of the best from visiting
cultures. To Naipaul, India's history is not one of continuity but of defeat, and against the background of Indira
Gandhi's declaration of Emergency, he sees India headed
for yet another upheaval, a prediction given substance
several times over by events since the publication of the
book. Naipaul retains an overwhelming vision of India's
distress:

> At the end of that bad evening it seemed barely imaginable
> — the huts of the landless along the Poona–Bombay road,
> the child labourers of Bihar among the blond hanks of jute,
> the chawls and squatters' settlements in central Bombay,

the starved squatters in bright cotton slipping in and out of
the stone ruins of Vijayanagar, the famine-wasted bodies
just outside Jaipur City. It was like a calamity that no one
could come to terms with. I was without the Indian defences,
which were also the attitudes that contributed to the
calamity. I could only wait for the morning. (IWC 140)

However, there is also now a deeper understanding of the
attitudes that contributed to the calamity, and perhaps, a
reminder of the imperial presence in ascribing English
blondness to the jute. In *An Area of Darkness* Naipaul expressed a sense of loss when he discovered that India did
not possess the unity he idealized. In *India: A Wounded Civilization* he moves past the simple racial nostalgia for the
Himalayas of his grandfather's pictures to a much deeper
understanding that "in myself, like the split-second images
of infancy which some of us carry, there survive, from the
family rituals that lasted into my childhood, phantasmal
memories of an old India which for me outline a whole
vanished world" (IWC 9). Like Ralph Singh, he feels the
beauty of sacrifice, the establishing of a link with the earth
and the totality of the past. Because he recognizes the
strength of this vision, Naipaul can appreciate the ease with
which it may overthrow reality and become a dangerous
obscuring fantasy. That is why his simile for his Indian
memories – "like trapdoors into a bottomless past" (IWC
10) – embodies a threat of oblivion.

A comparison of Naipaul's description of two visits to Vijayanagar reveals the way experience changes his response
to India. During his first visit Naipaul cannot see past the
squalor and degraded life of the people who inhabit the
ruins. He offers no detail of history, only mentions that a
noticeboard substitutes for history a legend of a "rain of
gold" in response to the Rajah's prayer. The most important
event of the visit is his own response to a beggar who shelters from the rain with him; ashamed of his dismissal of
the man, of his turning "fear and distaste into anger and
contempt" (AD 216), Naipaul gives him money and is doubly ashamed that he feels a sense of power with the act of

charity. Vijayanagar is offered as proof that India's history is a series of beginnings each of which ends in destruction, more ruins for the landscape. In *A Wounded Civilization*, Naipaul's memory is that the first sight of the temple avenue was "awesome" and that it spoke "directly . . . of a fabulous past" (IWC 17). This remarkable shift in viewpoint may be seen either as an uncharacteristic lapse in memory or as further evidence of the duality of experience, the two (or more) truths possible in any explanation of reality. We have been aware of Naipaul's increasing tolerance of uncertainty as we have traced the development of themes in his work, particularly in his fiction, but he is still seeking organizing principles, trying to order experience. So, although the ruins are still an inhabited slum and excrement still mixes with mud, Naipaul now appears to overlook the present degradation of the city and chronicles its history in detail. Instead of concluding, as he did in *An Area of Darkness*, that "each creation is separate, a beginning and an end in itself" (AD 216), Naipaul now appears to believe that there is a negative form of continuity in Indian history: "Life goes on, the past simply reasserts itself" (IWC 15). On this second visit Naipaul subjects the history of the city's repeated falls to rational analysis, and concludes that it was easily destroyed because it was itself only an imperfect reassertion of the past rather than an innovative or creative development. "India absorbs and outlasts its conquerors, Indians say. But at Vijayanagar, among the pilgrims, I wondered whether intellectually for a thousand years India hadn't always retreated before its conquerors and whether, in its periods of apparent revival, India hadn't only been making itself archaic again, intellectually smaller, always vulnerable" (IWC 18).

He goes on to mention the contradiction between the "archaism of national pride and the promise of the new" of which he had already been aware when writing *An Area of Darkness*. At that time he also portrayed the ways in which individuals were restricted by self-images dictated by caste and other social structures. What has been added

to the second book is more rational analysis of India's inability to cope with the contradictions and more sympathetic understanding of the "chaos and blankness" (IWC 103)
which results when individuals have to abandon the principles which have organized their existence for generations.
The character sketches of Ramnath, Malhotra and the
others in *Area* make Naipaul's point about the Indian sense
of degree; his study of Aziz expresses some appreciation for
the security it offers; but on the whole, he seems impatient
with the unquestioning acceptance of such limitations on
human development. In *A Wounded Civilization*, he even
turns to a psychotherapist in his attempts to offer rational
explanations for his observations. He is careful to establish
that Dr Sudhir Kakar has practised outside of India and so
has the credentials to compare Indian perspectives with
others. Kakar blames the highly "detailed social organization of Indian life" for the failure of Indian ego to develop.
Because individuals are never called upon to make decisions on their own, they do not learn to assess the world
objectively. In effect, they do not come to terms with reality
as something separate from themselves, something to be
evaluated other than by how individuals feel at the moment. "'We Indians,' Kakar says, 'use the outside reality to
preserve the continuity of the self amidst an ever changing
flux of outer events and things.' Men do not, therefore,
actively explore the world; rather, they are defined by it. It
is this negative way of perceiving that goes with 'medita-
tion', the striving after the infinite, the bliss of losing the
self; it also goes with *karma* and the complex organization
of Indian life. Everything locks together; one cannot be
isolated from the other" (IWC 103-4). When Mr Stone
founded the Knights Companion, he tried to fortify his
concept of self through outside reality, but the Western difference was that he attempted to manipulate outside
events; the Hindu turn the novel takes is that he comes to
accept the rush of external events and to find stability
(albeit temporary) within himself. For Naipaul the analytic
writer of nonfiction, *karma* is the killer, as the belief that

one is fated to an existence by a past life oppresses the sense of self. But Naipaul the novelist often writes of characters whose choices are limited by accidents of history and geography, or of transplanted characters who, like an Indian deprived of caste, also lose their identities.

As he did in *An Area of Darkness*, Naipaul turns to India's literature for understanding of how a religion which preaches self-realization can simultaneously deny the growth of individual identity. At this stage, Naipaul concludes that his early reading of Narayan failed to appreciate the Hindu perspective of the novels: "The novel I had read as a novel [which to Naipaul implies concern for the individual in society] was also a fable, a classic exposition of the Hindu equilibrium, surviving the shock of an alien culture, an alien literary form, an alien language, and making harmless even those new concepts it appeared to welcome. Identity became an aspect of *karma*, self-love was bolstered by an ideal of nonviolence" (IWC 27). The new concepts Narayan renders harmless are "independence and action" (IWC 26) which call on India to divorce herself from the past, from withdrawal into the irresponsibility of the Hindu sense of justice and balance in existence.

U. R. Anantamurti's *Samskara* (1976), illustrates for Naipaul the total failure of the concept of self in moments of stress and upheaval. The texts and his god fail to provide a Brahmin priest with a solution to a dilemma; as his external props are removed, the priest loses his concept of himself as a man of goodness. As he subjects himself to greater and greater pollution, he never, says Naipaul, sees the outside world as something to be reformed; he is only interested in trying to find out which is his true self — the man of goodness or the degraded and polluted thing he now seems to be. Naipaul finds it difficult to reconcile the author, an academic at Mysore University who has taught in the United States, with the novel.

> His academic background seems a world away from the society he describes in the novel; and it is hard to assess his attitude to that society. Knowingly or unknowingly, Anan-

tamurti has portrayed a barbaric civilization, where the books, the laws, are buttressed by magic, and where a too elaborate social organization is unquickened by intellect or creativity or ideas of moral responsibility (except to the self in its climb to salvation). These people are all helpless, disadvantaged, easily unbalanced; the civilization they have inherited has long gone sour; living instinctive lives, crippled by rules ("I didn't try to solve it for myself. I depended on God, on the old law books. Isn't this precisely why we have created the books?"), they make up a society without a head. (IWC 109)

Naipaul's use of the novel to advance his argument that the Indian (Hindu) idea of the self is hamstrung by the laws of caste and pollution, religious ritual, and an overly elaborate social structure seems perfectly legitimate but also somewhat limited. While I agree that the novel fully paints the decadence of the brahmins, it seems to me that Anantamurti transcends social barriers and writes in the existential tradition of the night journey into the soul. When Naipaul quotes the lines about turning to the law books, he neglects the rest of the passage in which the priest recognizes that individual decisions do affect the community:

... my dilemma, my decisions, my problem wasn't just mine, it included the entire agrahara. This is the root of the difficulty, the anxiety, the double-bind of dharma. When the question of Naranappa's death-rites came up, I didn't try to solve it for myself. I depended on God, on the old law books. Isn't this precisely why we have created the books? Because there's this deep relation between our decisions and the whole community. In every act we involve our forefathers, our gurus, our gods, our fellow humans. Hence this conflict. Did I feel such conflict when I lay with Chandri? Did I decide it after pouring and measuring and weighing? Now it's become dusky, unclear. That decision, that act gouged me out of my past world, the world of the brahmins, from my wife's existence, my very faith. The consequence, I'm shaking in the wind like a piece of string. (Anantha Murthy 1976, 106)

Certainly Naipaul is right that the Acharya is self-absorbed,

but he learns that in his own life he has been denying the
dualities his own Madhva sect stresses and he discovers
that a man does have a much more active role and greater
freedom of choice than he previously acknowledged. "Even
if I lost control, the responsibility to decide was still mine.
Man's decision is valid only because it's possible to lose
control, not because it's easy. We shape ourselves through
our choices, bring form and line to the thing we call our
person" (Ananta Murthy, 96). At the ambiguous end of the
book the Acharya is simultaneously whipping himself into
becoming decisive and begging God to take from him the
burden of decision, but the ambiguity raises no artistic difficulties nor does it seem a quality to which Naipaul would
be unsympathetic. Knowing Naipaul's concern for the individual's response to social pressures, it is surprising that his
reading of *Samskara* neglects the double significance of the
book's title for the protagonist. The word "samskara" means
many things in the Kannada language including "funeral
obsequies" and "preparation, making ready". Among its
many other suggestions for the novel, the title's first definition raises the possibility that at the end of the novel the
Acharya remains a dead man spiritually while the second
implies that he has been given the necessary knowledge to
begin life anew. The implication of the book as a whole is
that these readings may be simultaneously though paradoxically true. (See Nightingale 1978.)

To Naipaul, *Samskara* and *Mr Sampath* illustrate the tendency of the traditional Hindu view to deny any impulse
toward social reform. However, he sees that new pressures
on the society are creating new movements. With advanc-
ing industrialization and improved farming techniques,
many peasants are being pushed off the land and into the
cities, loosening ties by which individuals have defined
themselves and which have limited their ability to appraise
outside reality. Suddenly, Indians recognize the fact of Indian poverty and human distress as a cause for political
protest rather than as a reinforcement of the concept of
karma. However, he sees a danger to the force of these

movements. A section of Chapter 4 describes a visit to a village on the Deccan plateau where a cooperative irrigation scheme is beginning. Naipaul seems determined to report positively: "In India, where nearly everything waits for the government, a private scheme like this, started by farmers on their own was new and encouraging . . . " (IWC 73). Instead of being depressed by views of Bombay from the train windows or by the sight of a weary and sickly farmer working on his section of the irrigation trench or by a betel-chewing racketeer who guides him through the village, Naipaul emphasizes the solidity and permanence of the stone construction of buildings in the village, and the forward-thinking individuals of social conscience who support the scheme. However, when he reaches the Patel's house, Naipaul finds in a flourescent light tube and a shiny blue sofa the jarring note of modernity that speaks less of progress than of the reassertion of traditional privilege. His optimism dissolves: "It was necessary to be in the village, to see the Patel and his attendants, to understand the nature of the power of that simple man, to see how easily such a man could, if he wished, frustrate the talk from Delhi about minimum wages, the abolition of untouchability, the abolition of rural indebtedness. How could the laws be enforced? . . . The Patel . . . ruled by custom and consent. In his authority, which in his piety he extended backward to his ancestors, there was almost the weight of religion" (IWC 86). The descriptions that close this section are once again of beggars, muddy yards, sodden encampments beside the broken, rutted road, the homes of peasants forced off their land by men like the Patel and lacking a place to go.

Repeating the point made in 1967 when he wrote of his second visit to India in two *Daily Telegraph Magazine* articles, and again when he covered "The Election in Ajmer" for the *Sunday Times Magazine* in 1971 (all collected in *The Overcrowded Barracoon*), Naipaul states that over and over again old Hindu attitudes subvert the cause of progress. Since 1967, his condemnation of India has been modified, but he sees a similar danger in his most recent analysis to that he saw then. Then with his growing awareness of historical repetition, Naipaul saw a cycle of relapse into the simplicity and safety of ritual and magic being repeated again and again, even though reformers repeatedly try to teach the people that personal failure and national disasters have correctable causes, that they are not simply punishment for the sins of former lives. Naipaul's characteristic lack of faith in the possibilities of real progress through politics is reflected in the following passage:

> Individual obsessions coalesce into political movements: and in the last ten years or so these movements of protest have become wilder. Many of these movements look back to the past, which they reinterpret to suit their needs. Some, like the Shiv Sena in Bombay . . . and the Dravidian movement in the south . . . have positive regenerating effects. Others, like the Anand Marg . . . are the grossest kind of Hindu cult: a demonstration, like others in the past, of the ease with which Hinduism, striving after internal continuity and calm, stripping itself of intellect and the need for intellect, can decline into barbarism.
>
> A party which seeks a nuclear armoury for India, and combines that with a programme for protecting the holy cow (free fodder for cows, homes for old cows), might at first be dismissed as a joke. But it isn't a joke. This party is the Jan Sangh, the National Party. It is the best-organized opposition party; with its emphasis on Hindu power, it touches many Hindu hearts, and it has a large middle-class following in the cities; for some years it controlled the Delhi municipality. In the 1971 elections one of its candidates in Delhi ran purely on the cow issue. (IWC 114)

And he was correct that the Jan Sangh was no joke – this was the party that briefly unseated Mrs Gandhi and jailed her for "abuse of privilege".

The failure of Gandhianism embodies the most obvious case history of the desire to go back to a complete and integrated past leading to greater abuse in spite of a sincere wish for reform. When he wrote *An Area of Darkness*, Naipaul emphasized Gandhi's ability to see India, its filth, and

the need for the reform of the system as a whole with the
eyes of a new arrival, and his failure to impose that vision
on his followers. Seeking to explain Gandhi's failure in *A
Wounded Civilization*, Naipaul discovers Gandhi's weakness
in his autobiography: a self-absorption that says "the outer
world matters only in so far as it affects the inner. It is the
Indian way of experiencing" (IWC 101). Coupled with Gandhi's unusual sense of being Indian in a racial and national
sense, his concern for the effect of external forces on the
self led to fragmentation of his complex ideology. His
belief in service to the state and his concept of an Indian
identity are lost to Gandhians today, as they are to Narayan's Srinivas: " . . . Gandhian nonviolence has degenerat-
ed into something very like the opposite of what Gandhi
intended. For Srinivas nonviolence isn't a form of action, a
quickener of social conscience. It is only a means of secur-
ing an undisturbed calm; it is nondoing, noninterference,
social indifference. It merges with the ideal of self-realization, truth to one's identity. These modern-sounding words,
which reconcile Srinivas to the artist's predicament, disguise an acceptance of *karma*, the Hindu killer, the Hindu
calm . . . " (IWC 25). Naipaul sees in another Narayan novel,
The Vendor of Sweets, "a key to the moral bewilderment of
today" (IWC 38). His reading of the book stresses that Jagan,
a follower of Gandhi, is blind to his own moral confusion
which cheats of taxes the state for which he fought, which
allows him to abandon his son to a jail sentence, and which
asks only that he remain pure in the midst of pollution not
that social distress be alleviated. Present day politicians
are, according to Naipaul, very much like Jagan in their
desire to return to the "simplicity" of the past, to a pastoral
dream, that destructive fantasy with which this discussion
of *India: A Wounded Civilization* began. Vinoba Bhave, Gandhi's disciple and successor, is for Naipaul the ultimate
distortion, corruption and failure of Gandhianism, his
whole life a parody of Gandhi's and his effect on modern
politics totally stultifying. "It seems to be always there in
India: magic, the past, the death of the intellect, spirituality
annulling the civilization out of which it issues, India

swallowing its own tail" (IWC 166–67). This is why Naipaul can say that he is "not unsympathetic" to Mrs Gandhi in spite of her declaration of the Emergency "simply because I was appalled by the opposition people. I was appalled by their intellectual negligibility. I was appalled by the lies" (to Wheeler 1977, 537).

Despite Naipaul's harsh view of post-Gandhian Indian political life and, indeed, of Indian civilization as a whole, this book, in marked contrast to *An Area of Darkness*, ends with a declaration of hope: " . . . in the present uncertainty and emptiness there is the possibility of a true new beginning, of the emergence in India of mind, after the long spiritual night" (IWC 174). It is the hope he discovered with the "new morality" that recognizes the existence of poverty and of special abuses of the poor. It is the hope awakened by the Shiv Sena's self-help projects in the Bombay slums. Naipaul's description of his visit to a shanty town is of a descent into horror and degradation as he leaves behind the washing sheds and latrines near the entrance gates on the hill above a graveyard to come upon a vision straight from hell, of two starved women trying to pull two starved cows out of a bog of human excrement. Nevertheless, he does return to the city with "evidence of what was possible" (IWC 69) and a discovery of one group which is not dominated by the fantasy of the past. "For the Sena men, and the people they led, the world was new; they saw themselves at the beginning of things: unaccommodated men making a claim on their land for the first time, and out of chaos evolving their own philosophy of community and self-help. For them the past was dead; they had left it behind in the villages" (IWC 71–72).

Once again a bus becomes a symbol of civilization as Naipaul waits to return to Bombay from the slum. The white towers of Bombay as seen from that hillside become associated with the snowy Himalayan peaks of cinema posters and their promises of adventure and wordly satisfaction. While this might seem a false promise, to Naipaul India's hope does, in fact, reside in urban industrialization which makes possible self-help and a divorce from the past and from hereditary masters. The red double-decker which picks him up is dusty and oily, scratched and battered. India, too, has been crumpled many times; perhaps once again the civilization can be smoothed out and headed towards the white towers by these new men of the city fringes, and the city towers will replace the white Himalayan peaks which have symbolized the unity of old India for Naipaul since his childhood.

Naipaul finds a further cause for hope in the simple fact that he, who is "ancestrally of the culture" has written such a book of analysis of the civilization: " . . . the fact that I have written it might be taken as a sign of a mind at work" (to Wheeler, 537). Writers fill Naipaul's pages. Not only do they seek personal solace and better understanding of experience but also they order experience for others. They are not necessarily in possession of absolute truth, reality is far too complex for that, but they are obligated to offer the truth as they understand it at the time. So this time Naipaul may approach Vijayanagar differently, understand Narayan's writing differently or Gandhi; that does not negate the importance of his task. Perhaps even in his devotion to the word, there is an echo of Hinduism – the magical power of the word, of a *mantra* (see IWC 14).

At the Heart of Darkness: *A Bend in the River*

In his most recent novel, *A Bend in the River* (1979), V. S. Naipaul does not alter his vision of the destination of postcolonial society. Surrounded by darkness and despair, the narrator of *A Bend in the River* finally seeks only to survive – leaving all that he has built up in ruins behind him, he relinquishes any hope he ever had that history will provide explanations or the metropolis a future. Western civilization is disintegrating as the Arabs wait like vultures to pick the bones. But paradoxically, the narrator/protagonist of this novel is a stronger, more positive individual and the final effect of the novel is more tranquil than description of it would suggest.

Naipaul draws on his *New York Review of Books* article, "A New King for the Congo" (REP 171–204), for many details of background and political event, but just as Isabella is not Trinidad and the "free state" is not Uganda, the country of the novel is not identical with Zaire. Another less accessible publication allows us to participate in the development of both the journalism and the novel: in 1980, a limited edition titled *A Congo Diary* was released; it was apparently written during a visit to Zaire early in 1975. As he made the steamer journey up the Congo, Naipaul recalled Conrad's similar journey and the fiction it prompted; the horror uncovered by Marlow had its parallels in the town at the bend in the river which provides the setting for Naipaul's novel. At the end of the novel events seem to be moving toward a massacre similar to that which occurred during Pierre Mulele's rebellion at Stanleyville in which anyone who could read or write — or who wore a tie — is believed to have been shot. Kurtz reigned at this same site, but now "the man with 'the inconceivable mystery of a soul that knew no restraint, no faith, and no fear' was black, and not white; and he had been maddened not by contact with wilderness and primitivism, but with the civilization established by those pioneers who now lie on Mount Ngaliema, above the Kinshasa rapids" (REP 196). Astoundingly, *A Congo Diary* records, "no one, African, Asian, European, has heard of Conrad or *Heart of Darkness*" (CD 13). Naipaul and Conrad in real life; Marlow and Salim in fiction — Conrad's fiction shaping Naipaul's understanding of reality almost as much as his own observations; and Naipaul's fiction interpreting reality so that it captures a greater truth for his readers — and probably for himself — than the nonfiction. And yet at some stages the technique of the nonfiction is almost fictional: the material is allowed to speak for itself when Naipaul offers a detail such as the pitiful little dead monkeys strung up by their tails knotted around their necks and cooked over fires on the lower deck of the steamer. Naipaul does not need to tell us about the stench of the burning fur, nor does he need to comment that this scene is not colourful but nauseating.

Superficially, *A Bend in the River* is similar to *The Mimic Men* in that a narrator records political events at a time of turmoil and analyses his relationship to his postcolonial society. Singh abandoned his attempt to write history and found the order he sought in his personal past. Salim, however, finds that his family's history is virtually non-existent; there are no visions of Aryan horsemen and snow-capped Himalayas for him.

> My family was Muslim. But we were a special group. We were distinct from the Arabs and other Muslims on the coast; in our customs and attitudes we were closer to the Hindus of northwestern India, from which we had original-ly come. When we had come no one could tell me. We were not that kind of people. We simply lived; we did what was expected of us, what we had seen the previous generations do. We never asked why; we never recorded. We felt in our bones that we were a very old people; but we seemed to have no means of gauging the passing of time. Neither my father nor my grandfather could put dates to their stories. Not because they had forgotten or were confused; the past was simply the past. (BR 17)

Nor, a point we shall return to later, does history explain his people's place any better.

> All that I know of our history and the history of the Indian Ocean I have got from books written by Europeans. If I say that our Arabs in their time were great adventurers and writers; that our sailors gave the Mediterranean the lanteen sail that made the discovery of the Americas possible; that an Indian pilot led Vasco da Gama from East Africa to Cali-cut; that the very word *cheque* was first used by our Persian merchants – if I say these things it is because I have got them from European books. They formed no part of our knowledge or pride. Without Europeans, I feel, all our past would have been washed away, like the scuff marks of fishermen on the beach outside our town. (BR 18)

In *A Congo Diary*, the disappearance of history is a theme
to which Naipaul's thoughts return constantly. In discussions with people throughout his journey he notes that the
past does not exist except that which is within the reach of
their own memories. Or what history is known is distorted:
"(Even in the official handbook, *Profils du Zaire*, the Belgian
period is like something in a Belgian text book – about
institutions, etc. Passion comes later, where memory takes
over. So for many people here the history of the world
seems to begin in 1950 or 1960)" (CD 16). Another distortion
comes with the oral history of his Bantu people recounted
by a young geography teacher: " . . . he said; centuries ago
the land was empty. When his ancestors came they found
only pygmies, a primitive people, whom they chased away
into the deep forest" (CD 35). Obviously, colonialism is not
exclusively a white prerogative.

Although Salim seems to feel the lack of family and racial
history as a loss, he makes little attempt to make up for it
by recording events of his childhood and adolescence as
Singh does. He reveals only the history of his time at the
bend in the river, during which he draws what seem to be
his final conclusions about the meaning of life. Salim's
great illumination comes at the painful, violent and physically brutal end of his affair with Yvette, a sexual relationship that has brought him great pleasure as he abandons
the selfishness of brothel sex and tries to win a woman by
pleasing her. "It seemed to me that men were born only to
grow old, to live out their span, to acquire experience. Men
lived to acquire experience; the quality of the experience
was immaterial; pleasure and pain – and above all, pain –
had no meaning; to possess pain was as meaningless as to
chase pleasure" (BR 239). From this point on, that illumination dominates Salim's perceptions so that he now accepts
Indar's precept: where men are constantly on the move –
and that is in most of the world – they must learn to trample on the past because the past can only cause them pain.
There is no home to which men like Salim and Indar can
return; the life of their community is over.

Just as Salim draws no comfort from the past and very little from his relationship with Yvette, he also seems to fail to discover in the act of writing the pleasure that so many of Naipaul's characters have found. Ralph Singh is very conscious of himself as a writer, of the need to select the right place to begin his story so that it will be in the correct perspective from the start. He chooses not to follow a chronological order because the order he seeks is not simply of time but of relationships between events. Only on two or three occasions does Salim note the fact that he is writing, and then quite casually; one of these occasions coincides with his attempt to describe his first sexual contact with Yvette. "To write about the occasion in the manner of my pornographic magazines would be more than false. It would be like trying to take photographs of myself, to be the voyeur of my own actions, to reconvert the occasion into the brothel fantasy that, in the bedroom, it ceased to be" (BR 188). He tells his story in chronological order for the most part because he is unable to perceive the type of pattern Singh sees in events. Salim simply sees life as the substitution of one era for another; reflecting on the deterioration of the Domain into an African housing settlement surrounding a polytechnic, he comments: "This piece of earth — how many changes had come to it! Forest at a bend in the river, a meeting place, an Arab settlement, a European outpost, a European suburb, a ruin like the ruin of a dead civilization, the glittering Domain of new Africa, and now this" (BR 278).

Violence, only hinted at in Salim's accounts of atrocities during rebellions, surfaces in his own life and he describes in some detail his attack on Yvette. Since *The Mimic Men*, Naipaul has increasingly emphasized the violence of modern existence. He frequently asserts that after the first blow is struck, the first blood drawn, all succeeding blows are dealt easily, automatically. "It had begun as a squabble with some pavement sleepers who had barred off a stretch of pavement in a semi-permanent way with concrete blocks looted from a building site. And it could easily have ended as a shouting match, no more. But the officer had stumbled and fallen. By that fall, that momentary appearance of helplessness, he had invited the first blow with one of the concrete blocks; and the sight of blood had encouraged a sudden, frenzied attack by dozens of small hands" (BR 223). Recognition of a potential victim's vulnerability increases the chance of attack. Reflecting the quality of his society's relationships with its individual members, Salim, though not by nature a violent man, may be possessed by the same rage and fear that possess his society. So, feeling his own vulnerability as violence spreads through the town, and recognizing Raymond's precarious position as one of the President's former intimates, Salim thinks of Yvette as a defeated person as well. Believing that she is seeking new possibilities, that she is about to betray him, he attacks and humiliates her. When he has destroyed their relationship, like the people who destroy the town, he grieves for it: "I didn't want her. I didn't want her. That is what I can't bear. It's all gone" (BR 238).

Linked to the increasing emphasis on violence in Naipaul's writing is a theme which became apparent early in his career: the vulnerability of the flesh. Biswas, Stone, and Singh are aware of the weakness and corruptibility of the flesh, how easy it is to become a victim. In more recent works of fiction the emphasis shifts to the dehumanization and humiliation that physical fear and pain can bring, as Bobby and Peter Roche discover. On being imprisoned, Salim learns that although from the outside, the jail wall had seemed improvidently low, "A wall taller than a man is a high wall" (BR 286). Observing the torture inflicted on men and boys from the villages, Salim finds that retreat into the self is the only escape. "There was, with the prisoners as well as with their active tormentors, a frenzy. But the frenzy of the prisoners was internal; it had taken them far beyond their cause, far beyond thought. They had prepared themselves for death not because they were martyrs; but because what they were and what they knew they were was all they had. They were people crazed with the idea of who they were. I never felt closer to them, or more far away" (BR 288). Salim resolves not to provoke any physical contact for fear of any touch leading to "terrible things". He analyses the ambivalent attitude many of Naipaul's characters seem to have toward their bodies. "In a cell like mine you very quickly become aware of your body. You can grow to hate your body. And your body is all you have: this was the curious thought that kept floating up through my rage" (BR 287). Not only in jail or in physical danger but in all situations, Naipaul seems to say, man can be certain of nothing but his own physical existence and that in itself makes him terrifyingly vulnerable.

In *A Bend in the River* Naipaul seems to offer people no straw at which to clutch. Painfully aware of the falseness and fragility of civilizations, Salim is unable to invoke the vision of past civilizations leading inevitably to the present that soothed Ralph Singh. Through the missionary Father Huismans, Naipaul conveys the deluded confidence of the European who is certain of his place in the immense flow of history and of the continuation of his civilization. Perhaps with his "unfinished face" giving the impression of "incompleteness, fragility and toughness", he also represents the society itself — vulnerable and on the decline, but still strong enough to refuse to yield. Father Huismans' confidence is so great that "for him the destruction of the European town, the town that his countrymen had built, was only a temporary setback. Such things happened when something big and new was being set up, when the course of history was being altered" (BR 70). He collects the relics of Africa and reveres the spiritual qualities that make them live, but he also collects relics of the colonial past. "That past had been bitter, but Father Huismans appeared to take the bitterness for granted; he saw beyond it" (BR 71). He believes that each previous settlement at the bend in the river had "prepared the way for the mighty civilization of Europe". Salim records Huismans' confidence and expresses admiration for the priest, but notes at the same time that Huismans is self-absorbed, uninterested in the breakdown of one of his teachers, and unable to meet the eyes of another. When Huismans explains one of the mottoes that provide a varying refrain throughout the novel, Salim is staggered by the confidence of a people who have dared to tamper with the words of a god in such a way as to reverse their meaning. The Latin words on the monument to sixty years of steamer service, *Miscerique probat populos et foedera jungi* mean "'He approves of the mingling of the peoples and their bonds of union'", but in the original version the Roman hero was warned that the great god might not approve. Salim sees this alteration as tempting fate and believes that the almost immediate destruction of the monument is a natural result. The lycée motto also comes from ancient Rome and refers to Africa – *semper aliquid novi*, "'always something new'" – and reminds us that the Roman presence, like the Arab, is gone and that there is no reason to expect the European to last much longer.

Parallelling the European penchant for erecting statues and devising slogans is the Big Man's establishment of a cult of the African madonna, his distribution of his own portrait throughout the country and his dissemination of his own maxims on billboards. Both societies, the established and the developing, seem to require statues and slogans that will define and establish them in their own eyes. The slogan *Discipline Avant Tout* – in reality Mobutu's slogan – appears everywhere, but again it is a slogan in a language not of Africa and there is no reason to expect it to last. Salim is conscious of "an element of pathos in those maxims, portraits and statues, in this wish of a man of the bush to make himself big, and setting about it in such a crude way. I even felt a little sympathy for the man who was making such a display of himself" (BR 266). This, too, is a reaction Naipaul recorded in *A Congo Diary* " – sadness at the need of the African to assert himself, to give himself monuments, luxury, etc., everything other people possess" (CD 18). The rebels publish a leaflet entitled "The Ancestors Shriek" in which every propaganda cliché is trotted out once more, but Salim is aware of another shriek – that of the President, manifest in his statues and slogans which attempt to meet the "real competition" in Europe. The President seeks to combine the ideas of Europe and Africa, past and present, the bush and civilization, but as Salim flees down the river, it is certain that the Big Man's hold on the district is slipping. Already the statue of the African madonna has been smashed just as the steamer monument was smashed earlier.

Throughout the succession of eras at the bend of the river, the bush has endured unchanged. In daylight Salim can imagine the land being tamed, made part of the present and fit for the future, but at night, "if you were on the river, it was another thing. You felt the land taking you back to something that was familiar, something you had known at some time but had forgotten or ignored, but which was always there. You felt the land taking you back to what was there a hundred years ago, to what had been there always" (BR 15). So the cleared site of the Domain reverts to jungle practically overnight. Salim mentions frequently how small a space the town occupies, but on the last leg of his journey from Europe back to the town, he discovers just how inexorable and interminable the African bush is. His perception is sharpened by having discovered the falsity of his vision of Europe; the language, the goods, the trappings of modernity received from Europe made him believe in "great cities, great stores, great buildings, great universities. . . . But the Europe I had come to — and knew from the outset I was coming to — was neither the old Europe nor the new. It was something shrunken and mean and forbidding" (BR 247). Salim sees the loneliness and isolation of the girls from East Africa selling cigarettes in kiosks on London streets, but Nazruddin analyses the real threat, the cause for genuine dismay (and gives a hint of the attitudes behind *Among the Believers*):

> "I'm superstitious about the Arabs. They gave us and half the world our religion, but I can't help feeling that when they leave Arabia terrible things are about to happen in the world. You just have to think of where we come from. Per-

sia, India, Africa. Think of what happened there. Now
Europe. They're pumping the oil in and sucking the money
out. Pumping the oil in to keep the system going, sucking
the money out to send it crashing down. They need Europe.
They want the goods and the properties and at the same
time they need a safe place for their money. Their own
countries are so dreadful. But they're destroying money.
They're killing the goose that lays the golden egg.

"And they aren't the only ones. All over the world money
is in flight. People have scraped the world clean, as clean as
an African scrapes his yard, and now they want to run from
the dreadful places where they've made their money and
find some nice safe country. I was one of the crowd.
Koreans, Filipinos, people from Hong Kong and Taiwan,
South Africans, Italians, Greeks, South Americans, Argen-
tines, Colombians, Venezuelans, Bolivians, a lot of black
people who've cleaned out places you've never heard of,
Chinese from everywhere. All of them are on the run. They
are frightened of the fire. You mustn't think it's only Africa
people are running from." (BR 251–52)

The situation of every society, modern or ancient, is seen
to be precarious, subject to new threats; all that remains
constant is the bush with its primitive vitality. Ronald
Blaber (1986) describes the way Naipaul reverses the usual
imagery of light and darkness in this novel so that reality is
represented by the darkness of the bush and daylight in the
cleared area reveals only the transitory fantasies of humankind. Here again, fiction anticipates subsequent nonfiction,
for in *Finding the Centre* the night and the bush are again
equated with reality.

In *A Bend in the River* Naipaul seems close to recanting
his faith in the study of history. Previously he has argued
that knowing only the history of colonial masters, developing countries lack a sense of identity. However, in "A New
King for the Congo" Naipaul notes how little African history is recorded either from the European or the African
point of view: "The past has vanished. Facts in a book cannot by themselves give people a sense of history. Where so
little has changed, where bush and river are so overwhelm-

ing, another past is accessible, better answering African bewilderment and African religious beliefs: the past as *le bon vieux temps de nos ancêtres*" (REP 23). Aware that he has no sense of racial, national or personal past, Salim feels different from others in his Muslim coastal community because he is also aware that their way of life is ending. His resulting detachment could be the attribute of a budding historian, but Indar's anguish at his failed attempt to join his destiny to India's persuades Salim to accept the advice to trample on the past. His journey to Europe and the end of his affair with Yvette convince Salim that the quest for home is fruitless. The rôles are reversed, for Indar now longs to go home to some dream village, but Salim is certain that "there could be no going back; there was nothing to go back to. We had become what the world outside had made us; we had to live in the world as it existed. The younger Indar was wiser. Use the airplane; trample on the past, as Indar had said he had trampled on the past. Get rid of that idea of the past; make the dream-like scenes of loss ordinary" (BR 261–62).

Not only does it seem that the past will provide no comfort but also that it is unlikely ever to be fully known. Raymond, a historian himself, indulges in reveries about whether the truth can ever be known; at first his queries seem a pose, a way of demanding reassurance from his audience but as he continues with questions about what actually happened during the conquest of Gaul or about the truth of all the wars, rebellions, leaders, and defeats in Africa, he becomes more convincing. Finally when Indar summarizes a highly praised article about a rebellion, it sounds so much like nonsense that it sets up doubts as to whether the study of history can possibly reveal truth. The final seal on doubt is set when Raymond talks about Theodor Mommsen, the German genius who discovered the truth about the Roman Republic. "Discovered" is Raymond's word; he seems to see nothing strange in the idea of discovering "'The problems, the issues, the very narrative'" (BR 148) of events so long past even though he has just mentioned all the things that go unrecorded at the time they occur.

It might still be argued that Naipaul has not relinquished his faith in history's ability to explain and order, and that Raymond's failures are personal failures or failures of technique rather than of the discipline itself. However, the complex imagery surrounding the water hyacinth — the "new thing" in the river — also suggests that truth may not be consistent or discoverable. One of those real-world observations that Naipaul turns into a motif in his fiction, the water hyacinth offers a constant reminder of the bush that ceaselessly threatens to overwhelm attempts to establish civilization. "If the steamers do not fail, if there are no more wars, it is the Congo hyacinth that may yet imprison the river people in the immemorial ways of the bush" (REP 184). On the first occasion when Salim describes the hyacinth, he is at a look-out point which had been a park "with amenities" but has reverted to a fishing village. He has just abandoned an attempt to discuss a scientific advance with Ferdinand and muses on Ferdinand's return to his mother's village. Everything suggests the yielding of civilized European to bush African, and the hyacinth, though new, is natural, "as if rain and river were tearing away bush" (BR 52) and a threat to the river highway along which civilization pushes into the heart of Africa. Later the hyacinths are associated with another onslaught of primitive forces against the European. When Father Huismans is murdered, the canoe bearing his mutilated body is trapped in a tangle of water hyacinths (BR 89). Their presence is noted again when Indar, citing the nearness of the bush, expresses his doubts about the work going on at the Domain (BR 150).

The phrase, the new thing in the river, links the hyacinths to the lycée motto, *semper aliquid novi,* and its reminder of the many eras that have come and gone. The hyacinths themselves change from lilac to white and bring different messages to Salim: "The hyacinths of the river, floating on: during the days of the rebellion they had spoken of blood; on heavy afternoons of heat and glitter they had spoken of experience without savour; white in the moonlight, they had matched the mood of a particular evening. Now, lilac on bright green, they spoke of something over, other people moving on" (BR 170). In his use of this image, Naipaul seems to arrive at one of those conclusions to which fiction leads him even though with rational analysis he is able to deny it. Just as the hyacinths convey different messages at different times, so events of the past may be interpreted in various ways, depending on the perspective of the historian. History and hyacinths float inexorably on, but both, Naipaul seems to suggest, lack a totally consistent and discoverable meaning. Furthermore, because the study of history is associated with civilized people and the hyacinths with primitive, natural or bush forces which threaten to overwhelm the precariously sited outposts of progress, doubt is cast on the hope that history can provide enduring comfort by ordering chaos and explaining the present through investigation of the past.

Gradually Salim becomes aware that people construct their own truth. When Ferdinand tries to provoke Indar into condemning Christian missionary activity and making a statement about the relevance of African religion, Salim realizes that no one in the Domain is willing to discuss the Africa they knew. And again, comparison with *A Congo Diary* is interesting, for Naipaul visited a university class and had a similar conversation: "One was immediately taken by the open, bright faces; and the discussion was lively: language, religion, etc. They were very interested in the politics of Africa – Angola, Rhodesia, South Africa. One boy raised the question of people being *depersonalisés* by imperialism and I thought he was making the point that Christianity was an imported religion incompatible with African religion. I asked whether his feelings about African religion represented a need or was simply a sentimental attachment. I was sharply taken up by someone, an older student, a priest, about 40, I was told later, who said I was asking too complicated a question. I said I was not asking the question, but responding to the question that had been

put to me" (CD 14). For a moment Salim believes that to
return to the town from the Domain is "to grasp reality
again". He compares the way in which a bribe is passed as
he clears goods at customs with the way in which Africa is
discussed at the Domain – the bribe is never mentioned
though it is at the heart of the transaction. Ultimately he
questions the essence of reality and truth. "The Domain
was a hoax. But at the same time it was real, because it was
full of serious men (and a few women). Was there a truth
outside men? Didn't men make the truth for themselves?
Everything men did or made became real" (BR 135). In the
closing stages of his account of himself, Salim decides that
even the questions are pointless; all that matters is going
on. "Sometimes as I was falling asleep I was kicked awake
by some picture that came to me of my African town –
absolutely real (and the airplane could take me there
tomorrow), but its associations made it dream-like. Then I
remembered my illumination, about the need of men only
to live, about the illusion of pain. I played off London
against Africa until both became unreal, and I could fall
asleep. After a time I didn't have to call up the illumination, the mood of that African morning. It was there,
beside me, that remote vision of the planet, of men lost in
space and time, but dreadfully, pointlessly busy" (BR 257–
58). The continued use of the word "fantasy" in this narrative links Salim's questioning of reality to Naipaul's apprehension, very early in his career, that Trinidadians often
construct their reality out of the fantasy world of films.
When Salim recognizes that men make the truth for themselves, he approaches Naipaul's conclusion that truth may
be just another form of fantasy, that history and fiction are
often indistinguishable.

The river of this novel changes direction at an enormous
bend, a bend which obscures vision of its source as completely as the darkness hides the origin of the bus that hurtles past the boy outside his hut. In the Bengali novel,
Pather Panchali, Banerjee delights in the bends in the road,
in the onward movement of life/time toward unseen destin-

ations, but Naipaul captures the fear which arises when one cannot see around the corner. In other fiction he has fought against the Indian concept of *samsāra* (that existence is an endless sea of change). In *A Bend in the River* Naipaul seems ready to follow Stein's advice in Conrad's *Lord Jim* and submit himself to "the destructive element". Lacking explanations and stability, the individual is left alone with no aim but the simple one of continuing to survive. He does not even have much control over what is to happen to him. Salim tries to break free of his Fate, but Nazruddin has seen faithfulness in his hand, and finally Salim returns to his commitment to Kareisha: " . . . I had had my life of rebellion, in Africa. I had taken it as far as I could take it. And I had come to London for relief and rescue, clinging to what remained of our organized life" (BR 248).

Throughout the novel personal relationships are investigated in terms of dependence. The most complex is that of Salim and Yvette, a relationship in which, albeit briefly, selflessness leads to fulfilment so that being selfless is, in itself, selfish. Salim is aware from the first that the security he finds in Yvette's home is illusory: "It was make-believe – I never doubted that. You couldn't listen to sweet songs about injustice unless you expected justice and received it much of the time. You couldn't sing songs about the end of the world unless – like the other people in that room, so beautiful with such simple things: African mats on the floor and African hangings on the wall and spears and masks – you felt that the world was going on and you were safe in it. How easy it was, in that room, to make those assumptions!" (BR 139–40). In Salim's love affair there are elements that recall the behaviour of his family's domestic slaves who define themselves by connection with a reputable family and who, far from desiring freedom, cling to the family. Throughout the novel reminders of the African slave trade reinforce the notion that every dependency is a form of enslavement. The simpler association of Shoba and Mahesh parallels that of Salim with Yvette and helps to define the ways in which Salim feels stunted, as well as fulfilled, by being Yvette's lover. Mahesh is satisfied with himself and attempts nothing more than to preserve the person Shoba admires. Similarly, although through Yvette, Salim has broadened his understanding of world affairs, he looks at events only to estimate whether or not they threaten his life with her. Yet at the same time, he feels secure, certain that he will be returned to himself when their affair inevitably ends. As Salim's rage and despairing acts of violence parallel political events, so does the growth of his dependence on Yvette parallel the growth of the nation's dependence on the Big Man. In many ways the love of this coloured man for a white woman resembles the admiration of a colonial society for the metropolis. Both individual and society establish their identity through the relationships; both devalue others who resemble themselves; both fear the loss of whatever gives a sense of independent selfhood; both erupt in rage, demanding independence and yet fearing it and regretting the loss of the mistress. Salim is astonished to discover that his life with Yvette depends on the "health and optimism" of all parties to it: "I couldn't bear the idea of the lost coming together for comfort" (BR 232). As he comes to understand the anxieties that beset Yvette and Raymond, he begins to withdraw from her. A dependent colony's awe at the strength and glamour of the metropolis also wanes when familiarity increases or the metropolis itself is under threat. As Yvette is dependent on Raymond, so the metropolis is dependent on the larger world society, and when the relationship of an imperial power to the larger society weakens, so must the relationship with the colony. Since fulfilling associations cannot result when any of the partners lack "health and optimism", and since in Naipaul's world, health and optimism are rare states, it seems that both personal and political relationships are doomed.

Although Salim's relationship with Yvette provides the most complete metaphor for the colonial link between master and slave, ruler and subject, other personal relationships offer similar parallels. Salim discovers in his dealings with Metty that it is often more demanding to be master than slave. Not only has the master responsibility for the slave's physical well-being but he must also consciously maintain his position of superiority. In Salim's relationship with Ferdinand, he suffers the awkwardness and occasional fear that results from not being able to read an unfamiliar face, and he suffers the jealousy of a colonial who believes his protegé to be outstripping him. He also records Ferdinand's frenzy when the young man becomes aware that all his education and training are not sufficient to save him from the nightmares of executions, and that "progress" has deprived him of a haven.

All the characters of *A Bend in the River* share in this deprivation, but Indar is the one who articulates the sense of loss and its causes most clearly as he examines his experience at India House. The building itself represents not the real India but a British idea of India. Inside Indar finds cringing men, small in stature as well as in aspiration, who complacently define their virtue by their caste. Whatever their status these men have surrendered their manhood to enhance the heroic stature of Gandhi and Nehru. Indar resolves to be himself even if it means being alone – and it is likely that his words express most forcefully the sensibility of his creator:

> "I began to understand at the same time that my anguish about being a man adrift was false, that for me that dream of home and security was nothing more than a dream of isolation, anachronistic and stupid and very feeble. I belonged to myself alone. I was going to surrender my manhood to nobody. For someone like me there was only one civilization and one place – London, or a place like it. Every other kind of life was make-believe. Home – what for? To hide? To bow to our great man? For people in our situation, people led into slavery, that is the biggest trap of all. We have nothing. We solace ourselves with that idea of the great men of our tribe, the Gandhi and the Nehru, and we castrate ourselves. 'Here, take my manhood and invest it for me. Take my manhood and be a greater man for my sake!' No! I want to be a man myself!" (BR 163)

Here Naipaul's fiction seems to answer a question posed in
A Congo Diary: "I was thinking as I stood in the bows today,
about Mobutism. The cult of the personality; the green
book of thoughts; the mixture of all kinds of ideas. But
perhaps the idea of the value of the people, *le petit peuple,* is
the most important. Perhaps out of the *mélange* this is the
thing that points to the future. But I don't know. One is
clutching at straws now, because all the proclaimed ideas
deserve a better organized or more educated country. A
different country" (CD 31). Mobutism seems likely to de-
prive individuals of their manhood in the same way as
Gandhianism. Indar's tragedy is that he fails to maintain
his "colonial rage". He loses his idea of himself as someone
better, privileged, holy when he realizes he has exposed
himself to another who does not share in his vulnerability.
Without the rage, without the certainty of his own individual power, he feels the need to go home, to retreat to a
dream village, and this, of course, he cannot do.

Study of *A Bend in the River* can only reinforce admiration
for Naipaul's skill and increase awareness of the tension
between his words of despair and the act of creation which
orders them. The book is so unified that each detail is linked to the whole and contributes to the investigation of colonial dependency. Just as the relationship between Salim
and Yvette embodies many aspects of the colonial relationship, the steamer and its satellites, barge and canoes, stand
as a metaphor for the social and political development of
Africa. As Salim and Yvette begin their relationship, they
are on the steamer and watching dugout canoes riskily
approach to link up briefly with the steamer only to have
to paddle laboriously back to their village. Originally used
only by the colonial rulers, the steamer had attached to it a
barge on which "the people" were accommodated. Later
privileged local people, the President's new bureaucrats,
take over the steamer's first-class but it has become very
shabby, and the barge is still towed behind. The President's
elevation of the people is marked by lashing the barge to
the forward part of the steamer, but at the end of the novel,

the barge is cast adrift after an attempt by rebels to hijack the steamer. Again the imagination of Naipaul the novelist has converted the observations of Naipaul the journalist (and diarist) into images that illuminate not only the conditions of the characters in their own time and place but also the state of a world struggling through the chaos left by the breakdown of the old colonial structures.

A Bend in the River presents Salim's attempt to explore the aftermath of colonial rule, attempting to distinguish the direction in which the world seems to be heading, and to assess the implications of great events for the ordinary individual trying to make sense of life. In the end, like Santosh, Salim gives up the quest for meaning, for fulfilling relationships, for past and home, in order merely to live. The novel closes with an image that suggests restless, even frenzied activity continuing in darkness, the white moths which Bobby had also observed in "In A Free State". "The searchlight was turned off; the barge was no longer to be seen. The steamer started up again and moved without lights down the river, away from the area of battle. The air would have been full of moths and flying insects. The searchlight, while it was on, had shown thousands, white in the white light" (BR 296).

Earlier in the book Salim compares the secure cosiness of his lamplit flat to the protection and secrecy of huts at night.

> The gunfire went on. But it came no nearer. It was the sound of the weapons of the President's white men, the promise of order and continuity; and it was oddly comforting, like the sound of rain in the night. All that was threatening, in that great unknown outside, was being held in check. And it was a relief, after all the anxiety, to sit in the lamplit flat and watch the shadows that electric lights never made; and to hear Ferdinand and Metty talk in their leisurely old men's voices in that room which they had turned into a warm little cavern. It was a little like being transported to the hidden forest villages, to the protection and secrecy of the huts at night — everything outside shut out, kept beyond

some magical protecting line; and I thought, as I had
thought when I had had lunch with the old couple, how nice
it would be if it were true. If in the morning we could wake
up and find that the world had shrunken only to what we
knew and what was safe. (BR 86–87)

In the morning there is instead a fighter plane, "a killing
thing", "like a vicious bird that wouldn't go away".

Salim cannot retreat into the secure circle of light that
surrounds a hut at nightfall and neither, having traced the
journey of the bus back to its origins, and having ventured
to look down the road toward its destination, can his
creator. All that either can see ahead is the threatened collapse of society as they know it, meaningless activity, and
darkness. And yet, for many readers, there is some satisfaction in the fact that the post-colonial world has shaped
the lucid and ordering mind of V. S. Naipaul to play like a
powerful searchlight over the darkling plain. Helen Tiffin
(1986, 25) writes of the changing sensibility she discerns in
Naipaul and some other postcolonial writers:

> In *A House for Mr Biswas* and in *Voss* both Naipaul and
> White, in characteristically complex ways, couched their
> exploration of the postcolonial psyche in the house-build-
> ing and journey motifs, motifs which ultimately draw upon
> the ethic they sought to repudiate. In *A Bend in the River*
> and *The Twyborn Affair*, both published almost twenty years
> after the earlier works, these novelists seem to have moved
> away from the idea of the possibility and even desirability
> of indigenization (with its concomitant promise of personal
> and communal integrity) towards the notion that in the
> postcolonial world acceptance of fragmentation of person-
> ality and the abandonment of the idea of home might be
> often not a strategy for survival but offer a potential for
> creativity.

She believes that Naipaul's acceptance of fragmentation
leads to a more positive tone for this novel than its bleak
message would suggest. Salim is neither as "frenetic" nor as
"destructive" as Jimmy Ahmed or Ralph Singh; he remains
"resilient and humane". Here may be the resolution to

Meredith's dilemma, that if one sees too much one may simply retreat to a house on a hill. Naipaul's work has consistently walked this tightrope between creativity and involvement, withdrawal and passivity, but his most recent work, for all its despairing vision of human affairs, shows greater tolerance, accommodation and calm than earlier work, particularly that of the early 1970s.

A Dead End: *Among the Believers*

In *A Bend in the River*, being Muslim means little to Salim. He has no sense of community and no religious faith, nor apparently has Nazruddin who explicitly states his mistrust of the Arabs and his fear that they will bring Europe "crashing down" despite – or because of – their dependence on European goods and properties as a haven for their money. When Naipaul began his Islamic journey, these were the conclusions his fiction had led him toward, but in *Among the Believers* (1981) one feels little of the disturbing sense of threat or menace which contributes to the tension of the novel. *Among the Believers* reverts to the techniques of *The Middle Passage*, being a chronicle of an investigative journey through a number of countries. As did *The Middle Passage*, each of the major sections bears a carefully chosen epigraph which identifies Naipaul's main theme in the section. But the more recent book lacks the personal anger, the passionate rejection of what he considers second-rate and the result of the colonial experience. Overall, *Among the Believers* is an unusually calm book for Naipaul; though not unsympathetic, he simply does not seem to be fully engaged with the people or the countries he visits.

His distance results from a number of factors. One of the most obvious is language. Constantly engaging interpreters or struggling to discuss abstract and profound concepts with people whose command of English is limited, Naipaul often seems to give up the attempt to establish communication. A number of his contacts with the faithful result in

tortuously circular conversations where the other seems
simply to recite a litany. Naipaul tends to blame the simplifications of their faith for the breakdown in communication, and surely his inability to enter into that sort of belief
limits the exchange, but so must language. It is particularly
noticeable that only one novel is discussed in this book.
Believing that "People can hide behind direct statements;
fiction, by its seeming indirections, can make hidden impulses clear" (AB 17), Naipaul often turns to the fiction of
an area he visits to increase his understanding. He mentions
the Indonesian Pramoedya Ananta Toer, but Max Lane's
translation of *This Earth of Mankind* was not available until
1982. One cannot help wondering whether he would have
been more completely engaged with these societies if he
had had greater access to them through their literature.

In addition, Naipaul seems not to find in them a colonial
past with which he can identify, as he does in so many parts
of the world. Early in the book Naipaul compares his perspective with that of an Iranian student, Behzad, a communist with a strong sense of the injustice in his society and of
his own poverty. Naipaul sees Behzad as "emerged, even
privileged" in comparision with his own contemporaries in
Trinidad. "I had been born in a static colonial time; and in
Trinidad . . . I had known the poverty and spiritual limitations of an agricultural colony where, as was once comput-
ed, there were only eighty kinds of job. I therefore, in
places like Iran, had an eye for change. It was different for
Behzad. Born in Iran in 1955, he took the existence of
national wealth for granted; he took the expansion of his
society for granted; he had an eye only for what was still
unjust in that society" (AB 59). The societies he visits also
have colonial histories: Islam itself was "an imperialism as
well as a religion", but Naipaul lays less emphasis on the
outcomes of the various colonial periods than one might
expect. It would appear that Islam has imparted a greater
cultural stability in these areas than was available to Caribbean peoples in particular. As he portrays them, the Muslims he visits have a sense of their own identities that is not

dependent on a European metropolis. Nevertheless, he detects a profound contradiction in their rejection of Western values, for while Islamic publications renounce technology as evil, Khomeini sends Phantom jet fighters to attack insurgent Kurds. "Interpreter of God's will, leader of the faithful, he expressed all the confusion of his people and made it appear like glory, like the familiar faith: the confusion of a people of high medieval culture awakening to oil and money, a sense of power and violation, and a knowledge of a great new encircling civilization. That civilization couldn't be mastered. It was to be rejected; at the same time it was to be depended on" (AB 80).

Separating him even more from his subjects is Naipaul's inability to enter into their faith that Islam provides all the answers needed for living in the modern world. As he travels, he sees that the societies of believers are not converting their ethical ideals into institutions: Islam forbids usury but no one can come up with an interest-free banking system; Islamic law, to Naipaul, is about punishment not about justice, and such laws as have been enacted, in Pakistan, for example, become unenforceable because there is so much argument about the Koranic precedents. Again and again he is surprised by the simplistic belief that superficial changes reestablish the rule of Ali: "'What a nice thing it is now,' the man from Bombay said, 'to see the rule of Ali! Getting women back into the veil, getting them off television. No alcohol.' It was astonishing after the passion. Was that all there was to the rule of Ali? Did the Shia millennium offer nothing higher?" (AB 31).

The book is more a collection of characters than a chronicle of events; its effect is similar to watching a parade: a face or a costume catches one's eye, seems unforgettable, and is almost immediately lost again in the crowd. Only a few individuals stand out from the crowd of believers, and Naipaul's relations with them add to the feeling that he remained an outsider throughout his journey. While religious dialectic did not interfere with his communication with Behzad, the communist dialectic did. On the train from Mashhad a Revolutionary Guard forbids Behzad's card game, Behzad and Naipaul agree that he is exercising power to prove it is his; but Behzad cannot believe that a worker would behave this way, so he labels the soldier upper-class. When Naipaul questions Behzad's assumption, he equivocates by saying the army serves the upper classes, so they too are upper-class men. Not only this, but also the constraints of Behzad's culture close some avenues of discussion – of his mother or his girlfriend, for instance, and Naipaul comments on these constraints specifically and often enough for readers to remain aware of the doors that will not open to him. Most painful are the two occasions when individuals with whom he seems to have established friendships appear abruptly to change their minds about him and refuse further contact. Naipaul has no explanation for Ahmed's withdrawal or for Shafi's sudden refusal to meet him as he departs Kuala Lumpur; he recounts both incidents briefly, but clearly was wounded. The effect of his dispassionate statements of depression or unhappiness is to emphasize the author's isolation. It is not the sort of isolation that necessarily results in objective and penetrating vision, however; it is more the isolation of being behind a high barrier through which Naipaul is only able to see parts of the other side. Where Naipaul remains an honest and objective reporter is in portraying so clearly the barriers between him and his subjects.

While he is distant from the believers, Naipaul is not unsympathetic toward them. He responds to the sense of community that Islam imparts and would welcome the security it offers the faithful if it did not cut them off from political and economic realities: "Islam had achieved community and a kind of beauty, had given people a feeling of completeness – if only the world outside could be shut out, and men could be made to forget what they knew" (AB 137). Ever since he wrote of the vision of completeness in the tomb at Luxor, the theme of longing for a past in which the world was whole has recurred in Naipaul's work. The longing is not to reconstruct the historical past in order to

understand the present, but rather in a more mystical way
to reenter a time before societies became fragmented. He
realizes that that is also the goal of the fundamentalists, but
he knows that it is an impossible dream, that what has been
done cannot be undone. "The Islamic fundamentalist wish
is to work back to such a whole, for them a God-given
whole, but with the tool of faith alone — belief, religious
practices and rituals. It is like a wish — with intellect suppressed or limited, the historical sense falsified — to work
back from the abstract to the concrete, and to set up the
tribal walls again. It is to seek to recreate something like a
tribal or city state that — except in theological fantasy —
never was" (AB 157–58). In this realization lies the full significance of the first epigraph to the book, the quotation
from Polybius which states that from the rise of Rome on-
wards history has become "an organic whole . . . all events
bear a relationship and contribute to a single end". Michael
Neill's (1982, 48) comprehensive study of V. S. Naipaul's
politics concludes with an analysis of the importance to
Naipaul of "understanding of history, both private and
public, and the value of the special kind of 'vision' it
grants". Neill (50) notes that to Naipaul, in failing to accommodate the past, people reveal the intellectual deficiency
of their societies: the West Indian ignores the truth of the
slave period; in the Islamic world a selective history has
been fabricated "to serve the interests of theological myth".
Naipaul draws attention to the "more-than-colonial confusion" (AB 134) of people whose history must both abhor and
glorify successive waves of conquerors because eventually
the conquerors adopted Islam; in Pakistan it results in fabricated personalities and the pretence of being Turk or
Mogul or Arab so that one may participate in the glory of
the conqueror.

In Malaysia and Indonesia, particularly in Java, Naipaul
finds fragments of the perfect complete village life. The
Muslim organizer Shafi reveals the inconsistency between
longing for the pure village life and recognizing the backwardness of his people. In Malaysia where there is relative

wealth, the vision of completeness is erased by the racial divisions between Chinese and Malays. The discriminatory laws which favour Malays touch only some, for there is further division between villagers and city dwellers. Naipaul recognizes in Shafi the almost universal human desire to recreate the security of childhood; he comments that most of us, accepting responsibility for ourselves, accommodate ourselves to the grief, but that Shafi shifts the "whole burden of that accommodation onto Islam" (AB228). Java appeals particularly to Naipaul for the way the society has fused elements of many religions and cultures to evolve "an enchanted, complete world where everything . . . had reached a kind of perfection" (AB 320). Islam and Christianity complement the old faiths, animism and Hinduism; everywhere there is evidence of overlappings and borrowings. But gradually Naipaul reveals the problems and dislocations in the midst of such harmony: too many people, pressures to produce more rice disrupting the rhythm of village life, farmers going into debt, and Islam unable to solve problems of land tenure, unable to offer political and practical solutions to the injustices it brings to people's attention. What is most frustrating is that Islam need not fail, in Malaysia, Indonesia, Pakistan or Iran: "No religion is more worldly than Islam. In spite of its political incapacity, no religion keeps men's eyes more fixed on the way the world is run. And in the poetry of the doctor's son, in his fumbling response to the universal civilization, his concern with 'basics', I thought I could see how Islamic fervour could become creative, revolutionary and take men on to a humanism beyond religious doctrine: a true renaissance, open to the new and enriched by it, as the Muslims in their early days of glory had been" (AB 167). This is the lesson history could teach Muslims, that once Islam was a receptive philosophy of reformers open to ideas from any source.

As Naipaul continues to investigate the darkness outside the circle of light, it seems that he has reached a dead end with Islam. In *A Bend in the River* he seemed to suggest that the Arabs posed a threat to the centres of European imperialism, the former colonial metropolises, but after the analysis necessary to produce *Among the Believers,* it appears that Naipaul is unable to consider seriously a threat from this quarter. The return to the old order, to the faith of the past brings such superficial changes to the societies Naipaul observes and does so little to reconstruct political and economic institutions that there is nothing to fear, except continuing instability and the growing awareness of injustice fostered by modern Islam. "Step by step, out of its Islamic striving, Pakistan had undone the rule of law it had inherited from the British, and replaced it with nothing" (AB 159). Michael Neill (41) writes that Naipaul cannot accept Fanon's "simple conviction that the colonial world can and must be made anew" and quotes *The Overcrowded Barracoon* (OB 275): "'How, without empire, do such societies govern themselves? What is now the source of power? The ballot box, the mob, the regiment? When as in Haiti, the slave-owners leave, and there are only slaves, what are the sanctions?'" It is not that the British or any other imperialists were particularly enlightened or beneficent; it is simply that what they did cannot be undone so easily and that even if it could, people cannot exist in a vacuum. Writing before publication of *Finding the Centre,* Neill (54–55) finds "the vision of [the post-*Mimic Men* books] profoundly pessimistic; for, matching Naipaul's Fanonian indignation at the destructive legacy of imperialism, is a deepening despair at the seemingly irremediable confusion left in its wake. It implies, in its way, a critique of imperialism even more radical than Fanon's: for it asks us to contemplate the possibility of organic societies damaged beyond repair, of a world incapable, in any imaginable future, of putting itself together again". In strictly political terms, this seems to be a "correct" reading of Naipaul's work, but it fails to capture the increasing calm of recent books, particularly *A Bend in the River* but also *Among the Believers.* While Naipaul rejects the simplistic faith of the believers, he seems more tolerant of them as people despite their intellectual deficiencies and their illusions;

his impatience has been tempered considerably since *The Middle Passage* or *An Area of Darkness*. It is the difference in tone that, for all its bleakness and the basic consistency of political themes, makes *A Bend in the River* a more humane novel than *Guerrillas*.

Part Four

The Centre Recovered

A New Beginning? *Finding the Centre*

Of all V. S. Naipaul's nonfiction writing, *Finding the Centre* (1984) is the most consciously personal book he has produced. He says in the "Author's Foreword" that his intention was "to admit the reader to the process" of writing, a goal that may not have been strictly necessary since his work — fiction and nonfiction — is often about writing, and since his method, particularly in nonfiction, has always been transparent. But the book serves to confirm what readers have already discovered for themselves. The writing of it also seems to have brought Naipaul full circle, back to the clearing and the hut where he discovers that even in the most familiar surroundings with those people to whom one is closest, one's knowledge is incomplete. No longer does it seem his "bad blood" rising to the surface when he questions the nature of reality; now he is more comfortable with mysteries and the unresolvable in experience. Since *A Bend in the River* Naipaul seems to have found greater calm and greater acceptance of the way things are in the world. Speculation about future directions is probably foolish, but he has said (1983) he would like to return to comedy; perhaps he is ready for that now.

"Prologue to an Autobiography" states explicitly the importance of writing to Naipaul, confirming the themes of novel after novel in which the protagonists turn to writing for self-definition, for comfort, and for personal advancement. As he explores his own beginnings as a writer, Naipaul reveals that even in his incomplete knowledge — of Bogart, for instance — "I had divined his impulses" (FC 55). Again he asserts the power of fiction to capture truth — not that Bogart was, in fact, a bigamist (which he was not), but that he was vulnerable to being caught by the senses. The disturbing *asvamedha* episode in *The Mimic Men* was written without knowledge of the Kali sacrifice which so seriously unbalanced Naipaul's father. Again the fiction seems to capture truth where conscious knowledge is incomplete; the taste of raw flesh and tainted oil must express in physical terms the emotional and intellectual violation felt by Seepersad Naipaul. As fascinating as these revelations are, and as tenderly written as they are, the importance of "Prologue to an Autobiography" lies in its assertion of the power of writing to combat the fear of extinction.

What Naipaul has achieved and is continuing to develop is understanding of his own origins. Thoughout his work his emphasis falls on what societies, history, culture, religion do to shape people; people have little capacity to redirect their fate, but they can understand it better. The Indonesian poet Sitor Situmorang struggles to write autobiography but finds it impossible without an understanding of his tribal past: "he had lost touch with it; and he found that to write without an understanding of what he had come from was to do no more than record a sequence of events" (AB 286). Sitor's extraordinary personal history captures the essence of colonial events in Indonesia which took place over several centuries, but he cannot write of the changes in his own personality as he moved from tribal man, to object of Dutch colonialism, to subject of the conquering Japanese, to man of power, to political prisoner, to guest of Europe, and finally to writer of autobiography. Not only had he been cut off from his past by his Dutch education, but also — and Naipaul would be aware of his own privilege in this respect — "his early life had been oddly wordless: he had never had a conversation with his parents" (AB 295).

Finding the Centre suggests that the themes which are assuming greater importance in Naipaul's later work are rooted in his personal history and as his knowledge of himself has grown as a direct outcome of his writing, they have risen to the surface. Early in his career, one finds little nostalgia for "Indian village life, and the Hindu rituals that gave grace and completeness to that life"; yet he remembers his father's stories because they "gave a beauty (which in a corner of my mind still endures, like a fantasy of home) to the Indian village life I had never known" (FC 42). In addition, as we have previously noted, since recording the vision of a complete past in the tomb of Luxor, the search for people whose world is not fragmented has been a recurring theme of Naipaul's writing. In the second section of *Finding the Centre*, Naipaul seems to discover just such a place. "The Crocodiles of Yamoussoukro" records the stages of his discovery: from his arrival in hope that he was to investigate a successful postcolonial society, through the unsettled state of realizing that there is no finality in the ideas of the new world which are being superimposed on the old African ways, to the realization that in this society there is a greater and enduring reality from which people draw a sense of completion and wholeness. The difference between what he observes in the Ivory Coast and in Java (in *Among the Believers*) is that the African society is able to use the institutions of the modern Western world for its own benefit, increasing the wealth, well-being and stability of its people, without losing its understanding that reality may be found in the night world of sorcery and magic. As Naipaul's visit ends, he talks to Arlette who, though an expatriate herself, has "been converted" to a larger vision by her time in Africa.

> I asked her about Yamoussoukro. Why build that great city, if the world was sand?
> She said, "It is the president's attempt to integrate Africa into the modern world."
> And I thought she meant that to build a city like Yamoussoukro was not to accept what it stood for as the only reality. Ebony, the poet and civil servant, had hinted at something like that. Ebony's father had said to him, "I am not sending you to the school to be a white man or a Frenchman. I am sending you to enter the new world, that's all."
> (FC 188)

The first time Naipaul reports Ebony's father's words, the meaning is not entirely clear; they seem to contradict themselves, for how can one enter the new world without becoming at least a little "white" or "French", without losing part of one's identity as an African? Similarly, people Naipaul meets seem almost schizophrenic in their apparently contradictory acceptance of sorcery and scholarly discipline, of magic and sacrifices and international economics. A story which may be a joke presents an image of "technology at the service of old worship" (FC 184): a defective refrigerated container gives off an offensive odour and is found to contain severed heads "Sacrificial heads, for export". However, people like Mr Bony and Mr Niangoran-Bouah are not uncomfortably divided men; they are dignified, open, reasonable, whole. Naipaul finds himself "drawn into [the] spirit world", and surprisingly, he is not uncomfortable there. Perhaps, having stated (1983) that the process of writing seemed to require the exercise of magic, Naipaul is more willing to accept other people's magic than we might have expected him to be. In the concluding conversation with Arlette, Naipaul thinks at first that when she says "But the world is sand. Life is sand", she is saying what the Hindus say, that life is illusion. But he decides that the concepts are not the same, that the African culture imparts a different meaning: "The Hindu's idea of illusion comes from the contemplation of nothingness. Arlette's idea of sand came from her understanding and admiration of a beautifully organized society" (FC 187). Earlier Naipaul had been so disturbed by the impermanence of Abidjan and Yamoussoukro that he dreamed of a bridge melting under him and never to be repaired, but at the end of his journey, he seems to recognize that the preservation of institutions is not the most important thing, that given the security and order imparted by African acceptance of the reality of the night-time other world, it will not matter whether the day-time new world endures.

Though Arlette is a Martiniquan, she seems to have integrated her knowledge of Africa into her personality in a way that other expatriates have not. Her rejection of the pettiness of Martinique must, of course, appeal to Naipaul for whom this remains the most restricted and restricting of West Indian societies. Andrée, on the other hand, lives in solitude in the Ivory Coast and despite her association with Niangoran-Bouah, has been little changed by Africa, asserting her difference in a battle of wills with a waiter when she and Naipaul lunch together. In other work Naipaul has portrayed expatriates as failures fleeing from self-knowledge and exploiting the people of former colonies to feed their own egos. In the Ivory Coast, he finds or hears of some expatriates who remain in Africa for the "heightened sense of self" (FC 167) it gives. Others, like Busby, bring with them a cause — his is racial redemption — which seems to Naipaul an irrelevance, an antiquated import from "another continent, another past, another way of looking and feeling" (FC 131). They seem not to comprehend the enduring wholeness of Africa throughout its history. Still others, like Philip, start with few ideals and become good and conscientious people, "more knowledgeable and more tolerant", but they work to preserve the institutions of the new world, and no one has yet resolved the issue of whether there really is any "virtue in maintaining what had been given" (FC 150). In portraying these expatriates sympathetically, Naipaul is responding to them as "people I was attracted to, people not unlike myself. They too were trying to find order in their world, looking for the centre" (FC 11). He comments further that "especially after writing 'Prologue to an Autobiography' . . . I would have found equivalent connections with my past and myself wherever I had gone". An exile who has roots, who has found herself! The portrait of Arlette may well be the most positive Naipaul has ever offered readers, and suggests a possibility of discovering a centre which has in the past seemed unlikely at best. Arlette seems to have progressed past the acceptance of fragmentation which brought calm to Salim; she seems able to assimilate levels of experience, allowing them to co-exist without conflict and without seeking to integrate them. In her Naipaul captures that potential for creativity in the abandonment of an ideal of home identified by Tiffin (see above 220).

In many ways this book is about "finding the centre". Naipaul returns to his own centre of experience and learns that it still holds surprises, that new self-understanding will develop each time he undertakes a writing task. "Prologue to an Autobiography" emphasizes the significance of being a writer: "From the earliest stories and bits of stories my father had read to me, before the upheaval of the move, I had arrived at the conviction − the conviction that is at the root of so much human anguish and passion, and corrupts so many lives − that there was justice in the world. The wish to be a writer was a development of that. To be a writer as O. Henry was, to die in mid-sentence, was to triumph over darkness. And like a wild religious faith that hardens in adversity, this wish to be a writer, this refusal to be extinguished, this wish to seek at some future time for justice, strengthened as our conditions grew worse . . . " (FC 45). And Naipaul discovers that, incomplete though his knowledge of his father's illness was, he absorbed Seepersad Naipaul's hysteria, his fear of extinction and his faith that the word can protect. In returning to Trinidad and seeking the personal history which was missing from his earlier knowledge, Naipaul reassesses experiences he has already analysed. He becomes more aware of the discontinuity in his grandfather's life, aware that for him Trinidad was the illusion and India the reality to which he tried to return. And in learning the story of his father's grandmother's migration, Naipaul finally appreciates first, the wonder of his father's achievement in becoming any kind of writer at all, and secondly, how his father developed the ambition to be a writer, how it was a way of retaining the status of his caste in an environment where being a pundit was a meaningless ambition, how it preserved an essential part of his self-concept without forcing him to take up an unacceptable role.

Having rediscovered his personal centre, Naipaul is receptive to discovery of the centre of African knowledge. In accepting the dark side of experience, Naipaul has by no means thrown himself to the wolves of irrationality. He is still talking of how "it takes thought (a sifting of impulses, ideas and references that become more multifarious as one grows older) to understand what one has lived through or where one has been" (FC 13), and he is still seeking order. He still uses history to help him discover the organizing principles, even if history emphasizes that the creations of humans are impermanent – for instance, his repetition of the adjective "pharaonic" to remind us that as a monument Yamoussoukro may be as temporary as the monuments of pharaohs which provided the building blocks of the new pharoah's monument. Naipaul's acceptance of the reality of the night world is not really surprising; he was working towards it in *A Bend in the River* and maybe even somewhat unwillingly, as far back as *Mr Stone and the Knights Companion*. *Finding the Centre* emphasizes the persistence of Africa's old reality and the separation of European and African influences, where *A Bend in the River* suggested that the Big Man's attempts to create a new mythology lacked the power of the old. The centre of Yamoussoukro is not a recreation of the president's village but the village itself, and it is guarded by those dangerous, mysterious, totemic crocodiles. The Europeanization at the bend in the river differs from the Ivory Coast in that the trappings of Western modernity seek to replace the old, real African world, while Ivorians only use what is beneficial to them without abandoning the secrets of the night. Ferdinand merely took up roles and failed to retain the wholeness of personality of Niangoran-Bouah, but in the imagery of the novel, it is apparent old Africa endures while Europe's influence is transitory.

The goal of all Naipaul's writing, which arises from his personal need to explain his own dislocation and to triumph over its debilitating effects, is to order experience in such a way that readers discern the elements of fantasy which distort perception and understanding. Through most of his career, his attention moves outward through a series of concentric circles as his experience takes in more and more of the world on his continuing journey of social and self-discovery. Just as Salim in *A Bend in the River* is a much less inward-looking narrator than Ralph Singh in *The Mimic Men*, so Naipaul's second study of India, *India: A Wounded*

Civilization, is less an exploration of dark areas of the author's psyche than *An Area of Darkness*. But finally in *Finding the Centre*, Naipaul returns to the personal and to his own history and writes more positively than ever before.

Conclusion

When Naipaul wrote his first nonfictional study of a post-colonial area, *The Middle Passage*, he feared it would limit his ability to compose fiction. The fear proved groundless. In fact, throughout his career, the two forms feed each other. Obviously, *Guerrillas* draws on the experience of the journalist sent to cover the story of a murderer as his appeals against the death sentence reach the highest tribunal, and in most of Naipaul's novels, we can find elements of the nonfiction transmuted into character, plot, setting, imagery. But perhaps less obvious is the way Naipaul's fictive imagination leads him toward conclusions which shape and colour the way he perceives the reality he tries to capture in nonfiction. How different might *The Middle Passage* have been if Naipaul had not written first the tragedy of Mr Biswas? If it followed the comic novels, would the travel book have been so angry, so fearful and so rejecting? And if Naipaul had not undertaken the fictional study of Hindu family life in Trinidad which is an important element in *A House for Mr Biswas*, would he not have visited India in rather a different frame of mind? Fruitless speculation perhaps . . . At any rate, *Mr Stone and the Knights Companion* is the product of the disturbing visit to India; the most "fictional" of Naipaul's novels, it seems more subject to the metaphysical considerations Naipaul has told interviewers he seeks to suppress, but with which he seems more comfortable in recent writing. Drawing on many Hindu themes, this novel embodies most clearly the ambivalence and tension between Naipaul's statements of the futility of creative activity and his own continuing acts of creativity of the highest literary standard.

While we can find the "real world" antecedents of much of Naipaul's fiction – for instance, Guyanese politics inform the Isabellan situation in *The Mimic Men* and to these are added elements of autobiography – at the same time, fiction often suggests the preoccupations of subsequent nonfiction. Understanding of Singh's goals as a writer and his fascination with history greatly enhances study of *The Loss of El Dorado* in which Naipaul seeks to discover in the past the causes of the sterility, the chaotic lack of standards, and the self-denigration he believes to be characteristic of West Indian society. Lately, Naipaul's apparent success in this endeavour is questioned by his most recent novel, *A Bend in the River*, in which the narrator seems to reject the study of history as a path to peace of mind, and even more recently, *Finding the Centre* seems to turn much more inward once again, following Salim's lead. Naipaul's Author's Note to *The Return of Eva Peron* explains one of the functions of his nonfiction:

> These pieces, except for additions made to "Michael X" and to "The Return of Eva Peron", were written between 1972 and 1975. They bridged a creative gap: from the end of 1970 to the end of 1973 no novel offered itself to me. That perhaps explains the intensity of some of the pieces, and their obsessional nature. The themes repeat, whether in Argentina, Trinidad or the Congo. I can claim no further unity for the pieces; though it should be said that, out of these journeys and writings, novels did in the end come to me.

In the new postscript to "The Killings in Trinidad", Naipaul writes of the type of fiction which threatens both its author and his society, a fantasy which is turned into violent, insane fact.

> This was a literary murder, if ever there was one. Writing led both men there: for both of them, uneducated but clever, hustlers with the black cause always to hand, operating always among the converted or half-converted, writing had for too long been a public relations exercise, a form of applauded lie, fantasy. And in Arima it was a fantasy of power that led both men to contemplate, from their different standpoints, the act of murder. (REP 73)

Some pages later as Naipaul reconstructs Malik's elaborate plans for the day of Gale Benson's murder, he returns to this theme:

> That bathing party, with the fire on the riverbank: it was the crowning conception of an intricate day. Like an episode in a dense novel, it served many purposes and had many meanings. And it had been devised by a man who was writing a novel about himself, settling accounts with the world, filling pages of the cheap writing pad and counting the precious words as he wrote, anxious for world fame (including literary fame): a man led to lunacy by all the ideas he had been given of who he was, and now, in the exile of Arima, under the influence of Jamal, with an illusion of achieved power. Malik had no skills as a novelist, not even an elementary gift of language. He was too self-absorbed to process experience in any rational way or even to construct a connected narrative. But when he transferred his fantasy to real life, he went to work like the kind of novelist he would have liked to be. (REP 87–88)

Naipaul here enunciates the difference between fiction which reveals experience and that which cloaks it in dangerous fantasies: it must "process experience in a rational way". In his nonfiction Naipaul attempts to use reason to discover the patterns of experience, the cause and effect relationships between past, present, and future events. In his fiction he portrays the dilemma of the individual in a world his observations lead him to believe is disintegrating into chaos and violence. And yet the order in his writing in itself seems to suggest a positive, a cause for hope in the midst of chaos. In *A Bend in the River*, against a background of the events and setting depicted in an article on Mobutu's Congo, Naipaul's imagination creates a narrator who seems to reject the study of history and seek the stoic calm of Mr Stone. Although Salim is almost unconscious of his role as a writer, the reader cannot ignore the craftsmanship of his narrative which contains some of Naipaul's most extended and carefully constructed patterns of imagery and inter-related themes. As his imagination leads him towards acceptance of the reality in the darkness of the African bush in contrast with the illusions of civilization, Naipaul seeks a refuge which shelters many other postcolonials: words become the last line of defence against a vision of chaos.

> I met History once, but he ain't recognize me. . . .
> I confront him and shout, "Sir, this is Shabine!
> They say I'se your grandson. You remember Grandma,
> your black cook, at all?" The bitch hawk and spat.
> A spit like that worth any number of words.
> But that's all them bastards have left us: words.
>   (Derek Walcott 1979, 8–9)

References

Abdullah, Mena and Ray Matthew. 1974. *The Time of the Peacock*. Sydney: Angus and Robertson.

Achebe, Chinua. 1966. *A Man of the People*. London: Heinemann Educational Books.

Anand, Mulk Raj. 1972. *Coolie*. London: The Bodley Head (revised edition).

Anantha Murthy, U. R. 1976. *Samskara*. Translated by A. K. Ramanujan. Delhi: Oxford University Press.

Awoonor, Kofi. 1971. *This Earth, My Brother . . .* London: Heinemann Education Books.

Banerjee, Bibhuti Bhusan. n.d. *Pather Panchali*. Calcutta: Writers Workshop Publication.

Boxill, Anthony. 1976. The Little Bastard Worlds of V. S. Naipaul's *The Mimic Men* and *A Flag on the Island*. *International Fiction Review* 3: 12–19.

Blaber, Ronald. 1986. "This piece of earth": V. S. Naipaul's *A Bend in the River*. In *A Sense of Place*, ed. P. Nightingale, 61–67. St Lucia: University of Queensland Press.

Bryden, Ronald. 1973. The Novelist Talks About His Work. *The Listener* 22 March 1973: 367–68, 370.

Davies, Barrie. 1972. The Personal Sense of a Society — Minority View: Aspects of the "East Indian" Novel in the West Indies. *Studies in the Novel* 4 (2): 284–95.

Dayananda, James Y. 1975. Interview with Manohar Malgonkar. *Journal of Commonwealth Literature* 9 (3): 21–28.

Defoe, Daniel. c1963. *Robinson Crusoe*. Introduction by David G. Pitt. New York: Airmont Books.

Derrick, A. C. 1969. Naipaul's Technique as a Novelist. *Journal of Commonwealth Literature* 7 (July): 32–44.

Drodziak, William. 1978. Writer Without a Country. *Time* 27 February 1978: 21.

Forster, E. M. 1971. *A Passage to India*. London: Edward Arnold Ltd. (Pocket Edition).

Gilkes, Michael. 1974. Racial Identity and the Individual Consciousness in the Caribbean Novel. The Edgar Mittelholzer Memorial Lectures, 5th Series. Georgetown, Guyana: Ministry of Information and Culture (National History and Arts Council).

Griffiths, Gareth. 1978. *A Double Exile: African and West Indian Writing Between Two Cultures*. London: Marion Boyars.

Hamilton, Ian. 1971. Without a Place. *Times Literary Supplement* 30 July 1971: 897-98. Reprinted in Hamner 1977.

Hamner, Robert D. 1973. *V. S. Naipaul*. New York: Twayne Publishers, Inc.

———, ed. 1977. *Critical Perspectives on V. S. Naipaul*. Washington, D.C.: Three Continents Press.

Hemenway, Robert. 1982. Sex and Politics in V. S. Naipaul. *Studies in the Novel* 14: 189–202.

Henry, Jim Douglas. 1971. Unfurnished Entrails. *The Listener* 25 November 1971: 721.

Hume, Martin A. S. 1906. *Sir Walter Ralegh: The British Dominion of the West*. London: T. Fisher Unwin (4th edition).

Jhabvala, Ruth Prawer. 1971. Writing for Films. *The Illustrated Weekly of India* 21 March 1971: 25.

Klass, Morton. 1961. *East Indians in Trinidad: A Study of Cultural Persistence*. New York: Columbia University Press.

Lamming, George. 1960. *The Pleasures of Exile*. London: Michael Joseph.

———. 1970. *In the Castle of My Skin*. New York: Collier (reprint).

———. 1971. *Water with Berries*. Trinidad and Jamaica: Longman Caribbean, Ltd.

———. 1974. *Natives of My Person*. London: Picador (Pan Books Ltd).

Lee, R. H. 1966. The Novels of V. S. Naipaul. *Theoria* 27: 31–46. Reprinted in Hamner 1977.

Lessing, Doris. 1960. *In Pursuit of the English*. London: Sphere Books.

Lewis, Gordon K. 1962. The Trinidad and Tobago General Election of 1961. *Caribbean Studies* 2 (2): 2–30.

Lowenthal, David. 1972. *West Indian Societies*. London, New York: Oxford University Press.

de Madariaga, Salvador. 1947. *The Fall of the Spanish American Empire*. London: Hollis and Carter.

Maes-Jelinek, Hena. 1967. V.S. Naipaul: A Commonwealth Writer? *Revue des Langues Vivantes* 33: 499–513.

Malik, Yogendra. K. 1971. *East Indians in Trinidad*. London: Oxford University Press.

Malgonkar, Manohar. 1963. *The Princes*. London: Hamish Hamilton.

Miller, Karl. 1967. V.S. Naipaul and the New Order. *Kenyon Review* 29: 685–98.

Morris, Robert K. 1975. *Paradoxes of Order: Some Perspectives on the Fiction of V. S. Naipaul*. Columbia, Missouri: University of Missouri Press.

Naipaul, V. S. 1957. *The Mystic Masseur*. London: Andre Deutsch.

———. 1958. *The Suffrage of Elvira*. London: Andrew Deutsch.

———. 1959. *The Mimic Men*. London: Andre Deutsch.

———. 1961. *A House for Mr Biswas*. London: Andre Deutsch.

———. 1962a. *The Middle Passage*. London: Andre Deutsch.

———. 1962b. Trollope in the West Indies. *The Listener* 15 March 1962: 461.

———. 1963a. *Mr Stone and the Knights Companion*. London: Andre Deutsch.

———. 1963b. India's Cast-Off Revolution. *Sunday Times* 25 August 1963: 17.

———. 1964a. *An Area of Darkness*. London: Andre Deutsch.

———. 1964b. Critics and Criticism. *BIM* 10 (38): 74–77.

———. 1964c. Speaking of Writing. *The Times* 2 January 1964: 11.

———. 1967a. *The Mimic Men*. London: Andre Deutsch.

———. 1967b. *A Flag on the Island*. London: Andre Deutsch.

———. 1969a. *The Loss of El Dorado*. Harmondsworth: Penguin.

———. 1969b. Et in America ego! *The Listener*. 4 September 1969; 302–4.

———. 1971. *In a Free State*. London: Andre Deutsch.

———. 1972. *The Overcrowded Barracoon*. London: Andre Deutsch.

———. 1975. *Guerrillas*. London: Andre Deutsch.

———. 1977. *India: A Wounded Civilization*. London: Andre Deutsch.

———. 1979. *A Bend in the River*. London: Andre Deutsch.

———. 1980a. *The Return of Eva Peron with The Killings in Trinidad*. New York: Alfred A. Knopf.

_____. 1980b. *A Congo Diary*. Los Angeles: Sylvester and Orphanos.

_____. 1983. Writing "A House for Mr Biswas". *New York Review of Books* 24 November 1983: 22-23.

_____. 1984a. Heavy Manners in Grenada. *Sunday Times Magazine* 12 February 1984: 23-31.

_____. 1984b. *Finding the Centre*. London: Andre Deutsch.

Naipaul, Seepersad. 1976. *The Adventures of Gurudeva and Other Stories*. Foreword by V. S. Naipaul. London: Andre Deutsch.

Naipaul, Shiva. 1971. *Fireflies*. New York: Alfred A. Knopf.

Narayan, R. K. 1957. *The Printer of Malgudi*. Lansing: Michigan State University Press.

Neill, Michael. 1982. Guerillas and Gangs: Frantz Fanon and V. S. Naipaul. *Ariel* 13:21-62.

Ngugi, James (Ngugi wa Thiong'o). 1967. *A Grain of Wheat*. London: Heinemann Educational Books Ltd.

_____. 1972. *Homecoming: Essays on African and Caribbean Literature, Culture and Politics*. London: Heinemann.

Nightingale, Peggy (M. H.). 1978. Anantha Murthy's *Samskara*: An Indian Journey to the End of the Night . . . *New Literature Review* 4: 51-54.

Oxaal, Ivor. No date. *Black Intellectuals Come to Power: The Rise of Creole Nationalism in Trinidad and Tobago*. Cambridge, Mass: Schenkman Publishing Company.

Parrinder, Patrick. 1979. V. S. Naipaul and the Uses of Literacy. *Critical Quarterly* 21: 5-13.

Patterson, Orlando. 1967. *An Absence of Ruins*. London: Hutchinson.

Pramoedya Ananta Toer. 1982. *This Earth of Mankind*. Translated by Max Lane. Harmondsworth: Penguin.

Pritchett, V. S. 1963. Climacteric. *New Statesman* 31 May 1963: 831-32. Reprinted in Hamner 1977.

Ramchand, Kenneth. 1970. *The West Indian Novel and Its Background*. London: Faber and Faber.

_____. 1973. The Theatre of Politics. *Twentieth Century Studies* 10: 20-36.

Rohlehr, Gordon. 1968. Character and Rebellion in *A House for Mr Biswas*. *New World Quarterly* 4 (4): 66-72. Reprinted in Hamner 1977.

Rowe-Evans, Adrian. 1971. The Writer as Colonial. *Transition*. 40: 56-57, 66.

Selvon, Samuel. 1972. A Note on Dialect. In *Common Wealth.* Aarhus: Akademist Boghandel.

Singham, A. W. 1968. *The Hero and the Crowd in a Colonial Polity.* New Haven: Yale University Press.

Soyinka, Wole. 1965. *The Road.* London: Oxford University Press.

Thompson, Edward. 1935. *Sir Walter Ralegh: The Last of the Elizabethans.* London: Macmillan.

Thieme, John. 1975. V. S. Naipaul's Third World: A Not So Free State. *Journal of Commonwealth Literature* 10 (1): 10–22.

Tiffin, Helen. 1972. The Lost Ones: A Study of the Works of V. S. Naipaul. Dissertation, Queen's University, Canada.

———. 1986. New Concepts of Person and Place in *The Twyborn Affair* and *A Bend in the River.* In *A Sense of Place,* ed. P. Nightingale, 22–31. St Lucia: University of Queensland Press.

Trend, J. B. 1946. *Bolivar and the Independence of Spanish America.* London: Hodder and Stoughton (for the English Universities Press).

Walcott, Derek. 1965. Interview with V. S. Naipaul. *Sunday Guardian* (Trinidad) 7 March 1965: 5, 7.

———. 1979. *The Star-Apple Kingdom.* New York: Farrar, Straus and Giroux.

Wheeler, Charles. 1977. It's Every Man for Himself. *The Listener* 27 October 1977: 535, 537.

White, Landeg. 1975. *V. S. Naipaul: A Critical Introduction.* London: Macmillan.

Wyndham, Francis. 1971. V. S. Naipaul. *The Listener* 7 October 1971: 461–62.

Index